306090 08, Autonomous Urbanism

Untitled #5 (Skyways), 2001, Catherine Opie, IRIS print, ed. of 5, 2 APs, 13" x 19"

Untitled #22 (Skyways), 2001, Catherine Opie

Untitled #2 (Skyways), 2001, Catherine Opie

**306090, Architecture Journal:
From Every Angle**

Exploring contemporary issues in architecture from every angle, 306090 is dedicated to opening up architectural discourse across a range of places, people and practices. 306090 situates itself in this role out of a conviction that it is only through an expanded understanding of architecture's role in cultural production that architectural production itself may be challenged, redefined and enriched.

In an age of pluralism, how does an architect engage, or define, the meaningful issues of the day? The legacy of narrow arguments, exclusionary dialogues, and closed critical discourses that characterized the theorization of architecture in the late 20th century has left architects holding a weaker hand, less able than ever to affect the ever-broadening processes that dictate the built world.

Today, while some might still argue over whether architecture is better addressed through the disciplines of film, literature or mathematics, real cross-disciplinary exchanges, such as those explored in this volume, are changing the way architecture is practiced and the way everything from furniture to cities are built.

We propose a new regime of open criticism, which addresses contemporary conditions in political, technological and artistic disciplines, on the basis of what architecture can do with them—and for them. Comprising new work and untested ideas from around the world, the goal of this series is to suggest that a glance askew often leads to the discovery of a new idea.

**Emily Abruzzo
Alexander Briseño
Jonathan D. Solomon**

306090 08, Autonomous Urbanism
306090, Architecture Journal, vol. 8

Guest Editors
Alex Duval
Kjersti Monson

Series Editors
Emily Abruzzo
Alexander Briseño
Jonathan D. Solomon

Assistant Editors
Eva May Hagberg
Lynne DeSilva-Johnson

Graphic Design
O R G inc.

Advisory Board
M. Christine Boyer
Mario Gandelsonas
David L. Hays
Mark Jarzombeck
Paul Lewis
Michael Sorkin
Christian Unverzagt
Sarah Whiting

Acknowledgements

The guest-editors would like to thank the following people for their support and encouragement: Richard Peiser whose teaching and support provided the initial lens through which the city, in our line of research, is seen; Steven Plofker for his generous and practical guidance in understanding the real deals of urbanization; Marcel Smets for his scholarly and professional guidance and for providing the opportunity to undertake research related to this theme; our wonderful friends in New York for their aid during the editorial process—especially Walter Meyer and Matthew Soules; our colleagues who have discussed and debated these issues with us in a way that has helped to forward the dialogue, including Alexander D'Hooghe, Erik Van Hoof, and Kelly Shannon; Mark Wyse at A & I Digital Labs along with Lisa Overduin and Julie Hough at Regen Projects for facilitating our use of the Catherine Opie skyway photographs; the friendly and efficient people at John Portman's office, namely Emily Munnell and Judy Jones. Last but not least we would like to thank our family: Karen Monson and Donna Monson for their constant encouragement and Rosemary and Bertrand Duval-Arnould for all their love.

306090 is supported by a grant from the National Endowment for the Arts, and by a grant from the Graham Foundation for Advanced Studies in the Fine Arts. 306090 appreciates the continuing support of David L. Hays and anonymous donors.

Opinions expressed in 306090 are the authors' alone and do not necessarily reflect those of the editors. All reasonable attempts have been made to identify owners of copyright. Errors or omissions will be corrected in future volumes. No part of this volume may be reproduced without the written permission of the publisher, except in the context of reviews.

Published by 306090, Inc.
350 Canal St. Box 2092 / New York, NY 10013-0875

Distributed by Princeton Architectural Press
37 E. 7th St. / New York, NY 10003
1-800-722-6657 t / 1-718-504-5228 f

First Edition, 2005/ISBN 1-56898-522-3
Printed in Canada.

©Copyright 2005, 306090, Inc.
All rights reserved. Printed and bound in the United States. Contact the publisher for Library of Congress catalog-in-publication information.

306090, Architecture Journal, is published twice annually and accepts submissions year-round. 306090, Inc. is a non-profit organization registered in the State of New York. For information on past or future volumes, rights and permissions, or editorial submissions, contact 306090 at info@306090.org, or see www.306090.org.

For information on orders contact Princeton Architectural Press at orders@papress.com or see www.papress.com. 306090 does not sell subscriptions.

Other volumes by 306090

306090 07: Landscape within Architecture
David L. Hays, guest-editor 9/2004

306090 06: Shifting Infrastructures
Patricia Acevedo-Riker, Martha Mertzig, John Riker, Jeremi Sudol, guest-editors 3/2004

306090 05: Teaching + Building
Emily Abruzzo, Jonathan Solomon, editors 9/2003

306090 04: Global Trajectories
Jason K. Johnson, guest-editor 3/2003

306090 03: Urban Education
Alexander Briseño, Jonathan D. Solomon, editors 9/2002

306090 02: Student Discount
Alexander Briseño, Jonathan D. Solomon, editors 3/2002

306090 01: Where we are Now
Jennifer Ferng, Jonathan D. Solomon, editors 9/2001

14 DUVAL, Alex /
MONSON, Kjersti
Autonomous Urbanism

21 DUARTE, Gabriel /
CONTRERAS, Javier /
CABALLERO, Roberto C.
It's Not Just Grass!

30 HADDAD, Elie
Single-Owner Downtown: Reconstructing Beirut

35 HARRINGTON, Anthony /
LEE, Lina
Office Tower Infestation

39 JOACHIM, Mitchell /
ARBONA, Javier /
GREDEN, Lara
Nature's Home

44 KELLY, Caroline
Portman Space: An Interview with John Portman

51 LAIGU, Tonu
Estonian Megastructures Reuse

54 MARTENS, Charlotte
AVL-ville

66
MOSKOW, Keith AIA
Urban Hookah

67
PIPER, Michael
Capitalize on Your Context

78
SHAN, Wenhui
Market China Contestation: Purposeful Rationality Versus Value Rationality

85
SHAN, Wenhui
Developer Dialogue

91
SHANNON, Kelly PhD.
Shifting Norms— The Evolution of Real Estate in Vietnam

103
SHERMAN, Roger
If, Then: Shaping Change as a Strategic Basis for Design

115
SO, May
Pac Place

122
SOULES, Matthew
ON/OFF City Notes from Vancouver

123
SOLURI, Andre
SHoP Interview

130
THEUNIS, Katrien
The Rise of the Private Developer and The Fall of the Designer

140
VERBAKEL, Els
Space Blocks and Other Transnational Strategies for Urban Habitation

149
WALL, Ronald
Archinomics: An Investigation Between the Disciplines of Spatial Design and Spatial Science

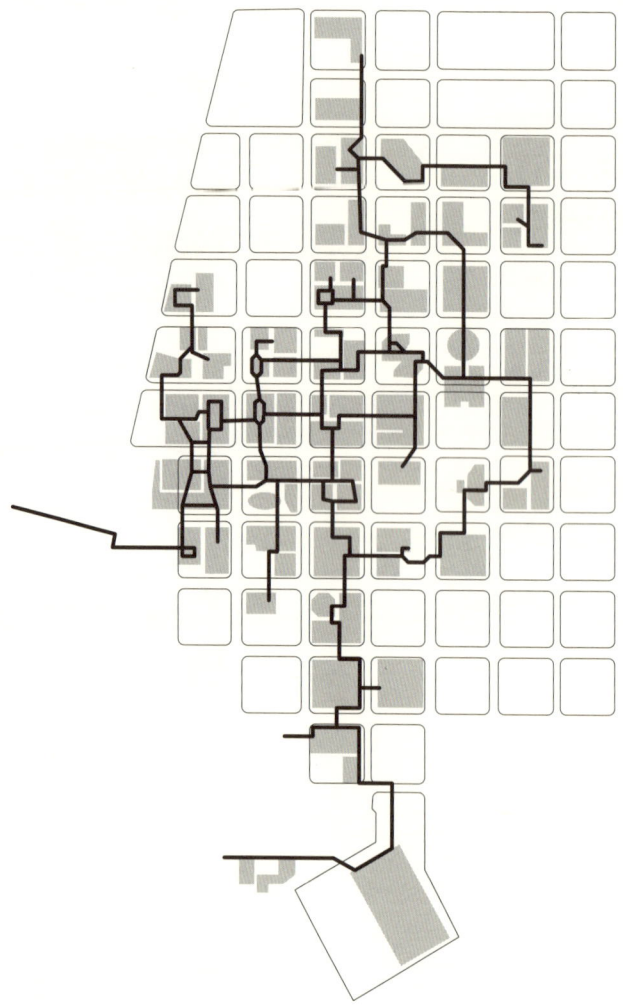

Minneapolis—5 miles of connected walkways

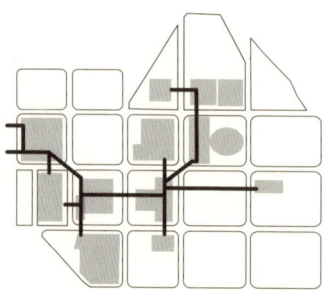

Atlanta—1 mile of connected walkways

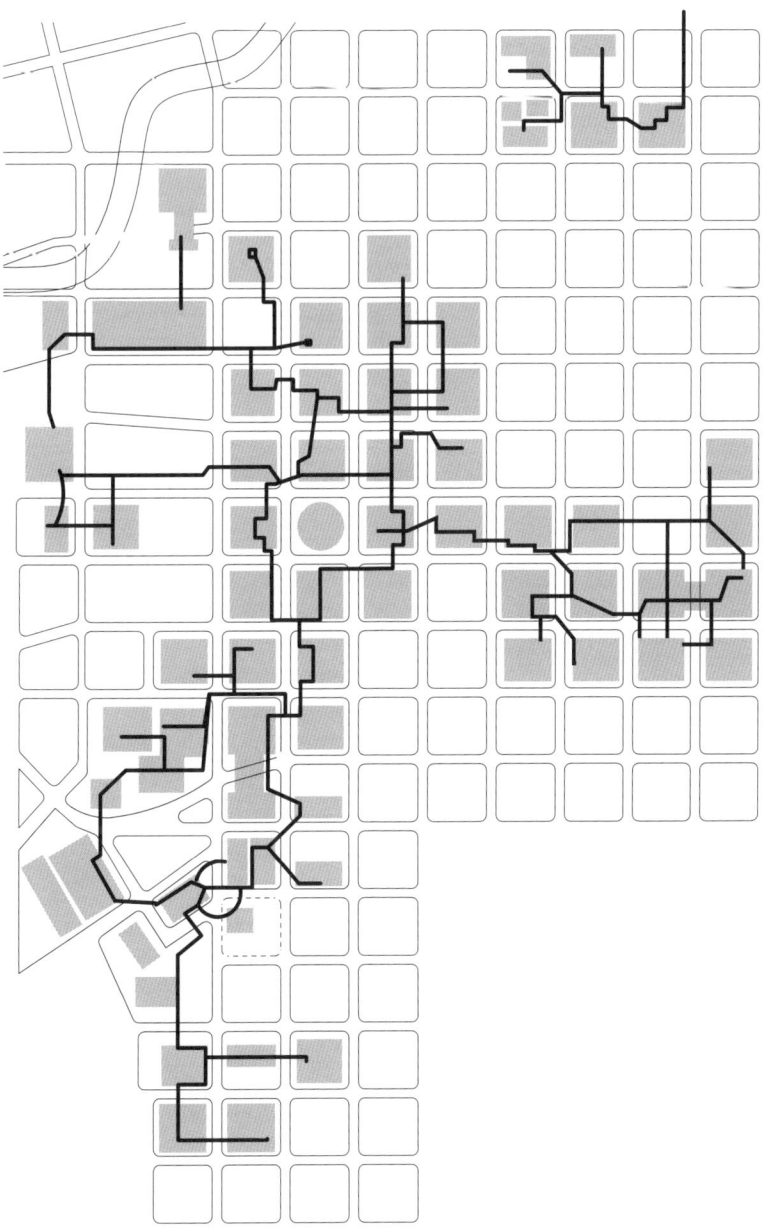

Houston—6 miles of connected walkways

DUVAL, Alex /
MONSON, Kjersti
Autonomous Urbanism

Autonomous Urbanism explores issues of privatization, individualism, and competition in the city. At stake is the way that we engage the built environment as designers, navigating these forces with the goal of establishing strategies for intellectual and professional practice.

In design discourse the term autonomy is used to describe the conceptual framework of a project that willfully resists the outside pressures of economy and politics. This work and the associated arguments are well known. The title of this volume of 306090 is intentionally paradoxical, as we mean to explore the implications of the idea that a project seeded in totalizing privatization achieves conceptual autonomy in its own right [1].

Privatization is a trend in cities and nations occurring globally, loosely defined for our purposes as the death of the welfare state in favor of market driven planning and development strategies and outcomes.

The basic characteristics and effects of privatization include: (1) public disinvestment in traditionally public goods; (2) private ownership or provision of formerly public lands, goods, or services such as policing or waste management; (3) emerging forms of public-private development; (4) reduced social welfare; and (5) increased entrepreneurialism and personal ownership.

Privatization can be observed as a process in its infancy in the form of transitional economies like Vietnam or Estonia just opening to the market and simultaneously as a matured process that has reached a hyperbolic extreme, for instance American covenant communities that are structured like shareholder corporations with a Board and a President rather than like a municipal government with a Mayor and a City Council [2].

The rise of individual interests invites a qualitative observation: namely, that privatization leads to the fragmentation of social goals, creating in its place a context of competing individual interests which may or may not generate good outcomes. Individual interests can be seen in the physical and social form of the city through the proliferation of consumer oriented patterns of urbanization.

Meanwhile, competition places increased demands in the corporate world and capital markets as well as directly on cities, which compete with one another. This environment increasingly rewards proposals for novel ownership structures that take advantage of laws and loopholes as well as those that generate persuasive arguments for regulatory variance in the name of responsive urbanism.

A discussion of privatization leads to questions of reification and the implicitly negative associations that follow. Reification, as understood in Marxist terminology, is the act of representing a person as a commodity, of describing people not in personalized terms but in terms of their value as labor commodity. A similar argument can be made about the reification of architecture and the urban landscape. In an increasingly exchange-based world culture, projects are defined less by their inherent qualities (function and program) and more by their commodity value (marketing an image for a client or a city).

The forces that drive the development of cities in an exchange culture—such as real estate interests, consumer logics, ownership, trade, commerce, and marketing—have traditionally been perceived as inherently in conflict with design theory and practice. Although we know that these forces drive built form at the meta-scale, they are not considered valid as an engine to drive either design intention or design theory. Defining the products of design in terms of these forces is therefore considered an act of reification itself.

Michael Hays—like most of the preceding generation of thinkers in both the United States and Europe—examines strategies of resistance that serve to advance the disciplinary strength of the design professions through theoretical texts. The material in this journal responds to Hays' speculation in the introduction of *Architecture Theory Since 1968* "that a different, younger audience, whose relation to consumption is altogether altered, may have to produce another kind of theory premised on neither the concept of reification or nor the apparatus of the sign."

The American Context

The death of the welfare state and the rise of privatization in America began with the liberalization of capital flows in the 1970s. The impact was immediately felt by cities, which began to suffer the effects of corporate flight and found themselves increasingly in competition with other cities around the world.[1] The real blow for municipal government, however, was the sudden dephysicalization of federal investment in cities that resulted from Ronald Reagan's New Federalist agenda in 1980–82[2]. Suddenly, dependable categorical federal grants became competitive grants administered by the State. With losses of $6.6 billion in direct federal investment in cities from 1981 to 1982 alone[3], municipal governments found themselves in a fiscal crisis of a magnitude they hadn't experienced since the Depression. The reduced capacity of public authorities to provide public goods and services under the burden of their newly constricted budgets[4] resulted in an increased dependency on the private provision of public goals leading to the emergence of public-private partnerships and quasi-governmental private entities like the Business Improvement District.

It should be stated upfront that physical investment by the federal government was somewhat problematic in America—it was born out of the Depression years with the first publicly built housing projects, and effectively ended with the outcry against the infamous Robert Moses style of clean-slate urban renewal[5]—especially the federal practice of paying 75% of the cost of demolition for urban renewal of those areas deemed "blighted" by local politicians. The urban renewal period generated immense criticism of federal physical investment in cities. The critique of the urban renewal era is well-known and will not be restated here. Suffice it to say that the impact of urban renewal ensured a wide base of support among typical citizens for the dephysicalization of federal investment in cities. Reagan's message of federal withdrawal from local development was therefore hitting ears ripe for hearing it—but the budgetary losses in areas of social welfare and public goods were significant.

In response to the crisis, most cities raised taxes and created new fees. Other creative means were invented for revenue generation and cost savings as well. Chicago began to buy land speculatively for later sale, Newark privatized services, and Los Angeles and Seattle postponed roads and bridges maintenance. In the City of Boston, several triage strategies kicked in as the city struggled to replace its lost revenue, including: taxation and fees, sale of assets, budget reforms, capital investment cuts, and new management techniques. Specific measures taken in Boston included a movement to raise property taxes; creation of new taxes on parking and condo conversion; creation of a new commercial fire service charge; sale of the Boston convention center asset to the state; implementation of personnel freezes and layoffs; reduction in soft program funding (job training, nutrition, recreation, lead paint poisoning prevention, and arts, for example); implementation of cuts to vital services including police, fire, health, and education; implementation of a full stop on all capital projects in midstream, leaving unfinished parks; avoidance of any new investment in infrastructure and disinvestment in maintenance; and the creation of a new contract relationship with an accounting firm. These facts come from a survey of eight cities conducted in the mid-1980's (presented at an urban symposium in 1985) by Robert Wood and Beverly Klimkowsky, who attempted to document and catalogue the effects on American cities as a result of New Federalist policies. "Viewed from the perspective of systematic financial strategy, the aggregate of city responses [to Reagan's New Federalism] becomes a shotgun approach, seizing at whatever instrument for increasing revenues and reducing expenditures lay immediately at hand."[6]

The rapid dismantling of the welfare state radically reduced the capacity of public planning agencies, whose stewardship of the built environment rested heavily on federal subsidies. Cities sought private partners because (1) federal aid to state and local governments was drastically cut, (2) federal grants were reformed from categorical grants to competitive block grants which could not be guaranteed, and (3) although cities were given expanded authority to levy local taxes, they could not easily utilize this power—struggling cities with a degraded tax base would risk losing population and worsening their situation with newly raised taxes, and most cities were also stymied by tax caps voted into law by residents (such as California's Proposition 13) when they tried to make up for their losses by raising local property taxes.[7] Since most cities cannot borrow extensively due to balanced budget or anti-deficit requirements imposed by the state, they were left with few resources at their disposal to overcome the revenue gap.

Interestingly, the Wood & Klimkowsky report made no forecast of the significant

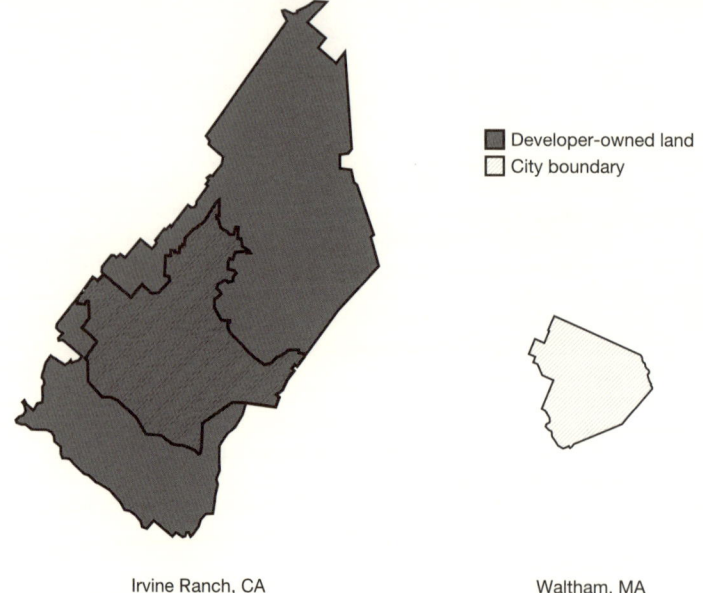

1. Irvine Ranch, CA is effectively owned by the single developer who conceived and built it. Compare this city/developer relationship to the more traditional scenario of a developer acting at the scale of the parcel and negotiating with the city (Waltham, Massachussets).

role to come for the private sector in the public realm. While they forecast private investment in terms of either nonprofit volunteerism or philanthropic effort, the study team did not anticipate privatization of traditionally public goods and services, or even the emergence of public-private development as we know it today. They did not foresee or perhaps even believe that private entities could fill the revenue gap—why would they? How would they? It was out of sheer necessity that cities invented incentive or exaction measures to motivate the private sector to participate in the provision of all of the goods and services that they had lost the capacity to provide themselves.

American cities have softened in the interest of incentivizing investment. Soft partnerships, soft money, soft costs, soft parcels, soft loans, and soft assets all imply a degree of flexibility, uncertainty, opportunity, and risk. "Softness" implies the existence of something outside of a given framework, uncommitted and unprotected. It implies negotiability. Soft coping mechanisms in American planning include developer empowerment through transferable development rights, variance, and special permit allocation; public benefit through exactions and linkages; opportunities for negotiation through public and private development, multipurpose public authorities behaving like private actors, expanded use of special zoning districts, and enabling business improvement districts.[8] These tools have been exceedingly important to the goal of meeting public needs by enabling and leveraging private investment.

The early involvement of corporate American in slum clearance and reconstruction during the urban renewal period may have provided a platform for expanded partnership on a much wider variety of public initiatives and projects when the need arose. City planners began to negotiate urban outcomes, including exactions and public benefits, with developers in much the same way as two businesses might negotiate a deal [Sagalyn]. In this framework, comprehensive planning can be understood as a way for the city to generate bargaining chips, as their primary power in negotiation rests in their ability to provide regulatory relief.

Implications for Practice

The increased reliance of government on private finance has resulted in an increasing disadvantage for architecture and design firms interested in practicing urbanism or urban design. In light of the expectations and the pragmatic needs of cities today, there

2. One example of extreme privatization in America is the unassuming covenant community. In Montgomery Village, MD, a city of 50,000 residents, the government is not comprised of publicly elected City Councillors and a Mayor—it adopts the structure of a shareholder corporation with a President and a Board. The city as a whole is a foundation, and the physical plan reflects the structure of the privately held homeowners corporations. In this city, only homeowners have the right to vote, although there is a resident population of renters.

are few firms who have the capacity to comprehensively design the most significant urban projects. The bar is high because cities expect financial guarantees, the projects are complex and long term, and the deal-structuring has to be customized per project, including strategies and benefits that are based both on planning logic and fiscal logic. A "win" on the public side is not always a simple question of revenue generation, and yet development interests require a profit.

Most firms who have the capacity to participate with the city on this level are contractors, banks, or very large developers. Katrien Theunis discusses exactly this dynamic in the context of Belgium, where the visionary architect/urbanist Renaat Braem loses out to a faceless corporation in a newtown development scheme—in spite of the fact that he and the town council who chooses the capital route are proclaimed socialists. It is also evident in the Solidere case in Beirut discussed here by Elie Haddad. Only recently, in the past ten years, have firms with a design focus started to grow in this direction. WILMA, a ten-year-old development company in Antwerp, Belgium, is headed up by one architect and one planner—both former students of eminent Belgian urbanist Marcel Smets and later trained in real estate development—who decided to specialize in large scale PPD projects, and have found their small firm in high demand by cities in a field of behemoth competitors.[9] The ten-person firm is now doing 50 million Euro PPD projects. In the United States we can look at our interview subjects at SHoP, an architecture firm in New York City that acts as its own development client. The firm is perhaps most well-known for their Porter House project in Manhattan's meatpacking district, a project that has been published in the journal *AD* among others [3]. The principle partners at SHoP embody not only architecturally specific professional knowledge (art history, structural engineering) but also professional expertise in finance and marketing.

We hypothesize that these first movers are leading the edge of a larger shift in practice on the horizon—and that a position of resistance to existing mechanisms of urbanization may reduce our capacity to find rich new veins of design theory. At stake is a growing marginalization of the design professions from the great task of envisioning urban futures. What are the alternatives for practitioners today? What are the rules of engagement? And how do we, as scholars, begin to rigorously define our territory of operation and inquiry in the market context—an increasingly pixelized landscape of competing interests?

The criterion for the selection of material in this volume was that it should deal with the aforementioned issues of privatization, competition, or individualism. The resulting selection of material can be loosely grouped into the traditional categories of historical analysis, built work, project, or interview. We asked ourselves and our contributors: How are the design professions engaging the forces that shape our cities today, and how can we understand these forces in physical design terms? We discovered three primary methods of engagement in the selected responses: (1) proposals for extreme autonomy—total privatization with no public component; (2) design entrepreneurialism—engaging market forces and bridging the gap between design and development; and (3) academic research—observing and documenting transitional economies or historic shifts relevant to the theme of privatization.

We are certain that this collection is only the tip of the iceberg, but in our estimation the following contributors have made an excellent start on what we hope is a growing dialogue.

The opening up of a competitive global marketplace with no international gold standard had significant implications for American cities. Businesses took advantage of the value discrepancy of the dollar between the developing and developed world. Companies were stripped of their national insulation of regulations and tariffs and exposed fully to global competitors. American companies, previously saturated with highly paid union workers and occupying valuable (and highly taxed) central city land, now looked to cheaper labor and cheaper land in order to speculate and better compete, moving to the periphery or abroad. This came at great cost to municipalities, whose losses went far beyond simple commercial tax revenue and employment base. In cases where the lost industry was in the city's basic sector, a multiplier effect kicked in. This alone was devastating for urban governance, but it was only the first blow.

Ronald Reagan and Margaret Thatcher were both proponents of the economic vision of Friedrich Hayek *(The Road to Serfdom)*, father of free market ideology. The Keynesian economics of social welfare, long assumed to be unquestionable, were fated to become history.

The losses of $6.6 billion occurred through the process of consolidating the existing federal direct investment in the form of 59 categorical grants into a new system of 9 block grants to be administered by the state—and these grants were to be competitive. A city could not assume that itwould receive money just because it needed it. Overall cuts to social programs and urban development reached into the tens of billions by the mid 1980s.

Business Improvement Districts, (also called Special Improvement Districts) were invented in Canada in the 1960s, but exploded in the U.S. in the 80's and 90's, with over half of the states in the U.S. passing enabling legislation. BIDs adopt traditionally public responsibilities such as waste management, security, and physical improvements to public space, and collect "taxes" from those properties in the established district in order to finance the operation. Effectively, the BID is a privatized and autonomous mini-government within the greater municipality.

Under the Depression-era Housing Act of 1937, the United States saw (1) the introduction of federal mortgaging programs through the creation of the Federal Housing Administration, and (2) the introduction of a social safety net through investment in public housing. In the 1937 legislation, federal investment was allocated to local housing authorities to physically construct social housing for the first time in American history. Federal physical investment did not end there. The post-war Housing Act of 1949 generated even greater means for federal intervention in the physical landscape of cities by ushering in the urban renewal era. The Act created the Urban Redevelopment Agency and authorized it to subsidize 75% of local slum clearance costs to facilitate urban renewal in cases where the local government determined an area was "blighted." The federal government thereby funded and managed local slum clearance and renewal projects at a local scale. Federal-to-local investment initiatives for the physical environment of cities became more subsidy-oriented and categorical (values-based) in the latter half of the 1960s, often in support of environmental planning. The creation of the Department of Housing and Urban Development (HUD) in 1965 stands out as the last significant effort of the federal government to empower an agent of physical investment. HUD was created as a Cabinet-level department comprised of several formerly independent agencies: the Housing and Home Finance Agency (HHFA), the Federal Housing Administration, the Federal National Mortgage Association, the Public Housing Administration, the Urban Renewal Administration, and the Community Facilities Administration. The federal government took an interest in subsidizing activities relevant to goals for the physical environment in two more significant Acts in the decade: (1) the creation of the

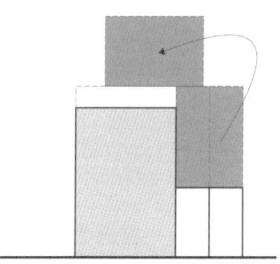

air rights transfer

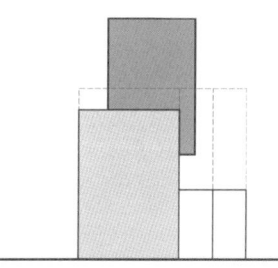

new buildable volume

3. The volume of the transferable development rights purchased by SHoP is clearly visible as a component of their design for Porter House. The project's financial strategy becomes present as architecture.

Model Cities Program in the Demonstration Cities and Metropolitan Development Act of 1966 to support coordinated metropolitan planning for open space, water, sewerage, mass transit, and the development of new communities, and (2) the creation of a Community Development Corporation in the Housing and Urban Development Act of 1970 to support "new town" formation by guaranteeing bonds for land acquisition and development. Predictably, Reagan launched an attack on the Department of Housing and Urban Development in the early 1980s and generated a simultaneous movement to introduce federal incentive measures rather than physical investment in cities (1982 Enterprise Zone Act, brought to Congress by Reagan). He pushed for further dephysicalization by forwarding the 1985 introduction of Section 8 vouchers to the management of affordable housing.

Notes

[1] *The opening up of a competetive global marketplace with no international gold standard had significant implications for American cities. Businesses took advantage of the value discrepancy of the dollar between the developing and developed world. Companies were stripped of their national insulation of regulations and tariffs and exposed fully to global competitors. American companies, previously saturated with highly paid union workers and occupying valuable (and highly taxed) central city land, now looked to cheaper labor and cheaper land in order to speculate and better compete, moving to the periphery or abroad. This came at great cost to municipalities, whose losses*

went far beyond simple commercial tax revenue and employment base. In cases where the lost industry was in the city's basic sector, a multiplier effect kicked in. This alone was devastating for urban governance, but it was only the first blow.

[2] Ronald Reagan and Margaret Thatcher were both proponents of the economic vision of Friedrich Hayek (The Road to Serfdom), father of free market ideology. The Keynesian economics of social welfare, long assumed unquestionable, were fated to become history.

[3] The losses of $6.6 billion occurred through the process of consolidating the existing federal direct investment in the form of 59 categorical grants into a new system of 9 block grants to be administered by the state—and these grants were to be competitive. A city could not assume that they would receive money just because they needed it. Overall cuts to social programs and urban development reached into the tens of billions by the mid 1980s.

[4] Business Improvement Districts (also called Special Improvement Districts) were invented in Canada in the 1960s, but exploded in the U.S. in the 80s and 90s, with over half of the states in the U.S. passing enabling legislation. BIDs adopt traditionally public responsibilities such as waste management, security, and physical improvements to public space, and collect "taxes" from those properties in the established district in order to finance the operation. Effectively, the BID is a privatized and autonomous mini-government within the greater municipality.

[5] Under the Depression-era Housing Act of 1937, the United States saw (1) the introduction of federal mortgaging programs through the creation of the Federal Housing Administration, and (2) the introduction of a social safety net through investment in public housing. In the 1937 legislation, federal investment was allocated to local housing authorities to physically construct social housing for the first time in American history. Federal physical investment did not end there. The post-war Housing Act of 1949 generated even greater means for federal intervention in the physical landscape of cities by ushering in the urban renewal era. The Act created the Urban Redevelopment Agency and authorized it to subsidize 75% of local slum clearance costs to facilitate urban renewal in cases where the local government determined an area was "blighted." The federal government thereby funded and managed local slum clearance and renewal projects at a local scale. Federal-to-local investment initiatives for the physical environment of cities became more subsidy-oriented and categorical (values-based) in the latter half of the 1960s, often in support of environmental planning. The creation of the Department of Housing and Urban Development (HUD) in 1965 stands out as the last significant effort of the federal government to empower an agent of physical investment. HUD was created as a Cabinet-level department comprised of several formerly independent agencies: the Housing and Home Finance Agency (HHFA), the Federal Housing Administration, the Federal National Mortgage Association, the Public Housing Administration, the Urban Renewal Administration, and the Community Facilities Administration. The federal government took an interest in subsidizing activities relevant to goals for the physical environment in two more significant Acts in the decade: (1) the creation of the Model Cities Program in the Demonstration Cities and Metropolitan Development Act of 1966 to support coordinated metropolitan planning for open space, water, sewerage, mass transit, and the development of new communities, and (2) the creation of a Community Development Corporation in the Housing and Urban Development Act of 1970 to support "new town" formation by guaranteeing bonds for land acquisition and development. Predictably, Reagan launched an attack on the Department of Housing and Urban Development in the early 1980s and generated a simultaneous movement to introduce federal incentive measures rather than physical investment in cities (1982 Enterprize Zone Act, brought to Congress by Reagan). He pushed for further dephysicalization by forwarding the 1985 introduction of Section 8 vouchers to the management of affordable housing.

[6] Warren, Charles, ed., Urban Policy in a Changing Federal System: Proceedings of a Symposium, "Cities in the New Federalism" by Robert C. Wood and Beverly Klimkowsky, page 228-253, The National Academies Press. This report can be viewed online at http://www.nap.edu/openbook/

[7] Taxation on land value was considered to be a reasonable way for cities to generate revenue, as well as an incentive to develop property to its highest and best use in order to not pay a high tax on a non-cash-flow property. U of CA economist Mason Gaffney published an argument in 1982 asserting that the shift of taxation off of wages and capital improvements and on to assessed property values would "so change the arithmetic of property ownership that virtually no government assistance would be required for urban renewal." Perhaps he would have been right if residents hadn't been so quick to vote tax caps into law—he inability of cities to easily raise taxes made the revenue gap nearly impossible to overcome.

[8] Although invented in the 1960s in Canada, enabling legislation for BIDs at the state level only exploded later—in the 1980s and 90s—in the United States.

[9] WILMA's primary competitors for projects in Benelux include ING Real Estate (Dutch real estate development arm of ING Bank), Heymans (Dutch contracting company with a development arm), Vinci (French contracting company with a development arm), Bernheim Real Estate (Dutch-Belgian development arm of Fortis Bank), KBC Real Estate (development arm of KBC Bank, and Euro Immostart (development arm of the Belgian railway).

Kjersti Monson (MUP, MLA Harvard University) lives and works in Shanghai, PRC. She and Duval are coauthors of Moody Street (forthcoming), a case study of a successful suburban downtown revitalization project in Waltham, MA. Monson recently completed a Fulbright fellowship at K. U. Leuven, looking at the emergence of large-scale public and private development projects in Belgium. Currently she is developing a planning and urban design company which will utilize strategies for private development projects with public interest components. The initial project site is in suburban Shanghai. She can be reached at kmonson@post.harvard.edu.

Alex Duval is an architect and real estate developer living and working in Shanghai, PRC. He received the Master in Architecture from Harvard University. He is a Research Associate of the Real Estate Academic Initiative at Harvard. Duval has worked for Preston Scott Cohen Architect and Nasser Nakib Architect. He and Monson are coauthors of Moody Street (forthcoming), a case study of a successful suburban downtown revitalization project in Waltham, MA. Duval helped to contribute research and writing for the second edition of Professional Real Estate Development: The Urban Land Institute Guide to the Business authored by Richard B. Peiser. Prior to his career in architecture and development Alex served as an Americorps VISTA Volunteer working with the homeless population of New York City. He can be reached at aduval@post.harvard.edu

DUARTE, Gabriel /
CONTRERAS, Javier /
CABALLERO, Roberto C.

It's Not Just Grass!

Subverting Legal Planning and the Reinvention of the Dutch Process-Landscape Agenda 2000 & The C2751

Rural areas in the European Union's territory are undergoing a critical shift in their fundamental functions, wherein agriculture is no longer playing a decisive role as part of the primary economic sector. Their weight in national economies and job markets is drastically decreasing, while their importance in preserving the landscape and cultural heritage, and as active bodies in national metropolitan development is increasing. A major share of EU rural regions are bound to become less productive entities, gradually turning into broader influential contexts, breaking up even more the already decaying binomial of town-and-country. The social and cultural profiles of numerous rural areas, especially of those nearby or within metropolitan regions, are entering a suburbanization process and starting to accommodate sprawl from surrounding cities.

These shifting conditions have forced the EU Common Agricultural Policy (CAP) to undertake radical changes in its directives regarding rural development, as the viability of these areas cannot depend on agriculture alone anymore. Over recent years, the EU has been turning its criteria for financing from supports to production achievements, which was already causing a certain level of unrest in the world agricultural market, towards the producers' income directly. In 1999, the CAP changed several of its agreements to reinforce investments in supporting multi-disciplinary approaches towards rural environments, and to equalize agricultural competition within the EU. This reform became known as Agenda 2000, and set the goals for the EU's rural development from 2000 to 2006 by unifying the new development measures in a single framework, and forwarding decision-making responsibilities to the Member States, providing them with unprecedented flexibility.

1. Less Favored Areas and Areas Subject to Environmental Constraints

Under the Agenda 2000, Member States were offered a sort of menu with 22 measures they could choose from to compose their own initiatives, which included subsidies to help change their rural and agricultural profiles in order to meet the unified goals previously set. Among these measures are: financing options for programes to encourage early rural retirement; shifts in land use and agricultural production; and rural landscape management and maintenance. These measures aimed at reshaping the social, economic, cultural and ecological profiles of the EU's rural environments. Through this process, on September 2000, the Netherlands approved the so-called Decision C2751, which set their priority actions, being strongly based on an Agenda 2000 measure for "less favored areas and areas subject to environmental constraints" (LFA). Such a definition could be assigned to areas affected by environmental restrictions related to the maintenance and protection of threatened landscapes. And this could not be more fortunate for the Netherlands, whose artificially built landscape is crucial for keeping the increasing water-level of the North Sea and of several rivers isolated from the lower parts of the country. The landscape's morphology is actively present in Dutch everyday life as part of an edge-relationship

1. *The rural is more than agriculture today.*

of potential flooding catastrophes. Not coincidentally, agriculture is the background for this protective and dangerous mechanism, stabilizing the soil and using excessive water for irrigation. Through the LFA, the Netherlands was entitled to receive compensatory investments, then, becoming embedded with concrete potentials to change the ways its ambiguous landscape evolves and maintains itself.

The C2751 purposefully allocated most of its budget (74%) to actions that prioritized the conservation of the landscape and water systems through agri-environmental measures. By using the term "agri-environmental," the C2751 denotes a crucial ambiguity in the EU's new rural policies: within the EU's legal framework, the concepts of rural and landscape are barely distinguished. They are often used as synonyms, consequently superimposing political interests and professional domains in this process—namely, landscape planning and design, and agricultural sciences. Nevertheless, should these domains be distinguishable at all in an EU of fast growing urbanization? Indeed, specifically in the Dutch situation, such separation is becoming less and less necessary.

Dutch agriculture is unsustainable without substantial national subsidies. Even though it has kept up good performance for the last decades, it is progressively becoming a burden and reason for complaint from fellow EU countries. Furthermore, although most unlikely, the intensive nature of Dutch agriculture is one of the country's main sources of environmental damage. The current tendency is to gradually decrease agricultural areas in the Southern, densely urbanized part of the country—known as Randstad—and to create specialized clusters of agricultural production in the Northern provinces of Friesland and Flevoland. This process will result in the generation of huge open areas within the Randstad, which, abandoned by their primary functions, will form conglomerates of highly geometrized meadows, bushes, and grass. The future of these areas mingles with the undefined state of rural, agricultural and landscape planning policies in both the Netherlands and the EU. What should be made of them?

2. Subvertion Is Not Manipulation

"If the delinquent exists only by displacing itself, if its specific mark is to live not on the margins but in the interstices of the codes that it undoes and displaces, if it is characterized by the privilege of the tour over the state, then the story is delinquent."—Michel de Certeau

This work was not about ways to disguisedly overlook legal barriers, but about reassessing their fundamental attributes in order to regain a certain level of domination over the design tools available in specific moments to architects and planners, and enable critical actions, even while being leashed by policies and regulations. In 2003, the planning authority of the Province of Zuid Holland invited the Delft University of Technology's Urbanism Department to develop a series of perspectives for the development of the Rijnland region, located along the homonymous Rijn river, which has the city of Leiden as its main urban cluster. Rijnland borders the so-called "Green Heart" of the Randstad, a low-density piece of land mostly regarded as rural and surrounded by the circular conurbation of Amsterdam, Utrecht, Den Haag and Rotterdam [2]. The Green Heart, and Rijnland consequently, are in the center of the discussions about rural and metropolitan development in the Netherlands, and their future is thoroughly linked to those envisioned by Agenda 2000 and the C2751.

This direct relationship triggered our design research as a means to explore alternative ways to subvert previous traditional notions of the relationship between the binomials of legislation/policies and planning/design, which we normally see as mono-dimensional, with one setting constraints for the other's actions. What would happen if legislation suddenly started to be literally treated as a design tool instead of its regulator? What if we could devise a new strategy to counter-balance private, collective and governmental interests for the dynamic development of the new Dutch metropolitan landscape?

We believed that the answer to these questions lay not in finding ways to sneak through legal breaches, but in understanding in depth its ambiguous nature, and to use it as the very basis of our argumentations and justification sources. It was a way to fight legal oppressions with the same measures that established them, therefore increasing the number of actual financing mechanisms available to us. We used the EU and the Netherlands' own inputs in financing tools and priorities to subvert their meanings, as opposed to using our own new design arguments in search for cohesion with the existing policies, or to change them. It was a matter of overtaking the legislator's vocabulary as our own, taking critical steps towards the policies' presets using its own tools. For that, we built a set of direct correlations between our design mechanisms and specific points of the policies, especially those set by the C2751. The design investigation simulated a series of plausible futures built-up through the policies' own restrictions, and proposed an alternative development plan for Rijnland's rural/green areas in order to rethink the modus operandi of current landscape design in the EU.

3. Rijnland, Terrain Vague

"The power of a landscape does not derive from the fact that it offers itself as a spectacle, but rather from the fact that, as mirror and mirage, it presents any susceptible viewer with an image at once true and false of a creative capacity which the subject (or Ego) is able, during a moment of marvellous self-deception, to claim as his own. A landscape also has the seductive power of all pictures, and this is especially true of an urban landscape."
—Henri Lefebvre

The relationship between the Dutch and their country's landscape is surrounded by a dichotomy between the idea of loss and re-invention. There is a growing awareness and concern about the transformation of the country's current natural and rural landscapes, even though they were the results of transformation processes as well. The country is too small and too densely inhabited to provide a clear distinction between the urban and the rural, and one cannot avoid the ubiquitous presence of man and the city. In many parts of the Randstad, the ex-

2. How to design across political boundaries?

pansion of its cities is taking over rural land to build new suburbs. Rural individualism provides nothing more than a pleasant attraction to city dwellers wiling to move away from the major urban centres, as a staged bucolism. Not even specific restrictions and guidelines to avoid urbanization within the Green Heart are able to retard this process. The only green areas to survive will be those purposefully designed and planned to do so.

Rijnland is not a case apart in this trend. Its share of the Green Heart is a vague terrain rather centrally positioned within the Randstad, being crossed by several national and local highways, and is defenseless against real-estate speculation. Although the national infrastructure connects Rijnland as a whole to the Delta Metropolis quite efficiently, the connectivity between and towards its rural/green areas is very poor. Moreover, the formerly agricultural/rural lands are essentially privately owned, and their administration is under the responsibility of a myriad of micro municipalities with distinct agendas. Consequently, large-scale consistent public planning and design actions, with which the Dutch are quite familiar, are fairly "leashed" while attempting to effectively intervene in this landscape. It is spatially open, but politically and economically closed. Not even its cultural relevance encourages a closer interest of the general public, who sees it as an important, but distant participant of their national daily life.

The Dutch landscape has an accumulative property of being at the same time in a constant process of transformation while simultaneously retaining history as scars of past attributes and cultures. It simultaneously resets and exhibits its shifting origins, developing an "archaeological dimension", in the words of Adriaan Geuze. It took just a quick survey of the area to discover that, if one traces an imaginary circle with a radius of 5.0Km from the center of Rijnland's rural/green area, a spot with the highest density of Dutch national landscape icons in the country, such as: windmills, lowlands, bulbs, are open green spaces will appear (image F), all within a range of 10 to 40 minutes away from the Delta Metropolis' main urban areas. This final discovery set off the development system we needed to combine the site-specific needs of Rijnland with the menu of options presented by the Agenda 2000 and the C2751–create an enclave of rural entertainment and preservation, diversifying territorial and social functions through the establishment of a large-scale park with both local and metropolitan reaches, the Rijnland Metropolitan Park (MetPark).

4. THE MetPARK

Common sense tells us that, while dealing with such a multitude of interests and action guidelines, diversified approaches must be used, with specific solutions and arguments towards each situation. However we actually approached this a different way. As it would be impossible to centralize the decisions regarding the MetPark creation process, and its action base would be completely fragmentary, it was more important not to establish individual approaches regarding the different institutions and stakeholders involved, but to devise a common structure for negotiation, debate and administration. In developing this common structure the biggest problem was not to find better ways to use the array of action set forth by the C2751, but how to transform these priorities into actual and palpable proposals, bridging the gap between governmental intentions and real life. The official priorities, as described below, set a list of pre-defined objectives that, in principle, were not elaborated in a way that they could super-impose and complement each other. The design mechanisms we created had to acknowledge this extreme stratification of the subject, namely the Dutch rural landscape, which separated the priorities into distinct and easily identifiable items. The new tools to be used by the several public and private authorities involved in the project had to be the same. Be they design or planning elements, the language spoken had to be the same; otherwise, the effort to bring together a series of local potentials into a coherent transformation plan would become dull and useless. In order to provide this coherent basis for negotiation and decision-making, we created a special planning and design vocabulary to directly link the C2751 with the desired effects for the MetPark. Aligned vocabularies were also necessary to more efficiently create links with the priorities set by the C2751, and to amplify the area's eligibility for further financing.

Priority 1: Developing sustainable agriculture
Promoting innovation, enabling farmers and growers to respond to market opportunities such as non-food crops and new food products using new agricultural methods, processing and marketing techniques. Providing training and services to farmers to aid diversification and business ventures that benefit society. Support for less favored areas through nature conservation. Agri-environmental measures, including organic farming.

Priority 2: Improving the quality of nature and the landscape
Using agri-environmental measures to conserve nature and landscapes, and introducing a network of protection areas. Increasing planting to improve land, for example along roads and watercourses. Re-parcelling of land to achieve environmental benefits. Promoting reforestation of agricultural land, both temporary and permanent, and the sustainable management of forests.

Priority 3: Sustainable water management
Subsidising projects to combat water depletion and optimize water levels for agriculture and nature. Improving infrastructures for water supply and drainage and supporting measures to recover water, such as dams and sills. Optimizing the sewer system to improve the quality of surface water.

Priority 4: Economic diversification
Encouraging new rural employment by diversifying activities within farming and expanding opportunities in other sectors.

Priority 5: Promoting tourism and recreation
Improving the infrastructure and amenities for rural tourism and recreational areas, such as footpaths, cycle paths, parking facilities, information boards and start-up aid for new services. Encouraging farm tourism and activities linked to cultural heritage and crafts.

Priority 6: Improving the quality of rural life
Improving the provision of and access to public services, particularly health care and public transport. Renovating historical buildings and features, such as market places and harbors. Developing rural infrastructure, including the adapting of roads and the improvement of road safety.

The core of this vocabulary was composed by three basic design mechanisms (Exo-Structures, Water+Housing and Space Boosters), which super-imposed several independent priorities into single actions, amplifying the area's eligibility for further financing and providing flexible solutions to tackle different solicitations within the project area, in distinct implementation stages and in adverse budgetary situations. These mechanisms represented organized but fragmented design solutions, which were organized to critically respond to different specific requests formulated by the C2751 at the same time. They set up concrete morphological propositions to the actions described in the C2751, creating hybrid results from mating its several priorities. These mechanisms group propositions to challenges in different territorial scales, that require different implementation periods and sources of funding. The hybridization of different priorities would also enable the collection of funding from different sources to achieve a single goal. The criteria for setting up these groups also highlights methods for their interrelations, representing different ways to complement and build favorable situations for each other.

Dead Investments
It is paramount to this p\ontinuous as possible. To attain an optimum situation, the implementation techniques of these mechanisms obey a very simple logic, in which there is always an initial public risk-investment (to which we refer as dead investments) to attract private interests to the area. Each dead investment phase only takes place when the possibilities of an already initiated cycle completely wears out.

Mediating Failure
Even though the best was made to ensure a continuity of the implementation cycles, there are no guarantees that the same pace will remain throughout the whole implementation process of the MetPARK, and the concept of dead investments are closely tied to this concern. By acknowledging eventual errors, the use of the dead investments must be maximized in order to make the most out of scarcity, while providing basic conditions for the existence of the MetPark. Another facet of the design mechanisms is that they are able to compose investments in different magnitudes, minimizing losses caused by abrupt or severe lacks of funds through an implementation dependent on sequential successes. Each implementation sub-phase is linked to the termination of a previous one to continue, as means to first guarantee a steady realization before taking a step further and introducing risk to the process again.

Exo-Structures (Priorities 5 & 6)
The current mobility network in the MetPark area has incomplete internal connections and insufficient links with the national highway system, causing a loss in potential users and investors for the area. Current roads and bike paths form dead-end circuits, creating maze situations where visitors and residents need to constantly avoid becoming trapped. Mostly composed by dead investment actions, these mechanisms intend to complete the

3. THE MetPARK, site plan

mobility network of the area by building new walking, biking and vehicular paths, as well as parking facilities. The remaining mechanisms cannot be implemented without the support of access structures.

Water + Housing (Priorities 3 & 4)
According to studies done by the Dutch Ministry of Transportation and Water Management, to avoid overloads to Rijnland's water system, its water surface area must be increased by 13% in the next 50 years. This increase forces the creation of new water structures in the rural areas, as Rijnland's cities cannot to contain enough extra room in their existing water system. However, new water structures alone are unable to enhance the use of the area, and would remain unseen as many other basic infrastructural works. For that, we decided to extend the programmatic scope of the new water and combine it with the development of new low-density residential areas. This extension is actually envisioning broader fittings with other C2751 priorities, which envision the creation of multiple economical, social and cultural possibilities within rural areas, and the creation of different sources of revenues for the project.

Space Boosters (Priorities 1, 2, 4 & 5)
This mechanism is the real flexibility cornerstone of the MetPARK, by concurrently overlapping the largest number of C2751 priorities. The Space Boosters are a sort of landscape furniture that can provide added activities and support to different regions inside the MetPark, each falling under different implementation and financing criteria. The idea behind the Space Boosters is to provide the material means for cooperation between private land owners/former farmers and our aim of wide-opening the Rijnland landscape for public use. To operate this mechanism, the implementation of Space Boosters in private properties was directly connected to the subsidizing schemes of the Agenda 2000, especially those related to landscape maintenance according to the LFA directives (Less Favored Area / Area Subject to Environmental Constraints).

The different sorts of Boosters were designed in a way that they could take advantage of the extremely parcelled and controlled surface of the Netherlands, and of specific situations within the area. Dimensioned to occupy a parcel unit at a time, they were aimed at creating a range of activities within that parcel, boosting existing activities or profiting from a differentiated topographic set. The choice to use the existing grid of the territory was made to increase the connection between the new MetPARK and the existing landscape as complementary entities. Their design used both industrially built parts and materials from the sites where they were to be implemented. This feature created a range of unique possibilities out of general modulated bodies, transforming the industrialized parts into specific and participating players in landscape dynamics and use.

Whenever a Space Booster was located in a publicly owned area, it could be turned into a self-supporting structure, by offering private sponsoring possibilities through corporate advertising. While, in private properties, whenever residents willed to house a Space Booster in their lots, they would be further entitled to receive subsidies for keeping it, or other advantages from programes such as the Early Agricultural Retirement Programe. The Boosters were made to provide the means to

4. A park with a façade? Located close to the highway, the plots will go on being for traditional activities, but also become the shop-window of the Rijnland MetPark towards the highway. Artificial boosters faking nature will configure the façade of the park and will provide the opportunity for advertising to the enterprises linked to the park.

multiply uses in landscape and enable some social and economical adaptations, which would be extremely hard and time-consuming to achieve through ordinary legal means.

5. Staged Pragmatisms

"Social delinquency consists in taking the story literally, in making it the principle of physical existence where a society no longer offers to subjects or groups symbolic outlets and expectations of spaces, where there is no longer any alternative to disciplinary falling-into-line or illegal drifting away, that it, one form or another of prison and wandering outside the pale."
—Michel de Certeau

As an exercise on how landscape and urban design can deal with restrictive conditions, this investigation strived to subvert the disguised vertical organization of such processes not by implying a conscious ignorance of the rules (it would be too naïve), but by creating a critical disobedience veiled by the rules themselves. Current planning practices believe in an algorithm for right choices. Be it in documented paradigms of urban laws and rules, or in the names planners create to render visible their fantasies. What we did was nothing more than falling into the same principles laws and guidelines are based on, those of implicit impossibilities of embracing the totality of a problematic (the future of EU's rural areas in this case) simplified by systems of orderings. It surely was not our intention to imply that orderings and plans are unnecessary (in anarchical terms). Indeed, we experimented with subversions of an imposed order through getting to know it literally, extracting our means to subvert establishments by using their own proposed tools.

The current pace of urbanization in the EU, especially in the Netherlands, and, consequently, the creation of new challenges and hybrid environments is overcoming the speed of the policy-makers. By the time policies and priorities are set and legally approved; their life-span before expiring as effective tools is getting shorter and shorter. Both unconsciously and inadvertently, urban and landscape designers become so tied to an imposed and excessively methodological system that they become unable to see real potentials and problems involved in a certain situation, and keep on being unable to change the very source of this problem. Unquestionably, governmental plans and policies, which directly influence the work of designers, are still done in a top-down way, and opposing responses to them are possible, but made as difficult as possible by all bureaucratic means available. Our reaction to this situation was not a dreamful opposition to the status-quo of planning in the EU, aiming at saving it by proposing an ideal horizontal perspective,

5. Alongside the paths of the park, there will be facilities for sports and special playgrounds for children. As there are already people living in the proposed park area, these boosters will be situated close to their villages, so that they can be enjoyed not only by the visitors of the park, but also by its inhabitants.

but to devise a way to re-insert a bottom-up, effective input in government planning. In our experimental case we re-combined and played with the possibilities offered to reach a desired effect, which we constructed from the specific needs and potentials of the Rijnland region. Furthermore, this work served to demonstrate that the creation of flexible structures and design tools have the ability to bend extremely generalizing and compartmentalized objectives. More importantly, it showed that governmental tools can and should be adapted and subverted to serve designers, not the other way around.

References

> Lefebvre, Henri; Nicholson-Smith, Donald (translation). The Production of Space. London: Blackwell Publishing, 1991
> Certeau, Michel de. Practice of Everyday Life. Berkeley: University of California Press, 1988
> Okasha, Samir. Philosophy of Science: A Very Short Introduction. Oxford: Oxford University Press, 2002
> European Commission—Agriculture Directorate General. Rural Development in the European Union. Luxembourg: Office for Official Publications of the European Communities, 2003
> European Commission—Agriculture Directorate General. Overview of the Implementation of Rural Development Policy 2000-2006. Luxembourg: Office for Official Publications of the European Communities, 2003
> European Commission—Agriculture Directorate General. Rural Development Programmes 2000-2006—Country Profile: the Netherlands. Luxembourg: Office for Official Publications of the European Communities, 2003
> Ministerie van Landbouw, Natuur en Voedselkwaliteit (LNV). The Netherlands: Horizontal Programme; Rural Development Programme for the Netherlands 2000-2006; Decision no. C(2000)2751; Date of Final Approval: 28.09.2000. Utrecht: National Coordination Office for Rural Development Planning, 2000. Article 33 of Council Regulation (EC) no. 1257/1999.
> Certeau, Michel de. The Practice of Everyday Life. Berkeley: University of California Press, 1988, p. 130.
> The Province of Zuid Holland is basically composed by the urban agglomerations of Den Haag, Rotterdam and Leiden.
> Lefebvre, Henri; Nicholson-Smith, Donald (translation). The Production of Space. London: Blackwell Publishing, 1991, p. 189.
> Jan Dirk Peereboom Voller. Het Hollands Landschap als Kunstwerk, in Forum 37/1, November, 1993.
> Ministerie van Landbouw, Natuur en Voedselkwaliteit (LNV). The Netherlands: Horizontal Programme; Rural Development Programme for the Netherlands 2000-2006; Decision no. C(2000)2751; Date of Final Approval: 28.09.2000. Utrecht: National Coordination Office for Rural Development Planning, 2000.
> Certeau, Michel de. Practice of Everyday Life. Berkeley: University of California Press, 1988, p. 130.
> Thomas Kuhn, in Okasha, Samir. Philosophy of Science: A Very Short Introduction. Oxford: Oxford University Press, 2002, p. 91.

Gabriel Duarte, DipArch, MSc, was born in Niterói (Brazil), and graduated as an architect and urban designer from the Federal University of Rio de Janeiro, where he held design teaching positions in the 2003 academic year prior to moving to the Netherlands with a fellowship from the Dutch Ministry of Foreign Affairs to engage on research at the Department of Urbanism of the Delft University of Technology, in the SpaceLab team. Apart from working in research and teaching, he established a small office in Rio, which is developing several urban design proposals for the City Government of Rio, and has received numerous awards, such as the Wolf Tochtermann Prize of the International Union of Architects, and the Takashi Inuye Award, from the International Federation for Housing and Planning.

Javier Fernanadez, Arch, was born in Granada (Spain), and studied architecture at ETSAM (Superior Technical School of Architecture of Madrid). Fernanadez spent a year in the Department of Urbanism of the Delft University of Technology with a research scholarship from the European Union. Working as an independent architect in both Madrid and Granada, he has already collaborated with the offices of Mansilla and Tuñón, and with eNRdos Arquitectos.

Roberto Carlos Garcia, Arch, was born in Salamanca (Spain), and studied architecture at ETSAM (Superior Technical School of Architecture of Madrid). Having spent a year in the Department of Urbanism of the Delft University of Technology with a research scholarship from the European Union, he participated in the research and design proposal for the Rijnland Metropolitan Park. His past professional activities include a collaboration with the office of Henk Döll, in Rotterdam, after which he returned to Madrid to work as a freelance architect.

HADDAD, Elie

Single-Owner Downtown: Reconstructing Beirut

At the end of a long and devastating civil war (1975–1991), the city center of Beirut became the focus of a reconstruction project, while the surrounding districts were left to the drive of market forces. In an unprecedented move, the government decided to entrust the entire process of the post-war reconstruction in downtown to a private company, Solidere, by a decree that allowed the expropriation and management of all land in the old city center by that company. In essence, the practice of eminent domain became a powerful tool of land assembly, allowing the entire city center to become a single site under the control of a single owner. This action was by itself controversial, and is still faced by contestation from the disaffected real estate owners, who became mere shareholders in a corporation, along with new international investors.

A number of controversial political decisions had preceded and paved the way for the establishment of this corporation, namely the abrupt demolitions of the market district near Martyrs Square in 1982, twelve years before the formal incorporation of Solidere and nine years before the end of the war. Ten years later, in 1992, the second market district comprising the historic Souk Ayyas was razed, beginning another cycle of demolitions that cleared up the old city and opened up its space, to be reconstituted according to a new image projecting a new city, cleansed of all its previous impurities.

The project of the BCD, Beirut Central District, would thus encompass 191 hectares (of which the old city covered 118 hectares, to which were added the areas of the landfill). Solidere determined that 98 hectares would be dedicated to public spaces, 59 hectares to roads, 39 hectares to open space, with the remaining 93 hectares left for development.

The first phase of reconstruction[1], spanning from 1994–2004, consisted of developing the infrastructures, restoring the old core, and initiating new building projects. The second phase (2005-2020) would basically complete Solidere's work in developing the Marina sector with the sea protection wall and the corniche, the rehabilitation of Martyrs square, and the finalization of real estate developments in the new sectors. The expressed goals of this real-estate mega-venture would be to turn Beirut once again into a prime destination, a "favored location for international businesses, financial and other specialized services and institutions, as well as a tourism destination and a prime residential area."

The first master plan produced by Solidere [2] proposed a pseudo Beaux Arts approach of grand axes, cutting through the urban fabric of the traditional city, framed by a hybrid, non-descript architecture. The images marketed in this first proposal suggested the possibility of reclaiming history through a pastiche of forms. Faced by a response of general outrage, the reconstruction company revised its formal strategy and developed a more balanced proposal, which replaced this pastiche vision of the city with a sensible, contextual approach, marketed as a synthesis between the "grand planning" tradition and the Anglo-Saxon contextual tradition of urban design. Yet the project maintained the same area of clearings as in the earlier proposal, with a few exceptions applying to particular landmarks. The second master plan also continued to promote the transformation of the city from a mixed city into a corporate metropolis. The "business-gentrification" of the core would reshape the image of the city.

Beirut would in a sense be the first city to make this transition from collective ownership to corporate ownership. Its architecture would be carefully tailored to project an image of apparent harmony, pretending to synthesize the contradictions of a modern age with the nostalgic demands for the recovery of a lost past. This is nowhere better reflected than in the new Saifi Village, previously a middle and lower class neighborhood of artisans, carpenters, and small retailers, now a secure enclave that appears to be an implant of a Parisian arrondissement, complete with its street furniture.

In retrospect, the reconstruction of the center had a dual effect: on the one hand a great number of historic buildings were restored to their original condition; on the other hand some districts disappeared or irreversibly lost their character, such as Wadi-abu-Jmil and Saifi.

On the positive side, important archaeological sites were uncovered, some of which were safeguarded for future inclusion in the urban plan. This is specifically the case of the old market near Martyrs Square, which was cleared in 1982, revealing the Cardo axis of the Roman city. [3] The historic Souk Ayyas, on the other hand, was demolished in 1992, simply to increase the surface exploitation area. Here, the archaeological finds exposed the foundations of an early Perso-Phoenician settlement, which was swiftly documented and then erased to make room for the new market district project. The demolition of the historic Souk Ayyas, which constituted one of the primary loci of the city's collective memory, was met by widespread condemnation and led the reconstruction company to mitigate this action by proposing an international competition to re-design the souks.

1. Beirut, first phase of reconstruction, 1994–2004

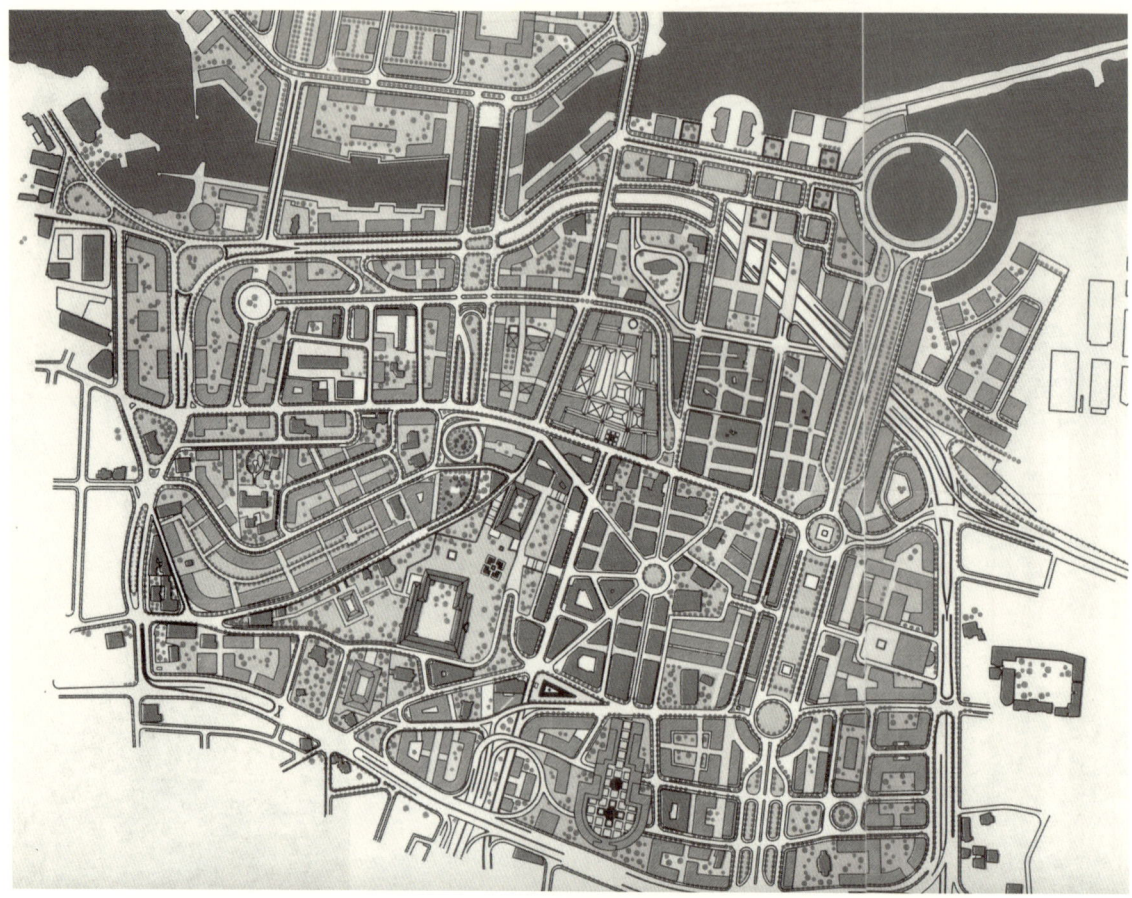

2. Beirut, first master plan produced by Solidere

The Souks Project

The international ideas competition for the Souks constituted the only open competition in the BCD from 1994 to 2004. More than 300 projects were submitted, representing a variety of approaches to the problem of urban reconstruction within a historic city center. The jury did not reach a decision on one winner, declaring a tie between the first three projects, all conservative proposals which failed to arouse general enthusiasm.

Among the more noteworthy entries, which received only mention, figured Aldo Rossi's project, which proposed the resurrection of the old street pattern to allow the city to gradually reconstitute the souks, while inserting a few characteristic Rossian landmarks [4]. Castillo & Gastano's project, in its restrained order, presented a radical approach by its minimalist reinterpretation of the souks as a series of parallel strips. Luciano Semerani proposed a collage of different elements, where the extension of the buildings along the eastern side creates an impermeable wall that seems to turn the souks into an enclave, reinforced by a large, fortress-type building at the southeastern corner. Zaha Hadid's proposal projected a series of sweeping lines translated into horizontal strips running along the north-south axis. Eventually the winning schemes of this ideas-competition were set aside, and the site was parceled among local and international architects, with Rafael Moneo receiving the commission to redesign the major parcel, the central souks [5].

3. From top: Cardo axis of the original Roman city; Perso-Phoenician settlement as found, and after construction

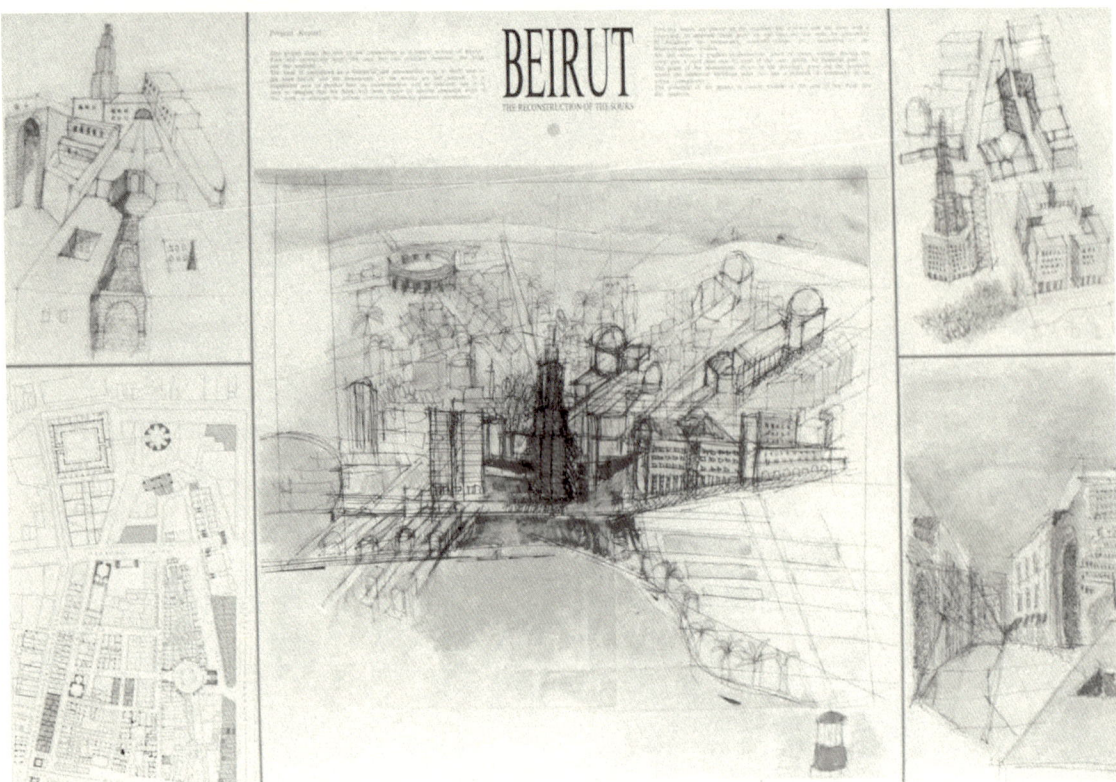

4. Aldo Rossi, entry, international ideas competition for the Souks

5. Rafael Moneo, commission for the central Souks

Architecture today is radically split into two distinct realities: on the one hand a practice which seeks, for better or worse, to cater to the demands of a society of the spectacle, by producing images which captivate the visual senses; on the other hand a reality of unbalanced growth that spreads across the landscape, constituting an aesthetic and environmental disaster.

The signs of an aborted modernity are too obvious. In the context of Beirut, this has manifested itself in a dual aspect: the reconstruction of the center as a corporate enclave on the one hand, and uncontrolled speculation outside the center which drastically transforms the social fabric of historic neighborhoods, leaving only traces of their past. Within this context, gradually emptied of its real sense of urbanity, architecture—in its various eclectic forms—is confined to serving the economic system, most of the time through an uncritical appropriation of forms, from the relics of the past to a reified deconstruction.

Beirut may not be so different in the end from Algiers, Bangkok, or New York City, except in terms of size, climate and geographical location. All cities share the consequences of a world folding into dense, overpopulated urban centers, levelled by the forces of globalization which thrive on these very architectural innovations that appear in retrospect as temporary divertissements from the painful reality. For in the reality of urban blight, the Modernist promise of a new world where decent housing, healthy working conditions, and entertainment spaces provides now only an occasion for nostalgia, which may explain the passion with which architects are re-discovering the appeal of those rationalist projects of the 1920's–30's, even the obsessively hygenic urban proposals of the same period.

Koolhaas is right in turning our attention to this reality driven by economic imperatives, yet this should not be taken as a cause for surrender or a psychedelic flight forward, but rather as an incentive to re-assess the possibilities of another modernist project that attends to the impending urban challenges.

HARRINGTON, Anthony / LEE, Lina

Office Tower Infestation

Enron was one of the world's leading energy, commodities, and financial services companies. At the turn of the millennium, Enron's revenues were $101 billion and the company had recorded $90 a share. One year later the share price dropped to below $1. The new Cesar Pelli Enron Tower in downtown Houston was nearing completion at the beginning of the company's demise. Intel purchased the tower for $102 million at a bankruptcy auction, which amounted to less than half of what it initially cost. The Enron Tower has not only become an icon of the rise and fall of the energy giant, but it has also symbolized the ensuing scandals that erupted nationwide in the business community, contributing to the downturn in the economy.

Events such as the collapse of Enron create a ripple effect that impacts the built environment. Local communities and the spaces they inhabit can rapidly change in the wake of financial disasters such as those epitomized by Enron. On the surface, to counter the enigma attached to the energy giant bankruptcy, Intel began to market to the "Enron Tower" by its street address: "1400 Louisiana." The 26-story, Class A tower remained nearly empty and incomplete until only recently. But as one of the most high-tech buildings in the world, it has maintained great potential in terms of its usability and functionality.

Re-Inhabitation

Cities in the United States are on the verge of a revolution. Already the artist's loft has been co-opted by young professionals in a post white-flight re-urbanization that is increasingly evident. The potential of this type

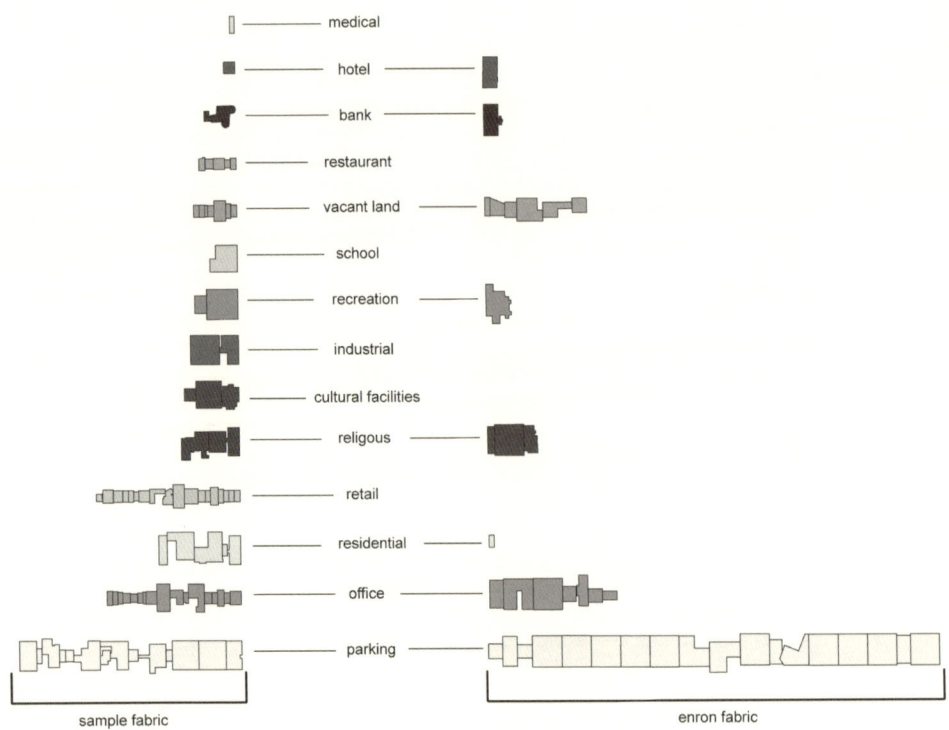
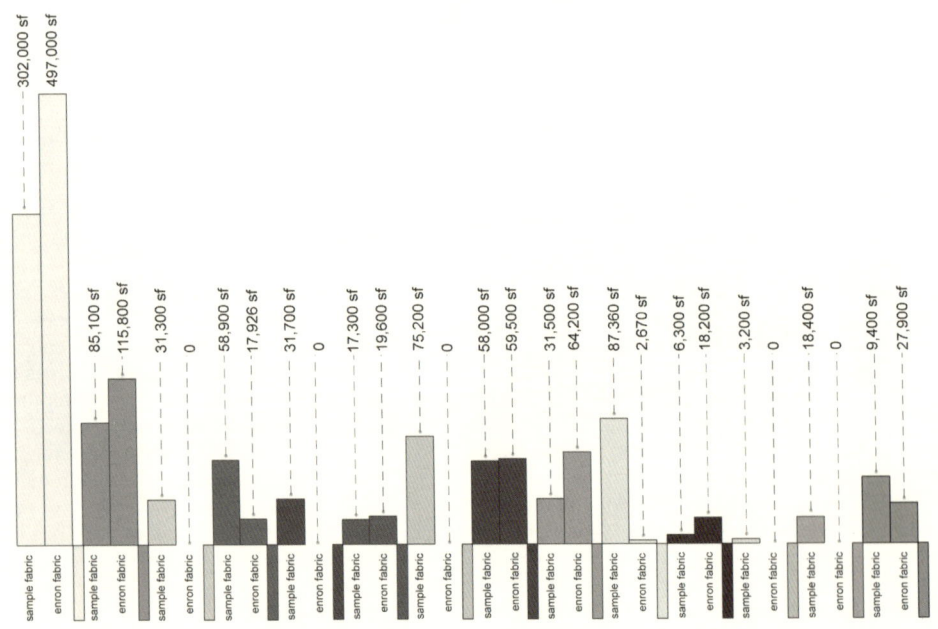

1. Sample fabric by program, Anthony Harrington and Lina Lee

2. Enron Tower brand insertion matrix study, Anthony Harrington and Lina Lee

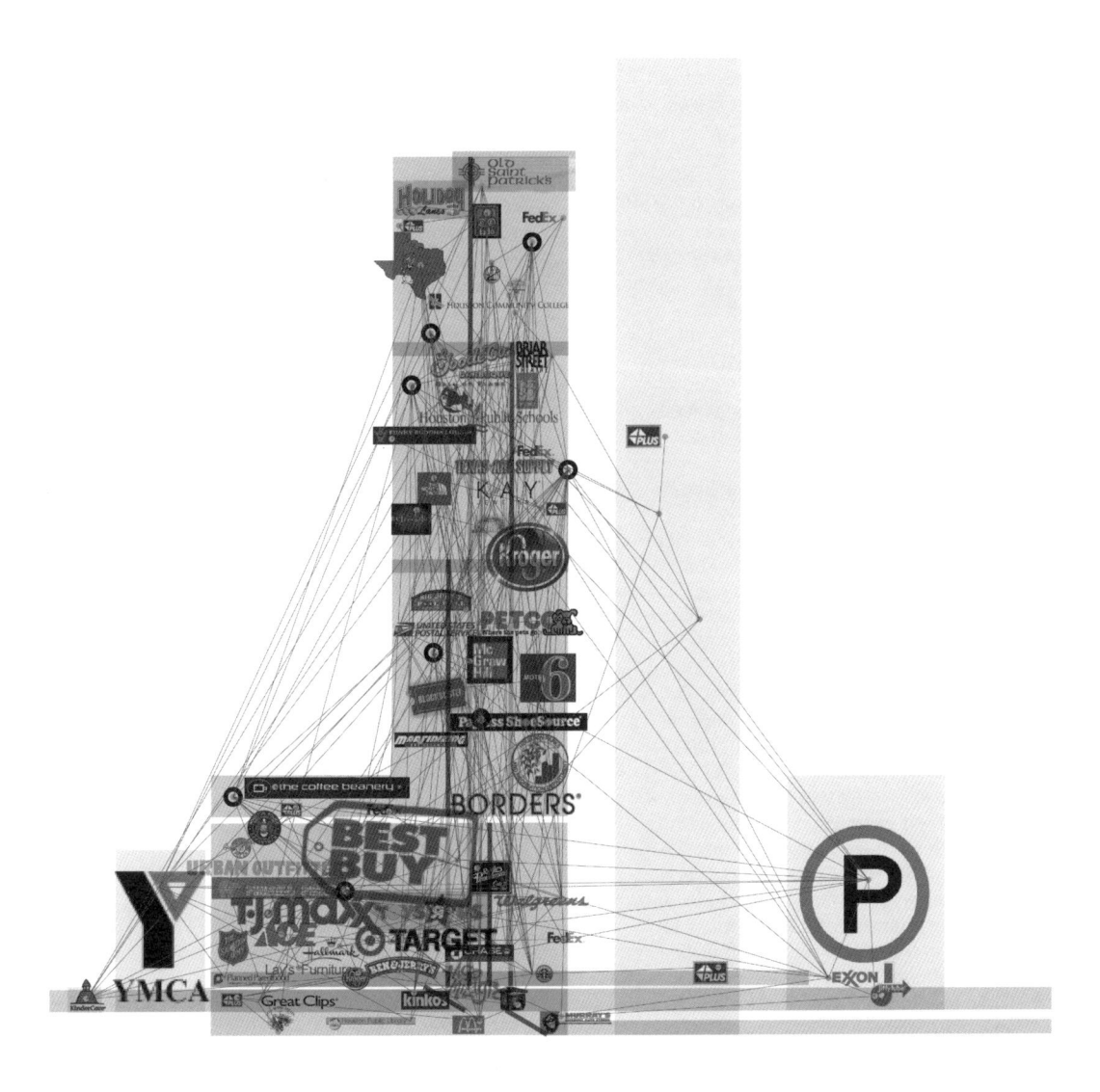

of adaptive re-use project is coming to a close as older brick industrial spaces are maximized. The new possibility for adaptive re-use development is now emerging in the conversion of old office space. New "Class A" office buildings are pushing older "Class B" and "Class C" buildings off the market, as they are no longer desirable to the larger space demands of today's business needs. In a market where office vacancy rates are at an eight-year high, 22% of downtown Houston's Class A office space remains empty. As a response to the growing office vacancy rates coupled with the high demand for housing in downtown Houston, we are proposing an alternate strategy for the vacant office tower: the introduction of a privately owned public network into the formerly single-function Enron Tower.

77002 Artificial Nexus

While Houston is the fourth largest city in the U.S. in terms of population, it is one of the least dense. Our design for the Enron Tower attempts to adapt the already radically privatized logic of Houston's infrastructure and amplify it in order to produce a more livable self-contained community within the tower itself. For example, Houston has an underground tunnel system that operates as a separate physical network and divorces itself from the rest of the city. Privately owned, it contains 6 miles of walkway that connect 55 buildings, 3 hotels, and 15 offices—yet there is no interaction with the street level. 58% of downtown streets are being rebuilt and do not take the tunnel into consideration.

It is evident that there is a physical and social lack of connection throughout downtown. The Central Loop of downtown Houston shares the recently renamed "Minute-Maid Park" and the new "Toyota Center" sports complexes, the Convention Center, and the Theatre District, but little has been developed in long-term housing. Parts of the city work well with a traditional urban model, such as Market Square in Houston. This is not the case a mile south and a few blocks west in zip code 77002, where the Enron campus is located.

It is unrealistic to see 77002 as an urban nexus. Understanding that housing cannot survive without the appropriate civic infrastructure, and observing that the Market Square neighborhood where most loft conversion has taken place on the north side of downtown functions with a successful level of urban activity, we propose to condense a similar mix of the scattered civic amenities and residential apartments within the Enron Tower. By creating a mixed use program, utilizing self-organizing tactics within those uses, and reaching out to the existing infrastructures, we wish to create a dynamic building program capable of a variety of roles as the downtown gradually matures.

Tower Housing Poche

In the effort to create a self sufficient micro-urbanism we realized that it was not the housing that needed to be designed, but rather the public spaces. Within the armature of the tower frame the infill housing would drop into the background and become poche. The tower acts as a vertical district where these extended urban nodes are organized into four zones: Attraction, Filter, Clustering, and Destination. Ultimately the proximity of these zones is based on their capability to attract pedestrians from the street and draw them up through the core to a destination. In turn, these zones formed a basis for the organization of the tower in terms of what kinds of programs could survive in these separate locations, how the existing elevator banks could be incorporated, and how housing could self-organize in and around these zones forming social networks.

Existing programs originally intended for Enron such as the cafeteria, trading floor, and the sky bridge could then be adapted into the matrix of organization developed by factors such as time based proximities and frequencies, subsystems, and relationships. Introduced programs vary in size from kiosk vendors to big box retail that could then be negotiated within the existing structure.

Housing emerges as a result of the matrix of negotiation. The relationship between retail and residential regulates the various programs introduced to the tower. Therefore, if we take the regularity of the base building structure, namely its shell, and infect it with another type of regularity, in this case the amenities of the city, there is an inevitable negotiation that emerges. Essentially, the urban model retains its traits, is then transformed and mutated into the tower where the repetition of larger programs filter through and collide with existing building systems. There is a constant interaction with programs, not just adjacencies, which also extend beyond the existing circulation network to the tower's exterior relationships: parking garage, underground tunnel, daycare center, YMCA and other civic programs in the immediate context area.

Anthony Harrington holds an M Arch from Rice University and a BS in Architecture from the University of Michigan. He is presently relocating to New York, but while in Houston he has been involved in several programs exposing high school students to architecture.

1. The Fab Tree Hab, clay study model. Mitchell Joachim, Javier Arbona and Lara Greden

JOACHIM, Mitchell / ARBONA, Javier / GREDEN, Lara

Nature's Home

The *Fab Tree Hab* concept resolutely accumulates the inscribed nuances that influenced the insurgent authors of the American Rustic Period: Thoreau, Emerson, Whitman, and Alcott. The writings stemming from this period represent an early mode of intention that was profoundly ecocentric. These authors' notions of dwelling were envisioned as retreats, poets' bowers, hermitages, and summer cottages in a Sylvan style. In 1847, the Rustic Period culminated in the assembly of a self-made, crooked cedar and honeysuckle summer home by Thoreau and Alcott for their friend Emerson in the midst of a cornfield. This peculiar house serves as our point of departure for the *Fab Tree Hab:* here, traditional anthropocentric doctrines are overturned and human life is subsumed within terrestrial environs. Here, home becomes indistinct and fits itself symbiotically into the surrounding ecosystem.

Our approach also draws from Jeffersonian ideologies, equalizing edification and ecology. In the mind of Thomas Jefferson, the measure of any single human gesture was its contribution to the individual's pursuit of happiness. He believed humans had natural rights and devoted most his life to a revolution ensuring the rights of agrarianism and education, considering such rights vital to a citizen's personal livelihood in an agrarian economy and nascent democracy. Universal access to education was critically linked to sustenance; thus, the "gentleman farmer." Jefferson advocated for ecological principles to be applied to human habitation so that each person could live off the land without detriment to it. It is thus in the Jeffersonian legacy that the Fab Tree Hab not only provides for a healthy biological exchange with its inhabitant, but also strives to contribute positively to everyone's quality of life.

Modern design has essentially left behind these principles of symbiosis. Although many individual and collective efforts towards the "sustainable" or "green" design of buildings are apparent internationally, derivative design cannot address the underlying systemic nature of sustainability. Fixing pieces of a puzzle fails to address the interplaying complexities of the whole, and innovation is stifled by the need to work within given contexts. Lack of certainty in cause and effect is often cited as a reason for not developing ecologically sound practices, most notably in the fields of greenhouse gas reductions and improvement of indoor air quality. However, the precautionary principle implies that protection should be embraced deliberately even in the face of uncertainty. Thus, instead of incorporating materials that may impart less impact to the environment

2. The Fab Tree Hab, rendering

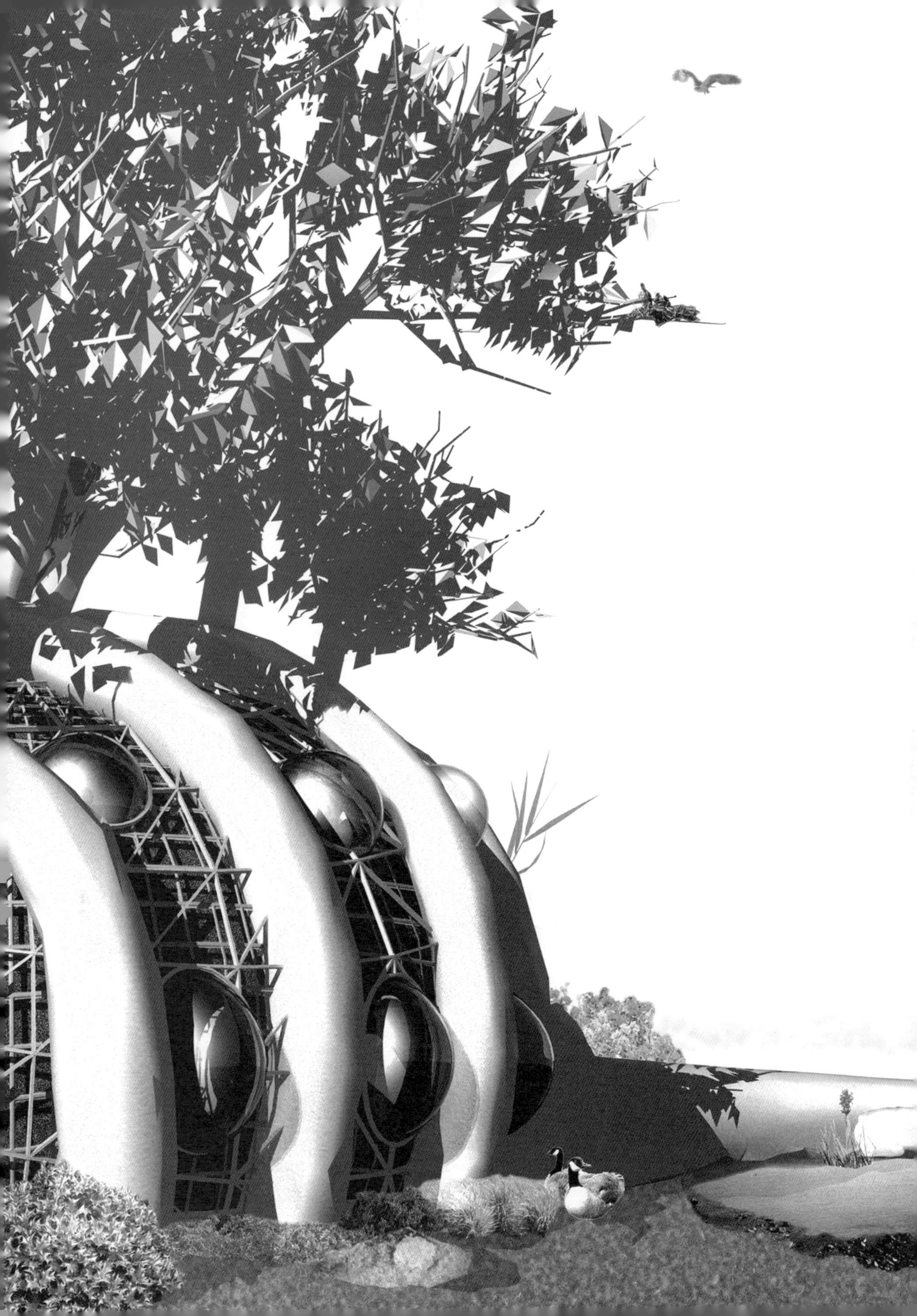

and human health—impacts which may remain uncertain in extent—the Fab Tree Hab design seeks to protect and embrace the ecosystem as a source of sustainability in the built environment. Just as the modern biotechnology revolution owes its existence to the intelligence of ecosystems at the molecular level, sustainable technologies for homes can also benefit from biological, natural systems. Starting at the molecular scale is not necessary, but, as this project explores, lumber maintained in its living form becomes a superstructure.

The Fab Tree Hab

The single-family home and encompassing ecology is a living structure. Tree trunks form the load-bearing structure which a weave of pleached branch stud support a thermal clay and straw-based infill. The Fab Tree Hab plan accommodates three bedrooms (one on the second level), a bathroom, and an open living, dining and kitchen area placed on the southern façade in accordance with passive solar principles.

Structure, Form, and Growth

Pleaching, a methodology new to buildings yet ancient to gardening is introduced in this design. Pleaching is a method of weaving together tree branches to form living archways, lattices, or screens. The trunks of inosculate, or self-grafting, trees, such as Elm, Live Oak, and Dogwood, are the load-bearing structure, and the branches form a continuous lattice frame for the walls and roof. Weaved along the exterior is a dense protective layer of vines, interspersed with soil pockets and growing plants. On the interior, a clay and straw composite insulates and blocks moisture, and over this a layer of smooth clay is applied like a plaster. In essence, the tree trunks of this design provide the structure for an extruded earth ecosystem, the growth of which is embraced over time. Living examples of pleached structures include the Red Alder bench by Richard Reames and the Sycamore Tower by Axel Erlandson.

Life Sustaining Flows

Water, integral to the survival of the structure itself, is the pulmonary system of the home, circulating from the roof-top collector, through human consumption, and ultimately exiting via transpiration. A gray water stream irrigates the gardens, and a filtration stream enters a Living Machine, where it is purified by bacteria, fish, and plants which eat the organic wastes. Cleaned water enters the pond, where it may infiltrate the soil or evaporate to the atmosphere. Water consumed by the vegetation eventually returns to the water cycle through transpiration, simultaneously cooling the home.

Fundamental to the flux of the water cycle is solar radiation, which also drives heating and ventilation. In the winter, sunlight shines through the large south-facing

3. The Fab Tree Hab, elevations and plan

windows, heating the open floor-space and thermal mass. The reverse is true in the summer, as the crown of the structure shades itself from extreme temperatures, instead using the sun's energy for photosynthesis. Two levels of operable windows set up a buoyancy-driven ventilating flow, drawing in cool air at floor level. An active solar hot water system heats the home through an array of radiant floor pipes. Technology inspired by nature also explicitly engages it to provide water and warmth to the habitat: a rooftop trough harvests water for human use; the plumbing system is positioned to provide for gravity-induced flow and gray-water reuse; and a composting system treats human waste and returns nutrients to the eco-system.

Renewal

The Fab Tree Hab is designed to be nearly entirely edible. While inhabited, the home's gardens and exterior walls produce food for people and animals. The seasonal cycles help the tree structure provide for itself through composting of fallen leaves in autumn. Bioplastic windows, which would flex with the home as it grows, would also degrade and return to the earth, as would the walls.

Rethinking budget

The compilation of a budget for this prototype opens a debate. For instance, it is widely acknowledged that life-cycle costing methods would provide more favor to conscientious home designs by including energy cost savings and, more abstractly, accounting for reduction or elimination of externality costs. However, this understanding fails to recognize sustainable housing as an interweaving of systems, and places too much value on benefits received today as opposed to tomorrow or hundred years from now. Only by rejecting the tendency towards immediacy and, likewise, first-cost dependency, can a true representation of sustainable value be achieved.

Realization of the living home is affordable. At the first stage of maturity, when the habitat is readied for human inhabitation, cost outlays are similar to those in traditional construction. Clay, gravel, and straw can be obtained locally; plants and vegetation, many of which can be started from seedlings when the structure is originally planted, will come at a nominal cost. The cost of installing heating, lighting, plumbing, electrical, and communication systems will be lessened due to systems integrated design features such as natural ventilation, gravity water flow, daylighting and passive solar power.

Additional operating costs and required expertise over the lifetime of the home include pest management and maintenance of the Living Machine water treatment system. Additionally, the time it takes for the Fab Tree Hab to reach livability is greater than that of traditional construction cycles, but the longevity of the home and family is also increased.

Experiment in time

With the realization of these homes as experiments, renewal will take on a new architectural form—one of interdependency between nature and people.

References

> Ahadu A. 2002. Tree House (p. 60-61). The Architectural Review: Emerging Architecture. AR&D Awards 2002. December 2002.
> Ashford NA. 2002. Incorporating Science, Technology, Fairness, and Accountability in Environmental, Health, and Safety Decisions. Adapted from "Implementing a Precautionary Approach in Decisions Affecting Health, Safety, and the Environment: Risk, technology alternatives, and tradeoff analysis" in The Role of Precaution in Chemicals Policy, Favorita Papers Jan 2002. Freytag E et al (eds). Diplomatic Academy, Vienna, pp. 128-140.
> Axelrod A. 2001. The Life and Work of Thomas Jefferson. Alpha Books. Indianapolis, IN.
> Bell A. 1991. Plant Form: An Illustrated Guide to Flowering Plant Morphology. Oxford University Press. New York. Excavated Rhizome System (p. 130).
> Doernach R. 1987. Pflanzen-Hauser Biotektur. Panorama Verlag. Munchen, Germany. Brunnen-Sitzlaube (p.77).
> Dougherty P. Dixie Cups (1998) and Headstrong (2002). (http://www.stickwork.net/dougherty/main.html).
> Elizabeth L and Adams C (Eds). 2000. Alternative Construction: Contemporary natural building methods. Wiley. New York, NY.

> Erlandson A. The Sycamore Tower (image). (http://www.arborsmith.com/treecircus.html). Grow Your Own House. 2000. Vitra Design Museum. Bent Bamboo (p. 214) and Composite Materials (p. 241).
> Living Machines, Inc. Open Aerobic Reactor. (http://www.livingmachines.com/htm/machine.htm).
> Maynard WB. 2002. Architecture in the United States, 1800-1850. New Haven Yale University Press, 2002.
> Nichols FD and Griswold RE. 1978. Thomas Jefferson Landscape Architect. University Press of Virginia. Charlottesville, VA.
> "Pleaching." (http://www.rainforestinfo.org.au/good_wood/pleachng.htm).
> Reames R. Red Alder Bench (image). (http://www.arborsmith.com/).

Mitchell W. Joachim is an architect and urban designer concentrating on ecological design. He is a Ph.D. candidate at the Massachusetts Institute of Technology in Architecture: Computation. Lara Greden, is a PhD candidate at MIT in the Dept. of Architecture, Building Technology. Javier Arbona teaches design and landscape studies at ArqPoli: The New School of Architecture, Polytechnic University of Puerto Rico. He also serves as the chief editor of Archinect.com.

KELLY, Caroline

Portman Space: An Interview with John Portman

John Portman's career has taken an unconventional path. With vision and an entrepreneurial spirit, he has pioneered design concepts, expanded the role of the architect, played an active role in city planning and helped open the door for international business in China. After graduating from Georgia Tech, Portman opened his own practice in Atlanta that has grown to a consortium of design, development and management companies with more than 1200 employees and offices in the US and abroad. Eager to implement his design concepts, he learned the real estate business so that he could combine the role of architect and developer, a practice once scorned. His first hotel, the Hyatt Regency Atlanta with its soaring 22-story atrium, revolutionized hotel design and introduced the grand atrium to the lexicon of modern architecture. Portman's strong commitment to urban planning was initially demonstrated by his participation as President of Central Atlanta Progress which produced Atlanta's first Central Area Study in 1970, laying out the plans for the city's rapid transit system, maintaining the airport close to the city center and focusing on parks and cultural components that bring life to the city. Over a 30 year period, he built AmericasMart, a complex of trade marts in the heart of downtown Atlanta, and is credited as being the catalyst for Atlanta's thriving convention business. His mixed-use projects, such as

Peachtree Center in Atlanta and Embarcadero Center in San Francisco, are a prototype for successful urban development. In the early 1980s, he was one of the first foreign architects to work in China, successfully adapting principles of urban design and architecture to China's rapid evolution as a world power. His architectural firm, John Portman & Associates, Inc., is headquartered in Atlanta with an office in Shanghai. The firm focuses on mixed-use, hotel, office, educational projects and master planning for clients worldwide.

306090: Talk about the strategy for structuring your company. It has become an international firm and we would like to know if this was your vision and if this is where you thought you would end up?

JP: When I started in practice, I wanted to determine my own destiny. I was eager to implement my ideas. I thought there ought to be a better way than standing in line with a lot of other architects to be interviewed for a particular job that only one would get. Too much depended on who you knew, your presentation and how you marketed yourself. I wanted to have a greater in-put on the process. So, I began to learn all that I could about real estate. I started a parallel course to understand all the steps that must be taken in the building process before the architectural stage; I learned about land acquisition and most importantly how to finance it. Capital markets are a big part of the building process. You might say capital markets drive real estate and consequently drive the whole building program. Since capital markets are constantly changing, this is an ongoing process. Secondly, after understanding how projects are financed, you need to understand how the real estate must function in order to be successful. A building is more than just a physical thing that you set on a site. The basic role of architecture is to create space that serves those who use it. This comes back to our focus on people throughout the design of our projects. So by seeing the big picture and becoming involved in the whole building cycle, I developed my firm by establishing separate operating companies to address the specific functions to be performed. The architectural firm provides design services for our sister companies as well as a large number of clients unrelated to our firm. Our development arm likewise works for outside clients as do our management companies. A few individuals, such as me, my son Jack, and a few others have a role in more than one company. I don't think I would have predicted fifty years ago that this is where we would be today, but I would have predicted that we would be—and still are—responsive to change. Change produces opportunities and challenges. It is one of the wonderful things about architecture.

306090: Can you talk about the structure of the

1. John Portman with John Street and Herb Lembecke, early 1970s

architectural versus the developmental part of your company and the synergies that exist between them?

JP: Our architectural and development arms work seamlessly together. We constantly have meetings where we go over the entire circumstances surrounding a project. We have a long history of collaborating with each other. Expertise from both camps helps drive a project. The architecture can often give impetus to the development side. Most importantly our architects truly understand projects from the owner's and developer's perspective. Building cost, schedules, operating efficiencies are genuinely important to us. Our third-party clients seem to appreciate the added value of this specialized experience.

306090: What kind of conflicts do you find exist when the architect is his own client?

JP: I don't know that there are conflicts other than the fact that it is always challenging to have a building respond to many concerns. It not only has to deal with aesthetics, but it also has to be economically viable to build and operate. We have the choices and the consequences. But that is part of what makes this such a great profession.

306090: So for the in-house teams that you create for different projects—could you take us through an example of a current project and some of the in-house teams and how things are divided up along the life cycle of the building process?

JP: In the development company, we have what we call field developers who put together programs, analyze need, analyze growth trends and try to expose opportunities for new projects. They work with the financial group that keeps track of what is happening in the capital markets: what companies, banks, institutions, pension funds, and equity investors are doing and how things are currently financed, which changes from time to time. Some financial entities are interested in certain types of projects and not interested in others. Our development group is focused on having a thorough understanding of the whole financial side of the equation. These real estate development and financial activities go on concurrently with design development. Once the project is identified, the architectural arm starts integrating the design aspects. Good architecture adds value to real estate development.

306090: Would you say that is the distinction of being developer AND architect?

JP: Yes. Most architectural practices do not participate in the development activities to the extent that we do. The exchange of ideas is helpful to our process. Others separate the roles of architect and developer and there will always be many who will continue to do that successfully.

306090: What is the competitive advantage for you to do it in the dual role, as opposed to the traditional division?

JP: Competitive? I never thought of it as a competitive advantage so much as an ability to have some say in the destiny of what I do. I like being able to pull all the factors together to be able to make decisions based on facts from a more global point of view. Some of our clients come to us because they prefer working with a company that has the design and development services all under one roof. It is easier and simpler for them and, in that light; arguably, I guess it may give us a competitive edge as both architects and developers.

306090: Another question we have is about outside forces, such as local government. Can you comment on local government, particularly here in Atlanta, but also as you are increasingly international and doing so much work in China?

JP: Governments all over the world are much more interested now than ever before in how their physical environment is developed. Their interest continues to increase, and rightly so. Good communication is important between us, as the architect or the developer, and the regulatory agencies with which we must work. Whether you are dealing with zoning, permits, licenses, building heights, or traffic issues, you need to understand their position and, if it differs from yours, seek ways in which you can work together. With rare exception, most communities want quality development. No one wants projects that are thrown up without regard for enhancing the quality of life of the community. Often it takes time and energy to communicate your goals with governmental entities. I have found most are eager to work for the improvement of their communities and will work in partnership with you to make things happen. However, you must clearly communicate to them your vision and what it can mean for their community.

306090: So, specifically in regards to China, what do you think is the most significant issue there in regards to its urbanization?

JP: Well, China is the country of the 21st century. What is happening in China is mind-boggling, to say the least. We began work in China in the early '80s with the development of Shanghai Centre which was the first large mixed-use complex with a 700-room hotel, 440 housing units, 300,000 square-feet of office space and a retail restaurant kind of village at its base. The project was filled with challenges. It was supposed to open in the fall of 1989. Because of the events at Tiananmen Square in June of that year, the opening was delayed. Many companies left China but we were committed to staying. We designed Shanghai Centre specifically thinking about what the international business community would need would as it explored the new business opportunities in China. So little had been built in prior years that we even had to incorporate our own telecommunications network and infrastructure components—things that we take for granted in the United States. The project proved to be a tremendous success and the mixed-use idea has really taken hold in China. The concept has evolved into single high-rise mixed-use towers which include office, hotel, housing and retail all in one building. Chinese cities have a very high density of population. You do not see the urban sprawl we experience here because they are less tied to the automobile. Yet in China, as well as in the US, our firm tries to focus on a pedestrian environment, bringing all the amenities one needs within easy walking distance. Additionally in China, we have tried to open public space, both inside and outside buildings, to create a release from the sense of confinement that one feels on China's crowded streets and sidewalks. We have tried to use architecture as a means to create a lifestyle—not as an imposition, but as an exposition. The architectural design process should expose all of the things one must deal with. As you let those things that are exposed lead you, you come to what the design solution should be. Universally, at the base root of everything it is people. The key to all architecture is how the built environment affects people and how they use it. Does it enhance their lives?

306090: Can you speak to how that has changed, or what you have seen in the last 50 years?

JP: Here it is urban sprawl. In this country, we continue to go hurdling down a dangerous cliff related to more roads and more cars. We are a society so dependent on the automobile, we are hooked. The freedom of the open road has been replaced by the congestion of round-the-clock rush hour traffic. For decades I have cited the value of the Coordinate Unit where you create communities within the city in which you have everything you need within walking distance. You could walk to work, to school, to church, to the grocery store, drugstore or retail shops. You walk to the tennis court or recreation center. It is pedestrian oriented. Isn't that a better lifestyle here or anywhere?

306090: How do you feel that that has played out here in Atlanta? I moved down here from New York where I walked everywhere, and then I came to Atlanta where I bought a car, and drive long distances to accomplish all those activities of daily living that you are talking about. Here, I see, on a day to day basis, where you come to work and have all these wonderful amenities, but still people are driving out to the suburbs to live. Could you comment on what you envisioned with the coordinate unit and how it practically exists here in Atlanta?

JP: Well, it goes back to how far people will walk before they think of wheels. Unless people are walking for leisure, in most cases people in this country will walk from 7 to 10 minutes. If it is beyond that, they are looking for a wheel. So, if you take a 7 to 10 minute walk and make that the radius, you could design things in such a way that within that area you put all the services you typically need—homes, offices, schools, shops, recreation, places of worship and so on. It becomes a coordinate unit. It has the quality of a small town within a big city. Because Atlanta has so much land around it, for years people have been choosing to live away from the city center in the suburbs even though they work in town. However, we have created such problems with urban sprawl and extraordinarily long, congested commuting times, that trend is beginning to change. People—particularly those without children—prefer to live in-town. There is a real boom in in-town residential building. I am optimistic that the elements that create coordinate units will continue to grow. It is already happening in many neighborhoods.

306090: Could you comment on Rem Koolhass' essay on Atlanta where he states that when it becomes a self-contained unit like that it doesn't have to be in the downtown—it could be anywhere, it could be placed in a non-urban environment?

JP: Some parts of Atlanta could be placed in a non-urban environment. In fact, they are. Atlanta is surrounded by open land in all directions. We have neither seacoast nor mountains that limit our expansion in any direction. Additionally, our ample rainfall makes the rolling hills beyond the city a beautiful and inviting place to be. Our city has an extensive expanse of office parks, retail malls, and hundreds and hundreds of subdivisions. Technology also enables people to work away from less centralized locations, inviting even wider urban sprawl. Yet, within the heart of the city certain activities occur that do not function elsewhere—government, sports, the arts, universities, conventions and trade. The central city will always play a major role in the region. But Atlanta, like many other cities, has to constantly work to be responsive to on-going change and find creative ways to make the city center a place where people want to be.

306090: You have been doing this (architecture and development) for 50 years and more architects are starting in this dual role. Is there anybody of interest, any new younger architects that are working today that are of interest to you? Are there any projects that have struck you as particularly compelling?

JP: Well, I say you have hit me with a high, fast one there. No one really jumps out. I am sure they are there, I am just not aware. I do have one concern about what I see today. Architecture has worked its way into an awkward situation by everything having to be different, everything having to be unique. Some architects seem to concentrate on the latest thing rather than concentrating on creating an environment that will end up contributing to a cohesive whole. Our job is not to create chaos but to bring our cities back together. It is not an easy task.

306090: What do you think architecture schools need to be doing to teach their students currently that may be a response to that problem? Are there any particular essentials that students need to be coming out of architectural school with, beyond their personal expression of making something new and different?

JP: I think you start by asking, "What is the essence of what architecture is all about?" The essence of architecture is to serve the human being. How? We create a physical environment that enhances people's lives and what life means to them. That means that architects have to better understand society. We have a society that is the most eclectic and the most time sensitive that the world has ever known. Those two things create quite a problem because we have no patience. Everyone is jumping, jumping, jumping. We have 500 television channels. From fast food to fast information, everything is fast. We want it now. We don't want to plan; that takes too long. Add to that the fact that everyone wants to be an individual even though in some ways they think collectively. People want to define themselves by their clothes, their home, and their car. They don't want to be like the neighbor next door. This has created an eclectic society. It adds interest to life but it also gives architects a greater challenge. We first have to understand the society in which we live, and then sort through what is happening so we can make meaningful changes. Our architecture students need to know their work will make a difference. It needs to be a plus not a negative.

306090: Having an international practice and being about lifestyle—the United States versus China,

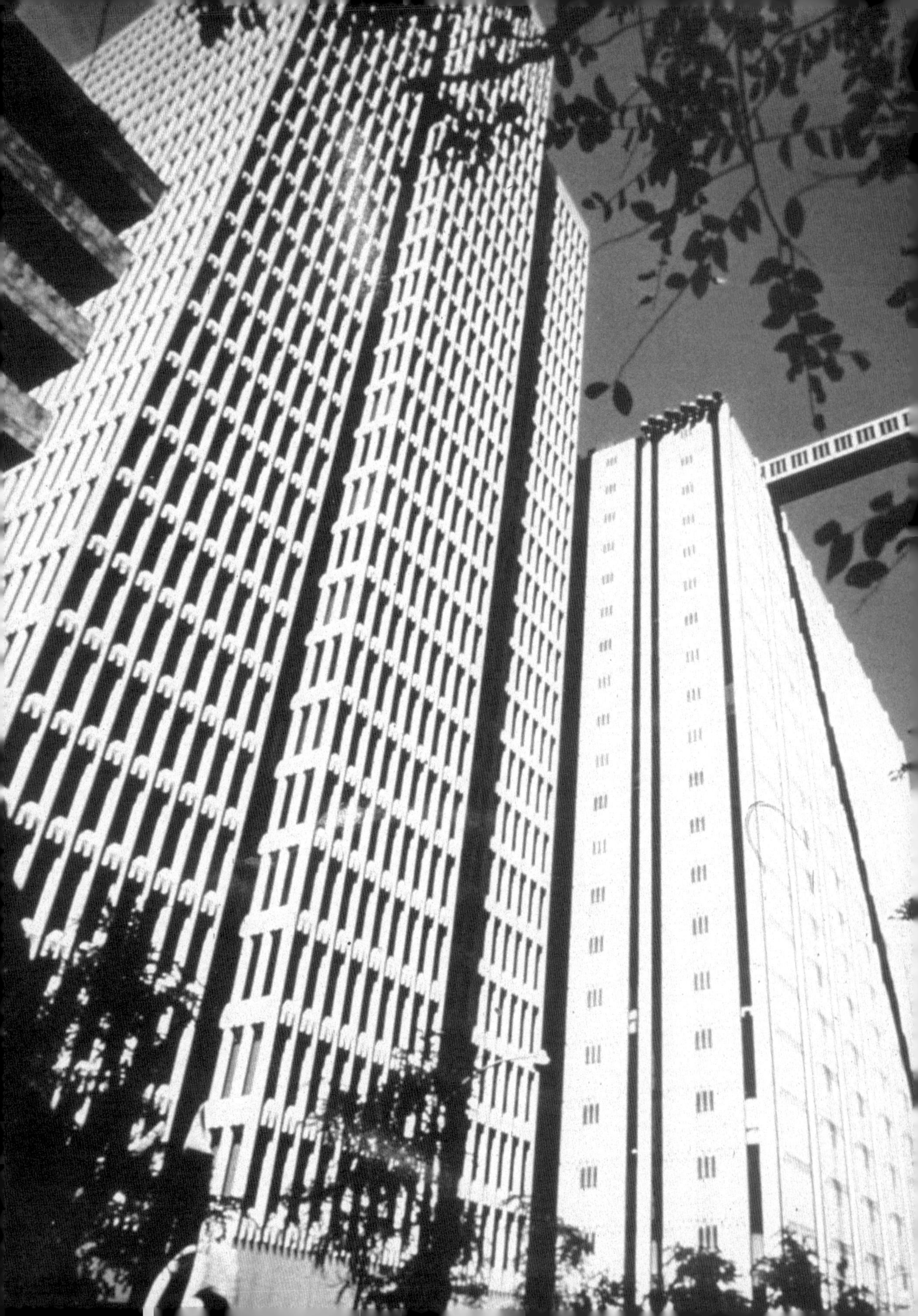

2. Peachtree Center, Atlanta, John Portman & Associates Inc.

3. Hyatt Regency Atlanta, atrium, John Portman & Associates Inc.

Europe or other parts of the world, how should an architect prepare for the sensitivities needed toward the different cultures?

JP: I think that the common denominator is that we are all human beings. We have the same feelings, the same desires even though we might speak differently or like different food. At the basic human level, we are more alike than we are different. However, each society or culture has characteristics and history that makes them unique. Landscapes are different, indigenous building materials vary, even local art forms express the uniqueness of various cultures. The more we learn about these things, the better we will be in creating an environment that is right for that specific place. However, we do not need to be shackled by the past, copying what has gone before us. Our role is to bring each community forward in a positive way.

306090: One last question that I have, in a bit of a jump, is about the story of the creation of the Pritzker Prize and your involvement and any recollections you might have.

JP: My relationship with the Pritzker family goes back to the original Regency hotel. The Pritzker's owned the Hyatt House Motels, a small chain of low-rise motels on the West coast, and were not involved with the Regency when we first began the project. Originally, we were going to operate it independently, but when construction got up to the fourth level, the investor group got a little nervous and we decided to get a hotel operator. Many of the larger, better-known hotel companies didn't think the idea of the 22-story atrium lobby would fly. They rejected us, but the Pritzkers were intrigued by the idea. They came on board. The hotel was a tremendous success and it turned the Pritzkers on to architecture. They became the operators of our next two hotels, one at O'Hare in Chicago, the other at Embarcadero Center in San Francisco. Both used large atrium lobbies that attracted local people as well as hotel guests. They began to realize that a hotel that people want to be a part of would be a lot more successful. They became interested in what architecture could do to contribute to better business. From that enthusiasm for architecture came the idea of the Pritzker Prize, which we of course support.

Caroline Kelly is a graduate student at the Georgia Institute of Technology College of Architecture. Prior to her return to academics, she was the assistant director of the Max Protetch Gallery in New York City.

LAIGU, Tonu

Estonian Megastructure Reuse

In 1991 in Estonia, the Soviet state-driven system of housing production was discarded in favor of a laisserfaire system founded on values of privatization and restitution. New principles of property reform were passed into law, including the two major aspects of housing privatization: (1) restitution of illegally expropriated properties, and (2) privatization of dwellings built during the pre-war period and state and municipal owned housing stock built during the post-war period. Privatization in Estonia was very similar to other countries in Eastern Europe: it was based on a system of voucher-privatization (so-called EVP), meant to ensure that social aims prevailed over economic aims throughout the process. By 2001, 94% of living space was privatized, leaving only 6% in the ownership of state or local government.

While the new ownership system has quickly taken shape and the process of privatization and restitution is largely complete, market-driven development is relatively new in Estonia, which has a long history of state-mandated social experiments through urban housing construction. The impact of privatization on city form is yet to be seen. This discussion is intended to explore some of the implications of the old Soviet megastructures on the Estonian city as well as to examine their potential reuse.

Privatization

Privatization implies a city built in the context of competing interests, while the welfare state project for public housing can often be traced to a single author. Private developers will always reference comparable development projects (absorption, returns, and so on) in the bid to get bank loans. Private development looks to the urban and market context for clues about program, often seeking variance from the public authorityís zoned land use in order to more accurately respond to market forces. In order to provide a counterpoint to the radical competitive contextualism of urbanization driven by private interests, we look to the massive social housing experiments by the Soviet Union in Estonia, and how these projects are being reconsidered since Estonia shifted to laissez faire economics and privatization of property in the 1990s.

The development of the Estonian city shifted from its pre-war course after World War II as a result of Soviet occupation. Life, culture, and politics were ruled from Moscow. Wartime devastation had created a great need for reconstruction, while simultaneously, forced migration in the interest of "Russification" had resulted in significant population growth in the country. Tallinn grew to 1.6 times its pre-war size by the 1960s, necessitating significant new urban fabric to accommodate the expanding population. The new construction, which would house non-native forced migrants and "party soldiers," was guided by the use of Stalinist housing principles.

These developments covered the ruins of war with visions of a new Soviet society in Estonia. The construction of spacious apartments in houses with showy architecture for important comrades flourished in city centers. The working class was to be housed in Stalinist standardized architecture—utopic projects designed by Soviet architects whose ideological mission was to design the "palace" of the Soviet citizen.

The ideal model of communist housing in Estonia was cohabitation—several families sharing the same dwelling. As a rule, identical plans for the cohabitation units were used to construct numerous buildings along a street. Construction methods were based on the handicraft of individual workers, which is why "standardization" must be understood not as a modular material building system but rather as the standard distribution of the plan itself, the resulting similarity of building structures, and standardized decorations (columns, chapiters, rosettes, and other festive items) that were glued on the street side facades of the houses [2].

After the death of Stalin, the political and cultural landscape of Estonia remained the same, but the attitude toward innovation changed. An objective was set in the 1950s to use new construction technologies to design the ideal home for the Soviet citizen—a project which must also be understood as a reaction to Stalinist national architecture.

From 1956 to 1958, the standardized Series 1-317 section type residential building was designed, intended for widespread use in Estonia on the basis of a Soviet Union-wide model—the so-called Khrushcev House. The 1-317 type is characterised by a flexible modular construction method that allows for the changing of partition walls in the apartment over time or to achieve different spatial types. For this reason these apartments are valued and viable even today as homes for small families.

During the Khrushcev era, a number of residential building clusters based on the 1-317 standard type were established. However, they influenced cities and towns only in limited areas. The next period of state housing was much more massive [3].

The Soviet utopia of the social-organisational effect of mass housing through standardization is realised most extensively in the so-called mäe regions of Estonia, established in the 1960s and growing rapidly. Mäe is a popular nickname for these megastructural giants. The name is derived from the suffix mäe (hill), metaphorically characterizing these massive "houses" as constructed hills. Extensive capacity for construction in Estonia became possible due to the establishment of the housing factory of Tallinn in 1961, followed shortly afterwards by operations in Tartu and Narva. These plants produced large panel elements for housing construction. Their Union-wide funding was part of the Russian population policy.

Within one generation the city districts of Mustamäe, Õismäe, Lasnamäe in Tallinn, Anne district in Tartu and Mai St. district in Pärnu were established. Mass construction is also extensive in the northeastern towns of Narva and Kohtla-Järve. The most serious failure of Estonian urban development is considered to be the construction of Keldrimäe in the Tallinn city centre as well as the erection of similar standardized residential buildings in Estonian small towns and rural towns. A paradoxical fact is that today, about half of the total number of city residents live in these areas [4].

The two most cohesive residential megaprojects are Väike-Õismäe and Lasnamäe in Tallinn, where in addition to the section type residential buildings with a standardized height of 5, 9 and 16 stories, they propose a clear urban design and planning idea. But perhaps due to the radical simplification of modernistic ideas through single authorship, these districts feel and function like large dormitory districts, lacking the pleasant street-life that is characteristic of a more diversified city [5].

Väike-Õismäe

Architects M. Port and M. Meelak planned Väike-Õismäe in 1968. It was a project for 40,000 people. The rapid construction of the new urban region over ten years took place when funding was plentiful and the Soviet high-volume production mechanisms were running smoothly. Väike-'ismäe was planned as a perfectly circular town, in the centre of which there is a regional recreation and resting area surrounding a circular man-made lake. The innermost ring includes schools and kindergartens surrounded by a belt of nine-story residential buildings. The outermost zone consists of five-story buildings. Following the concentric structure, fourteen- and sixteen-story residential high-rises are located between lower housing blocks. Two circular highways that in turn are connected to radial roads provide access to buildings. Väike-Õismäe was considered to be a masterpiece of citymaking—a symbol and a badge of honor for the entire Soviet Union.

Not surprisingly, for individuals living there the city is less than a masterpiece. The most impressive views of Väike-Õismäe are distant aerial perspectives accessible only from a helicopter. Small apartments of the region are relatively spacious but they are totally inflexible compared to type 1–317. However it is interesting to note that today there are no serious social problems in Väike-Õismäe. A large shopping, culture and sports center has been established not far from it in Rocca-al-Mare. The two megaprojects seem to work together symbiotically to meet residents' needs.

Lasnamäe

The territory of Lasnamäe is 30 km of which the region of panel residential buildings constitutes about one half. The authors of the plan of Lasnamäe, including M. Port, M. Meelak, I. Raud, O. Zemtsugov, H. Sepp and V. Herkel, foresaw an urban region with a population of 200,000 people. A comprehensive plan for the region was completed in 1976. The plan of Lasnamäe proposed two parallel highways that linearly join eleven smaller city districts, each with 12 to18 thousand inhabitants. These were the so-called "micro-districts." Each micro-district was to have a center where a school, a kindergarten and a commercial and cultural centre would be located. Micro-districts were to be bisected by a highway; the plan was for pedestrians and cars to have access to both sides of the highway via bridges. The highway has in actuality been sunk in flagstone rock, separating cars and pedestrians to different levels (5).

The construction of Lasnamäe panel houses started at the end of the 1970s as planned, beginning with micro-district I. As an enormous new construction site, Lasnamäe became a storage site for the products of the Tallinn housing plant, and the conveyor was put to work at full capacity. The buildings that started to go up were of the same type as those in Väike-Õismäe, although the apartments were a bit more spacious.

The project was destined to remain unfinished—mass construction came to an abrupt halt when Estonia regained its independence. This was a blow to the socialist economy as well as to national housing projects. A total of only 650 apartment houses were erected in Lasnamäe. In micro-district X, underground infrastructure was installed and construction sites were prepared before the project came to a full stop. Today Lasnamäe is an unfinished residential district without fully developed services or leisure. Forgotten city space lies between standardized houses in this place where people live only temporarily and leave as soon as possible.

Today more than 112,000 people live in Lasnamäe of whom about 60-70% are non-Estonians. Paradoxically, despite shortcomings in social life, there are no empty and abandoned properties in Lasnamäe. All residential space is liquid and can be sold or leased for a good price. Perhaps this indicates that today there is not enough residential space in Tallinn. Because it is in use, there is no apparent will to demolish Lasnamäe as was done with a similar but smaller urban region in Ballymun, Dublin. Thus, the future of development in the area is a question for private interests.

New housing development projects are occurring at seemingly random locations throughout the city and suburbs, according to market potential. Neither private development interests nor the state have not been active in the state-built housing districts from the 1970s and 80's. However, another kind of bottom-up activity driven by what is known as the third sector has taken place. Owners themselves have formed administrative associations in order to improve their buildings and neighborhoods using their own resources. This is not unlike the phenomenon of homeowners associations or business improvement districts in the United States.

Attention has also been drawn to these areas by interested architects, landscape architects, sociologists, urban geographers, and some politicians, who see an interesting urban history and a potential for redevelopment. In 1998 a three-year project called "Urban Renewal of Lasnamäe—Windows into the Future" was launched through cooperation of academic institutions and the ministries of Finland and Estonia. Unfortunately, the project remained an academic exercise. Lasnamäe was also a subject of international study as a site for the Europan 7 competition; however, the competition site (a void of 35 ha in the district Paevalja) is quite small in the context of all of Lasnamäe. The competition winners were A. Atela (E), M. Andriau (F), and I. Morshedi (F), who proposed a simple but powerful strategy to cover the territory with a regular grid, moving away from the open planning street system.

Another competition, organized by the public authority in 2003 and called "Stone City is a Habitat as Well," looked at the Mustamäe district in Tallinn and the Anne district in Tartu. The Mustamäe competition was won by I. Järve and T. Sild, who proposed to program the large neglected voids between buildings with outdoor exercise and park activities, designed lighting schemes, and parking. Architectural proposals include new low-story structures to facilitate public activities and the addition of penthouses on top of existing apartment buildings. A similar strategy was put forward by P. Mättas and R. K̦bar in the Anne district competition in Tartu.

Despite academic and design interest in these areas, little has been done in practical terms to reclaim them. One exception is a social housing cluster built in 2003 in Lasnamäe, designed by architects P. Pere and U. Muru. The project stands as a regular quarter of dwellings, alone in the void and far from the surrounding settlement of the city. When will a continuous city be established here? The government's five-year housing program, "5000 residences in Tallinn," initiated three years ago, is a ghost that many doubt will be realized.

While the solution is not yet clear, we know that academic and government interest is not enough to ensure implementation. Amassing the capital and other resources that were allocated to housing production during the time of the totalitarian Soviet regime is no longer possible present-day, and the scale of action that is needed to mitigate the sheer amount of emptiness is daunting considering the logics of urban development in a privatized system. We must continue to engage the question, do the research, write the books, host the competitions, and encourage the vision to present itself.

> *The vision of Lasnamäe corresponds almost one to one to the Antonio Sant'Elia's La Citta' Nuova.*

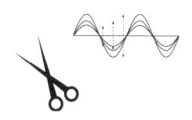

1. AVL-ville I site photograph

MARTENS, Charlotte
AVL-ville

The goal of this Free State is to create a place of its own in a land that is becoming more oppressively over-regulated by the day, a place where anything is possible. AVL-Ville has its own flag, its own constitution and its own currency and is spread out over two locations within the City of Rotterdam: Keilestraat 43e (AVL-Ville I) and Vierhavenstraat 15 (AVL-Ville II).

AVL-Ville I is the main site. Here you'll find the atelier where all the products and works of art are designed and produced, the Hall of Delights, the AVL Academy and the area where you can live and build without needing a building or residence permit and where there are no zoning laws.

1. Graz Container
This container was commissioned by the Grazer Kunstverein for Expo 2000 in Hanover. Complete with podium and bar, this was where performances and happenings presented by a number of international artists could take place. In reaction to the political situation in Austria at the time of production, the decision was made to give the container a hard military look. Thus the artists were provided with their own armed outpost. The happening that AVL organized also served as the starting signal for the founding of AVL-Ville. The plain was occupied by a variety of tents, mobile homes, fires and parties. After three days, this oasis of freedom within an over-organized and respectable world exposition was christened "Hangover 2000".

2. Avl-spitaal
This field hospital was built in 1998 in a 40-foot transport container. The interior is completely furnished with all the necessary facilities such as a waiting room, a consultation room for the doctor (???) and his assistant, an operating room with the requisite surgical instruments and anaesthetic equipment, plumbing and a recovery room. The hospital can be used in AVL-Ville as well as during times of war and emergency. [2]

3. Racing Car
Joep van Lieshout raced this souped-up Opel Ascona in the Dutch championships at the Zandvoort racetrack from '91 to '95. He won a 2nd and a 3rd place. The car was sponsored by various art institutions, galleries and magazines who successfully held their own against the usual big commercial sponsors.

4. A-portable
This abortion clinic was commissioned by the Women on Waves Foundation (WOW). They fight for the legalization of abortion in countries where abortion is prohibited, since approximately 70,000 women die each year as a result of illegal practices and poor hygiene. The A-Portable is very functional. The clinic is furnished with all the necessary medical equipment and has its own electricity and water supply. With a hired ship and the abortion clinic on board, WOW sails to the countries in question. Arriving in the harbour, the organization provides information on family planning, safe sex, abortion and related matters. Women who want to have a safe abortion can board the ship and be treated in international waters under Dutch law. When WOW is not at sea, A-portable is kept on the AVL-Ville grounds. [3]

5. Big Avl Man
This work from 2000 is an enlarged version of a dying AVL man who is using his last bit of energy in a struggle to right himself.

6. Modular Mobile Home
This mobile home from 1996 consists of four parts: the chassis; the functional unit, with all the facilities needed by the user such as kitchen, heating, hot and cold running water, sleeping area and the like; the cargo space and a toilet and shower unit. The third part is a section that can be used as a dining room and office but can also easily be cleared to serve as a cargo area. In this set-up, the doors of the cargo section have been replaced by the toilet and shower unit, which can be opened like a big door.

7. The Sex Container
In the future, the container will provide space for almost every sexual fantasy that the human mind can imagine. Morality is something that each person must determine for himself or herself and therefore is not the business of the state.

8. Fisherman's House
This house was designed in 2000 by AVL and measures 2.10 m by 2.90 m. This very simple dwelling was inspired by cottages that stood around the IJsselmeer until the 1950s and served as weekday shelters for the local fishermen. Although the form of the house is traditional and small, the dwelling is very pleasant to stay in. Many of the works of AVL are attempts to combine simple solutions from the past with modern applications and materials.

9. Favela House
Designed for an exhibition in Sao Paulo, Brazil. After several visits to the slums (favelas) of Sao Paulo, AVL developed the idea of entering into a working relationship with the favela dwellers. Five façades with windows and doors were made for this purpose in typical AVL style. The plan was to give the façades to the future inhabitants and let them finish building the house on the site with locally available materials. The organic way of building that is characteristic of the favelas is very appealing; the houses are built on top of and next to each other in a haphazard fashion, with no account being taken of streets, infrastructure or building accessibility. The form of the houses and the city is determined by the acute need, the available materials and money. Unfortunately, the project was discontinued for lack of funds. This house was built in a single day with waste materials from the atelier.

10. The Plain Of Independence
This was set up on 28 April 2001. Around it, AVL members can build their own houses without having to contend with any technical, aesthetic or residential regulations. Anything is possible, as long as it's portable.

11. Autocrat
This is a survival car made in 1997. The Autocrat is meant to enable survival in places that are remote from the civilized world. Actually it's just a big kitchen with a sleeping area. There's a kitchen outside as well for the heavier work. The design and manufac-

4. AVL-ville I, with Big Avl man in midground

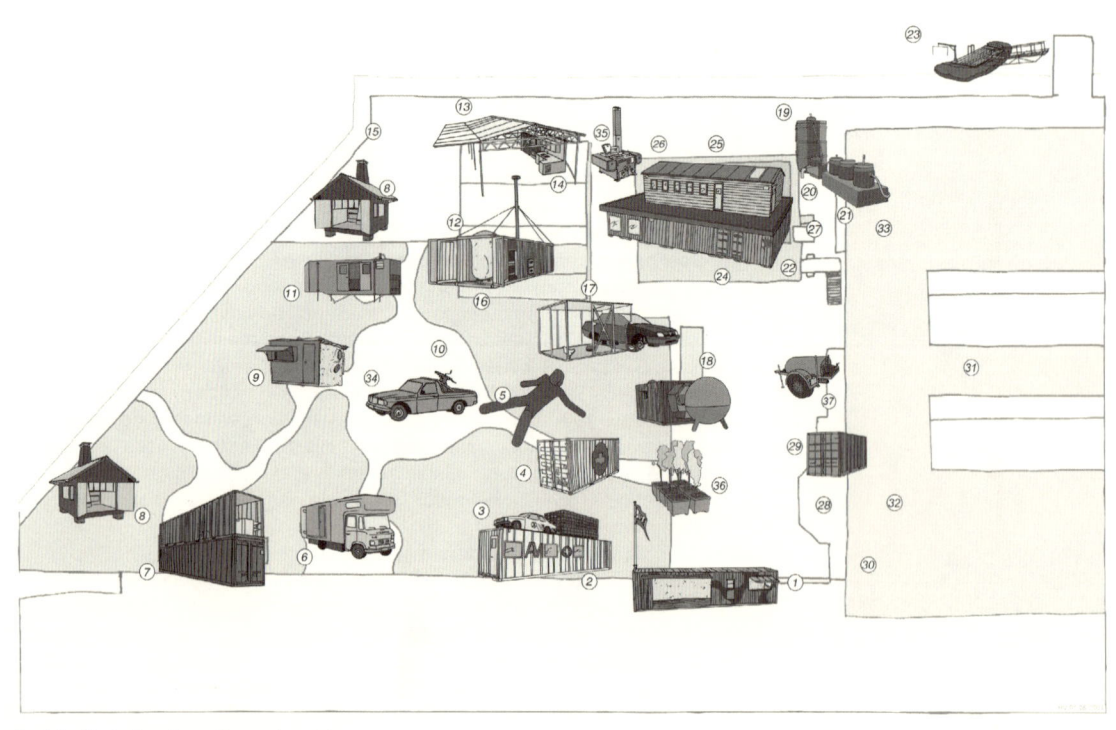

5. AVL-ville I, site plan with numbered key

Constitution AVL-Ville

In a constantly developing society, the artist plays an important stimulating role. Development implies breaking away from existing structures. To reach optimal artistic expression, it is crucial for the artist to be able to deploy himself or herself without being subject to the restrictions of civil morality. The objective of AVL-Ville is to create an environment where this is possible. To reach this goal, the rights formulated below are to be seen as absolute, without any exceptions. Living at AVL-Ville can be experienced as a hard and confrontational artistic life. However, this is the ultimate consequence of an honest and uncompromising existence.

1) Everyone has the right to freedom of artistic expression and design.

2) Everyone has the right to freedom of expression, which is to say revealing and receiving thoughts or feelings other than artistic.

3) Every participant of AVL-Ville is equal and is entitled to be treated without discrimination on account of race, colour, sex, language, belief, political, artistic and philosophical ideas, nationality, possessions, or any other ground.

4) Everyone is entitled to gather with others and to demonstrate.

5) Everyone has the right to freedom of religious expression, including idolatry, polygamy and forming a sect.

6) Everyone is entitled to have an education, including an artistic education.

7) Everyone has the right to immunity in privacy and artistic lifestyle, as well as communication in any way with third parties.

8) Everyone is allowed to wander freely within the AVL-Ville area.

9) Everyone is entitled to create independently his or her own housing within the AVL-Ville territory.

10) Everyone has the right to have immunity over body and spirit, which also includes being able to dispose of one's body and spirit according to one's own wishes, with or without help of artificial means.

11) All AVL-Ville participants are obliged to treat any other member with absolute honesty and respect; it is compulsory to solve any conflict within AVL-Ville.

12) A) All AVL-Ville participants accept that management will be decided by the general committee, which is composed of an as of yet unspecified supervising board, to be formed by members of the general committee along with others. B) The general committee is qualified to expel participants, if no amicable settlement can be agreed upon in conflicts.

ture of the car were also carried out with autocracy in mind: every effort was made to use homemade items and to avoid ready-made products as much as possible. The suspension and locks were made this way, as was the cooker.

12. Power Station

Made in 2001. The building of the AVL-Ville power station was begun in these two containers. The power station is a combination of traditional and alternative power generators. Ultimately, AVL-Ville would like to provide most of its own energy. The emphasis will be placed on renewable sources of energy such as wind and solar power.

12a. Heating Boiler

This boiler was completely designed and constructed in 2000 by AVL and is equipped with a water jacket and heat exchangers. All the rubbish from the atelier can be burned in it. The incineration is efficient and complete. All the warm water produced is stored in the water buffer. The boiler contains a complex installation of pumps, valves and electronics partly sponsored by Wolters en Dros. During heating season the boiler is fired only one day a week; on the other six days the heat from the buffer tank can be used.

12b. Buffer Tank

Made in 2000. All the heat and residual heat that is produced in the boiler, generator and solar panels is stored in this 300-liter buffer tank. The enormous amount of water, the relatively small surface that comes in contact with the open air and the effective insulation keep the contents of the tank warm for months at a time. The heat from the tank can be used for producing interior warmth and hot water and for process heat for the biogas installation and the beer brewery. This last is still in progress. Because of the buffer tank, heat can be provided independent of the time of production.

12c. 80-kw Generator

In 1999 this generator was made from the turbo diesel engine of the Alfa Romeo that now serves as a chicken coop. The sexy Italian engine is connected to the thoroughly Dutch Heemaf generator. The Heemaf is not made of the customary cast iron but, in typical Dutch fashion, is constructed entirely of tubing and plate. The gauge and control block, which provides current at a continuous voltage and frequency, is made by AVL in improvised style. The generator produces enough electricity to provide the entire village with power. The engine's cooling system is connected to the water tank.

12d. Windmill

This work is in progress. A windmill will soon be erected on the roof of this power station. The windmill will be about 20 meters in height, with a 10-KW capacity and a 7-meter vane span. The current generated will be used in the village or fed back into the supply system. Ultimately AVL would like to erect a very large windmill able to produce an abundance of energy.

12e. Solar Panels

Work in progress. The most efficient way of extracting energy from the sun is with solar panels. When the sunlight hits the panels it is converted into heat; when the temperature of the panel exceeds the temperature in the buffer tank, the pump switches on. The water in the buffer tank can then be used for heating and hot water supply.

13. The Roof

This is part of the Hall of Delights and is used as an outdoor kitchen. It also creates a space that can be used as a dining area. In the winter this is where firewood is sawed and stored. The place is also ideal for slaughtering and boning our farm animals.

14. Modular Building System

This system, dating from 1996, consists of wall and function modules. The modules conform to a standard size of 284 or 584 cm and can be connected in a simple manner. With the addition of a floor and roof panels of 300 x 600 cm, both small units as well as large dwellings and a utility area can be built.

15. Sportopia

This is still under construction and will provide physical and mental excitement and relaxation.

16. Reed Filter

This is a work from 2001. Mildly contaminated water from the kitchen and bathrooms, from which the fat and coarse particles have been separated out, is pumped over the reed filter. This is an organic filter that works according to two principles. Impurities are filtered through the sand. The reeds introduce a great deal of oxygen into the soil through their hollow stems and roots. This helps the bacteria in their conversion of harmful substances. The reeds also absorb a variety of waste products as fertilizer, which causes the plants to grow. At the end of the filter, clean water is produced that can just be released into the surface water. A well-constructed reed filter is able to produce drinking water.

17. Alfa With Chicken Coop

This car had put in a considerable amount of time as a company car before its engine was taken out to serve as a generator. The body was then lovingly restored in 1999 and converted into a chicken coop. In order to arrive at the current design, a thorough study of chickens was first undertaken. The findings concerning their health and psychological behaviour were processed, and the proper adaptations were made. The eggs can easily be gathered by opening the boot, which now serves as the nest. This convenience for AVL is happily united with chicken welfare in the Alfa.

18. Workshop For Weapons And Bombs

This work of art from 1998 consists of three parts: a metal shop, a chemical laboratory stocked with easily obtainable chemicals and instructions, and the freedom fighter's residence in the back, with office space for writing manifestos and a spherical bedroom. Actually, this workshop is a sort of ode to individual working terrorists who have announced their decision to take on the rest of the world.

19. Septic Tank

This installation consists of three connected tanks, each with a 4500-litre capacity. The so-called black water is pumped through the faeces pump to the first tank. Part of the mass settles, another part keeps floating and the middle part flows on to the next tank. Following the same pattern, it flows on to the last tank. While the sewage remains in the tank the water is purified by means of fermentation and bacterial culture. Finally it is pumped to a reed filter, where it produces clean water once again. This is a temporary solution and will remain in operation until the biogas installation is in place

20. Feces Pump

In the feces pump, the pieces of excrement are broken up by means of a number of blades, after which they are pumped away by a normal plunger pump to the septic tank

21. Fat Separator

The fat separator consists of three connected trays which receive the so-called grey water. This is sewage from the kitchen, showers and sinks. The intake, lead-through and drain are set at different heights so that both the fat and the heavier particles can be separated out. When the pre-purified water enters the last tray, it is pumped to the reed filter for further purification. After a period of time, the fat is skimmed off, filtered and added to the tractor's diesel oil or simply incinerated in the boiler.

22. Rainwater Collection

This work in progress is to be completed in 2001. The rainwater that falls on the roof is collected, filtered and transported to this receiving tank. It enters the tank as smoothly as possible to avoid any turbulence, so that the small particles that are difficult to filter out can sink to the bottom. In the tank hangs a pump, which begins operating whenever a 'rainwater tap' is opened anywhere in the building. The water is drained off by means of a floating intake hanging 10 cm beneath the water's surface. Rainwater can be used for flushing toilets, laundry, cleaning and, after additional filtering, even for drinking water. Not only are these techniques good for the environment, but the installations also make it possible to copy the AVL-Ville concept anywhere.

23. Marina

The marina consists of an inflatable raft and scaffolding pipes and is used for mooring AVL-Ville's pleasure and touring boats.

24. Hall Of Delights (Or Zdg, Zaal Der Geneugten)

This is the clubhouse of the Society of the Inner Self (or VIM, the Vereniging de Innerlijke Mens). Everything that tastes good is meant to have a place here. Every day, delicious and healthy meals are prepared in the ZDG. For a modest fee, visitors can partake as well. A variety of guest cooks are also being invited, running from artists and five-star cooks to specialists and regional fanatics. The ZDG was created in 2001 from seven sea containers that have been welded together and whose interior dividing walls have been removed.

25. The Constitution

Unique and especially made for a free state, the constitution guarantees many rights and freedoms. It makes it possible for every individual to create his own life and environment and renders judges, lawyers and police superfluous. The constitution, as drawn up by lawyer Gerard Spong, can be found in the Hall of Delights.

26. Avl Office

Like all AVL structures, this building can be disassembled and moved. It is based on

6. The Pioneer Set, farmhouse exterior

wooden frame construction, a very common building method. A unique feature of this building is that the furniture, working surfaces, closets, gutters, etc., are all part of the construction. They keep the walls rigid so that the gable roof requires a minimum of braces. This results in a more open area and a more pleasant sense of space. Most of the designs are created in this office. It provides a place for the support personnel and also has a library. The designers work according to the flexwork system: you occupy a room when you need it and leave it empty when you're finished. In this way the space is used in a very flexible way, which promotes cooperation and keeps the projects manageable.

27. Compost Toilet
The compost toilet was made in 2001. It is a low-tech way of processing solid human waste. Instead of flushing, you throw a handful of straw into the toilet. The toilet functions when excrement comes in contact with straw and oxygen producing compost. After about a year, the flap beneath the toilet can be opened and the compost—which now has a fresh woodland smell—can be removed and used as potting soil. The composting tank contains an air circulation system and exhaust fan to guarantee complete and odourless composting. This technique was developed in cooperation with Schie 2.0, a bureau for urban development and Eco systems. This process, which is normally in the hands of a governmental monopoly and is hidden beneath the ground, is here run by Atelier van Lieshout itself and has been rendered visible.

28. Music Studio
Built by several AVL members and intended for rehearsals and musical recordings for the AVL label.

29. Workshop For Alcohol And Medicine
This work of art from 1998 is all about right and wrong. Part of it can be used for the illegal distillation of alcohol, while the other part can be used for making medicines for treating physical and mental ailments from the same alcohol and medicinal herbs.

30. Avl-ville Office
Here you can obtain more information about AVL-Ville and walk through to the overhead bridges in the atelier. Please take special note: the bridges are absolutely unsuitable for children, pets and people who are unsteady on their feet.

7. The Pioneer Set, farmhouse interior

31. The Atelier
The beating heart of AVL-Ville is the Atelier, where works of art and other products are made. Atelier van Lieshout has about 30 employees, most of whom have different creative backgrounds and are of different nationalities. The designers are either closely involved in the manufacturing process of each product or the product is made by hand. This gives rise to intense contact between the maker and the product, which is one of the hallmarks of AVL style. AVL is organized as a business where horizontal communication is encouraged. Although the value of money and the opportunities it offers are recognized, profit is not AVL's primary objective. Rather, the chief concern is to make special, innovative and challenging products. The atelier is not open to the public. AVL-Ville is the name of the free state and is organized in a fundamentally different way. Here the focus is on individual freedom and the providing of space and possibilities.

32. Drawing Gallery
This gallery features a selection of the colored drawings that were made in past years.

Some drawings have to do with the genesis of AVL-Ville, others are about machines and weapons or the designing of works of art. Others concern the position of the individual in the midst of life, work and longings.

33. Avl Academy
This is AVL-Ville's educational institute, where tailor-made training programmes and courses are given for a wide range of individuals and groups. The Academy programme is intensive, innovative and practical. The experience gained here enables participants to generate creative ideas and quickly solve problems in the future. It is a school for communication, experience and the art of living. For further information, fill in the application form or speak with one of our staff members.

The furniture is among the first pieces made by AVL, the so-called hard-edge furniture dating from 1988–1989. The pieces were made according to a strict designing system; tables and storage cabinets built based on a modular concept with increasing sizes and fixed proportions and colors.

34. Mercedes With Canon
This is Atelier van Lieshout's old company car. It's an ordinary Mercedes converted into a pick-up truck and equipped with a 57-mm canon designed and made by Atelier van

8. AVL-ville, site axonometric drawing

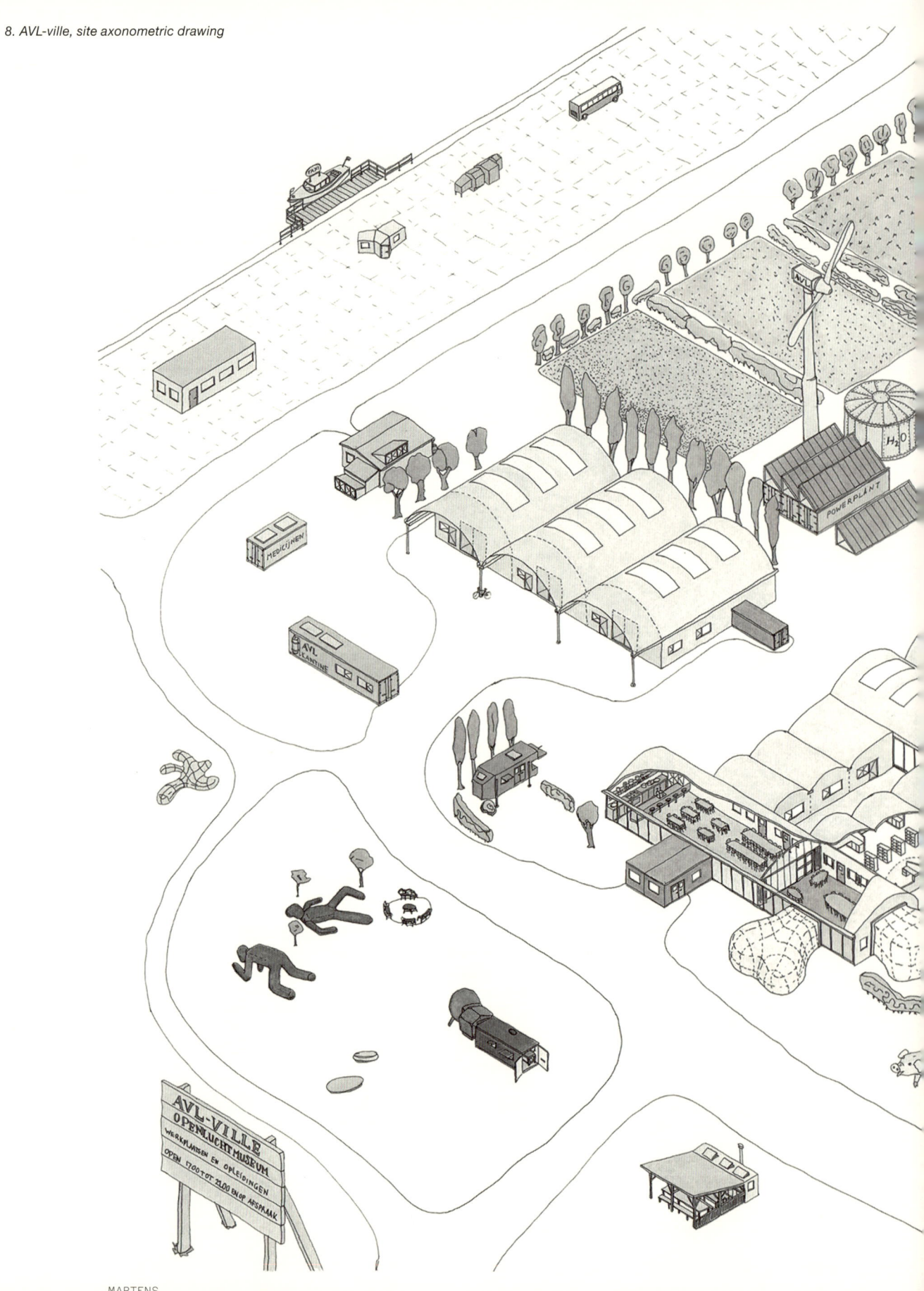

63

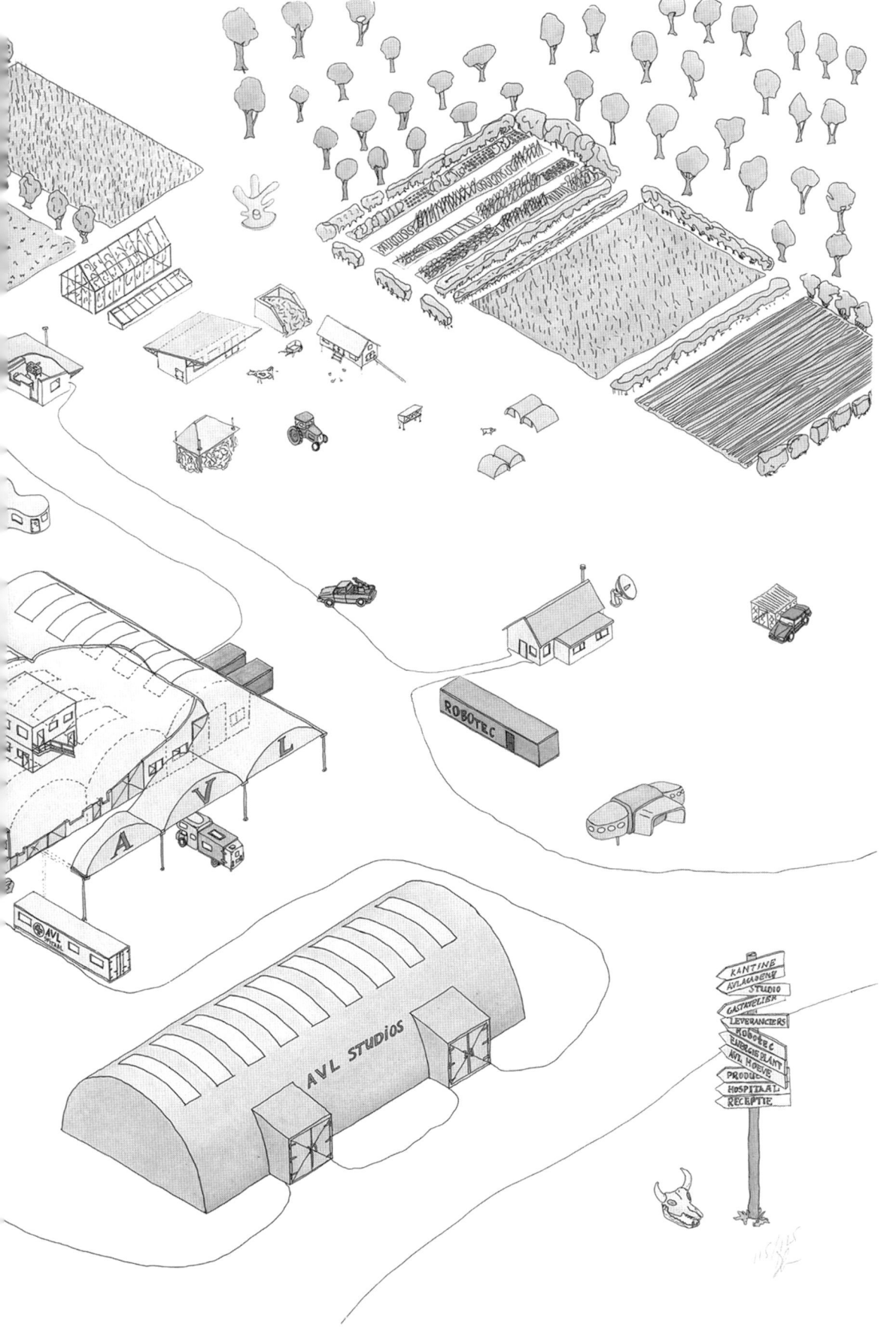

Lieshout out of everyday materials. The Mercedes was part of the exhibition The Good, The Bad and The Ugly, presented in Rabastens in 1998, and produced the usual commotion when the exhibition was banned by the mayor.

35. Goulash Canon

This army field canon is suitable for cooking large meals. It can be heated with diesel, petrol, turf or wood. Two of the mess tins are double-walled and filled with paraffin so the food won't burn. AVL loves good, hearty food and plenty of it.

36. Mobile Orchard

Like the pioneer set, this orchard can be set up anywhere. The boxes are extremely strong and the fruit trees, bushes and soil are all certified organic with the Eko mark of quality. The boxes—trees and all—are available for purchase. Ask the staff for further information.

37. Water Wagon

The water wagon also originated in the army. In the event of emergencies, water can be pumped from the river by means of the hand pump. The water wagon is used on the farm to provide drinking water for the cattle and, along with the goulash canon, can be used when AVL cooks on location.

Avl-ville II

This part of AVL-Ville is the home of the pioneer set. The pioneer set is the easily dismantled farm which, along with all its tools and equipment, can be transported in a shipping container and unpacked anywhere in the world so a new farm can be started. Cultivation is to be carried out according to organic principles and the products are intended for private consumption. This summer, a small workshop is being set up to convert railway carriages, and the AVL will be open for snacks, pleasant recreation and special events.

9. Canteen

38. Hay Barn

This is the container that has been used since 2000 for transporting the pioneer set. When at rest, the container functions as a barn. It is used to store fodder and tools. These are traditional tools that are still being made. The ergonomics, design and materials have been determined by generations of farmers and their experience with this kind of handiwork. The ideal tool has stood the test of time.

39. Cattle Stable

The stable is a fine place for cattle. AVL's stable was made in 2000. As with the other parts of the pioneer set, the stable was chosen on the basis of functionality and soundness.

Reliability and durability are of vital importance, certainly if the pioneer set is to be used in remote areas.

40. Avl Transport Horse

The AVL-Ville workhorse, Kereda, is a Gelderlander. She was born in 1993 and is in the best of health. The horse has been specially trained to pull wagons. Please be considerate of the horse and driver when riding in the big city. Do not feed the horse, do not shout and do not frighten her. The maker of the carriage is unknown. All passengers riding in the wagon can enjoy a range of AVL liqueurs.

41. Chicken Coop

After an extensive study was carried out of chickens, their lives and habits, this chicken coop was constructed. A good living area and nesting place has been made for the chickens as well as a separate maternity ward and perches with integrated manure collection that is easy to clean from the outside. A choice was made from a range of feeds, and the feed trays can be filled from the outside as well. The eggs can easily be gathered through special hatches on the sides of the coop. In short, a utopian accommodation for chickens combined with convenience for the farmer.

42. Rabbit Hutch

A single pair of rabbits can produce 200 kilos of meat per year.

43. Greenhouse

Unfortunately this is not made by AVL, but it's still inexpensive and can easily be moved, so it fully complies with AVL style. In the future, more greenhouses will be provided for cultivating good varieties of plants. These in turn will produce very good vegetables from which honest and delicious dishes can be prepared. The greenhouses, in which vegetables are cultivated according to organic principles, are not artificially heated.

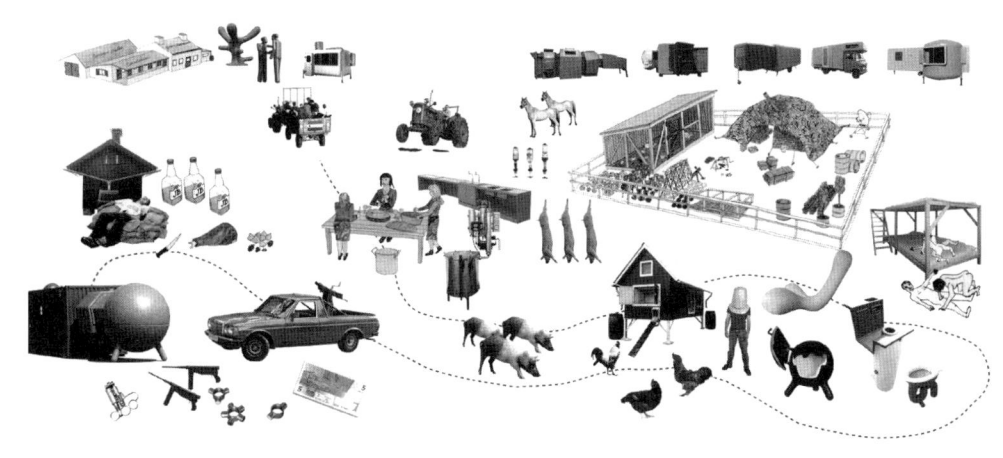

10. AVL-ville, elements

44. Pig Sty
In their natural setting, pigs are family creatures. They build their own homes and keep them clean. They care for their children and pay visits to their family and neighbours. It's important for the animals' well-being and for the flavor of the meat that they be allowed to live as 'true to nature' as possible. With these simple stables, the pigs can live quite natural lives; they can accommodate a pig family and provide shade in the summer and sufficient shelter in the winter. The shape of the roof prevents the piglets from being accidentally crushed by their wallowing mother. All the animals on the pioneer set have room that exceeds the norms stipulated by the Eko mark of quality.

45. The Farmhouse
This is the farmer's home. It is identical in shape and size to the cattle stable. After all, humans and animals are somewhat equal. The farmer's house, however, is equipped with a multi-woman bed, a wood stove and a kitchen. As usual, everything in the workshop is made by AVL. [6, 7]

46. Outhouse
Even the farmer's manure is valuable.

47. Canteen
A kitchen and eating area for 16 people originally made for an exhibition in Bourneville, UK. Bourneville is a village built in the early 20th century by the Cadbury chocolate company for its factory employees. The purpose of the founders was to provide good homes with large gardens—spacious, dry and light. Common facilities were also made such as the men's recreation grounds, which were austere athletic fields with the occasional dressing room. The women's recreation grounds, on the other hand, consisted of an idyllic park with little brooks and hills, hermetically sealed off from the men. Bourneville is still an idyllic place and the ban on alcohol is still in effect. Is AVL-Ville the Bourneville of the 21st century? [9]

48. Avl Transport Tractor
The tractor is a Nuffield Universal 4, produced in 1965, and up until recently was used for ploughing contests. It has a 56 HP engine and the maximum speed is 35 km per hour. The tractor is equipped with a hydraulic system, a lifting device and a power take-off for connecting all sorts of other tools such as ploughs, mowing machines, tippers, lifting masts, excavators, etc. The tractor normally runs on diesel fuel but also has a hankering for a bit of processed frying fat. The tractor is used on the farm but it is also used to pull the AVL transport trailer. The trailer has room for a maximum of 60 persons, or 5000 kilos of cargo.

Atelier Van Lieshout *is an arts collaborative in Rotterdam. Joep Van Lieshout's work has been exhibited and collected by the Museum of Modern Art in New York, the Walker Art Center in Minneapolis and numerous other institutions.*

MOSKOW, Keith; AIA
Urban Hookah

Architecture is a heavily regulated industry. Building codes and zoning regulations dictate shape, program, materiality and countless other aspects of the building process. As a result, architects have responded to, skirted around, subverted and played games with these codes in the pursuit of emergent spatial conditions. Occasionally, legislation is drafted that is not directly intended to control the production of built space, and architects respond to this change in the law in an effort to sustain activities that are being regulated out of the public sphere or produce new urban artifacts, spaces and activities.

A massive change in attitude towards public health concerns surrounding cigarette smoking has swept the United States. The federal governments began eliminating smoking areas in all federally owned or operated buildings and soon state government followed suit. Recently cities, such as Los Angeles, New York and Boston have instituted bans on smoking in privately owned and operated restaurants in the interest of public health.

While the world around us changes rapidly in terms of technology, culture and economics, the built environment responds to new issues at a perilously slow pace. This is especially true in the public domain. This is in part due to the cost and the lifespan of public infrastructure. But it is also the result of widespread perceptions of ownership and management of this domain. Legislated out of restaurants, offices and public buildings, smokers now form a displaced constituency. They also contribute to a new form of socialization on the sidewalk and around building entrances.

In much the same way that the cafes and restaurants of Paris capture sidewalk space for patrons to eat and drink outside, the Urban Hookah is an attempt to address this new forced congregation by creating a positive amenity that serves both smokers and non-smokers alike. Experience has shown that the most successful urban sidewalks are those that combine both public and private uses and thus generate a much greater level of social activity. While we expect that the costs of the fixture will be born, in most cases by private interests, the opportunity for the Hookah to generate income through advertising space may make it attractive for public entities as well. The Hookah uses city infrastructure in order to sustain itself. It adopts a host/parasite logic similar to that of Korteknie Stuhlmacher Architecten's project Parasite in Las Palmas Rotterdam. The Parasite building attaches onto a former industrial structure and draws power and utilities. The syntactical arrangement of Korteknie Stuhlmacher's project creates the appearance of a parasitic relationship. In fact, the building is managed by a single owner. By contrast, the Hookah completely relies on pre-existing lampposts that are owned by the city as the primary structural member. Power is also tapped from the lamppost in order to run heating elements and air filtration equipment. This parasitic relationship reduces unit production costs. The design of the Hookah perceives the city as a site of underutilized public resources, namely seeing lampposts not as lampposts but as structural masts in a yet-to-be architectural form.

1. Urban Hookah, Moskow Architects, Boston Massachusetts. Keith Moskow AIA, Gordon Stott, Robert Linn, and Mike Moorehead

PIPER, Michael
Capitalize on Your Context

Architects and urban designers typically consider context as something to be different than or similar to.[1] As this either-or logic offers marginal value to the developer driven logic that seeks to profit from property, I propose a third alternative that describes context as something to take advantage of. Building on the idea that spatial specificity is of growing importance to both the economic and physical change going on in cities today,[2] the following project proposes an opportunistic analysis of context that seeks to understand it as a depot of physical assets that may yield economic benefit when engaged through a strategic reconfiguration of its patterns. Formulating an analysis for capitalizing on assets in such a way provides the real estate developer incentive for engaging social and physical contingencies within a context that are otherwise more lucrative to ignore.

Occupational Analysis

Figuring out how to make use of resources in a context, this analysis and subsequent method of building design focuses on how the space of the city is occupied. Occupational analysis combines two familiar but typically unrelated forms of contextual study: physical/aesthetic and programmatic. Physical descriptions, like figure grounds, characterize the shape of a place. Programmatic ones, like a Koolhaasian-styled enumeration of activities, highlight what goes on in space. Occupational analysis describes how the physical environment facilitates the activities that take place within it.[3] It does not suggest the end of figure grounds nor of bold text of programs on a map, but rather uses them as a first step. Consider for example describing the context of a strip mall parking lot. Physically it has concrete islands with small buildings floating in a sea of asphalt. Programmatically, there might be a drive-thru restaurant, a photo development booth, or a laundromat located on the islands. Occupationally, you hop between these programmatic islands that are physically and programmatically suited to a point to point experience of the city. Where form is a noun, and programs are verbs, occupation is understood as an adjective and so aptly suited to the project of description.

Understanding occupation provides a means of describing a context in a way that enables a project to capitalize on it. In order to make use of something, you have to understand how to get to it and how it is inhabited. The following design project, a high school situated in San Diego, CA at its border with Mexico, proposes this method as a way to think about and engage the developer driven logic that dictates the change and growth going on in today's cities.

Opportunistic Urbanism: The Case Of The District Lasso

Shaped to take advantage of its border with Tijuana, Mexico, San Diego provides a subject for understanding the relationship between urban form and the opportunism that drives its shape. Though transnational manufacturing, shopping, educating and medicating dominate the discussion of these border cities it is perhaps most interesting to understand how these programs have produced and resulted from the physical form of the cities that share them.

In order to capitalize on its proximity to Mexico, San Diego wished to incorporate the border community of San Ysidro without, however, assuming responsibility for the largely low income township of Chula Vista that separated the two. However, in San Diego districts must be physically contiguous in order to be legally incorporated. In order to get San Ysidro and not Chula Vista, San Diego invented what I call the district lasso. The district lasso is a thin stretch of land that runs under the San Diego bay establishing physical adjacency between the two disparate halves of district 8. The peculiar shape of the city with its lasso is shown on the following page.[1]

San Ysidro, a small residential community, is of great interest not only to the city but also to its various developers and institutions who view the land as viable real estate. Along with this redistricting a slew of development ensued in San Ysidro that seeks to take advantage of its proximity to the border. The negotiations between these land developers and the local community is the impetus for the following contextual analysis and high school design.

Library—Community College—Playing Fields, Negotiating For The Depot Of Assets

The programs listed above are the result of real and proposed negotiations made between developers, the local community, and my would-be high school.[4] An extroverted attitude of exchange is a growing tendency within public high schools throughout the United States: in Boston, MA, a high school uses MIT's athletic fields and media center during the institute's off hours. Such arrangements represent a hybrid form of funding and operation that involve multiple private and public interests. Rather than resort to the standard school format, a single site set back from the city, this design proposes an open campus dispersed in the city, arranged to capitalize on the above mentioned programmatic assets. How the space in which these programmatic resources are located is occupied will be the focus of the subsequent analysis and design.

When developer Ed Marasco proposed his border hugging mall "Gateway of the Americas" the local community protested until they all settled that Marasco, as a sort of concession, would build a community library on an outparcel in the corner of his mall parking lot. In exchange for the use of the library and its surrounding parking lot, I propose that the school's adjacent cafeteria, shown in images 3 & 4 be given to Marasco for development of eating establishments that would extend the pattern of outparceled restaurants located

2. Island hopping

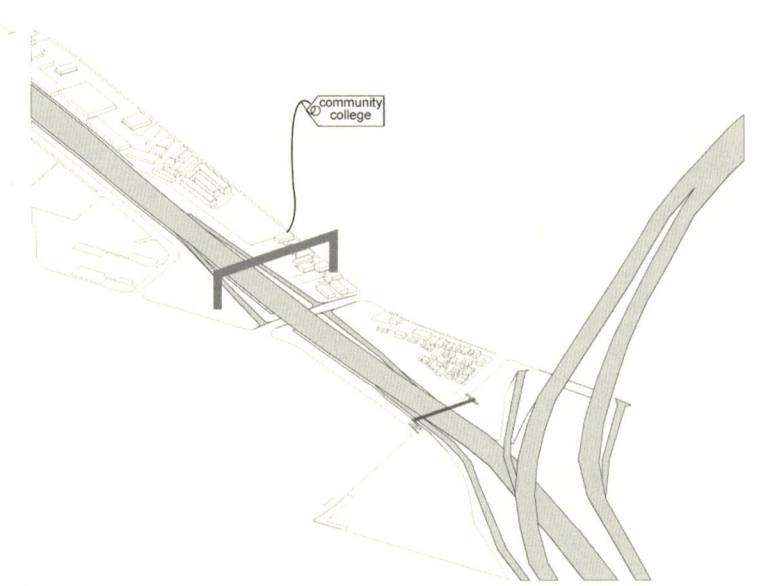

3. Obstacle skipping

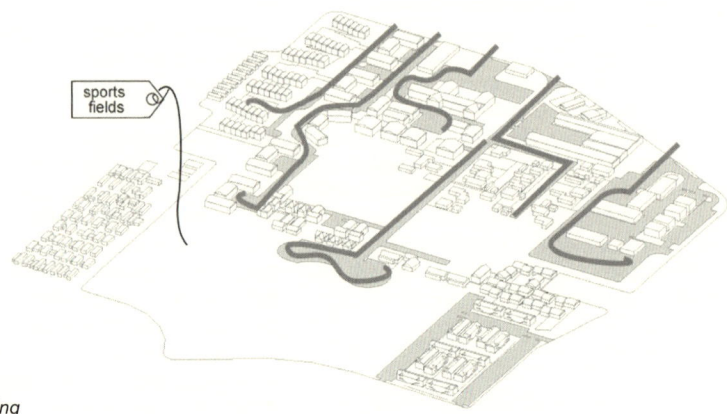

4. Fabric moseying

1. Lasso

in his parking lot.

San Diego State University has an existing satellite campus in San Ysidro. I propose the expansion of this campus, using my proposed public high school's unlimited development rights, to provide further facilities for the study of international affairs and trade.

Located in the middle of a residential neighborhood a local community center owns baseball and soccer fields. I propose that for the use of these fields that the high school provides bonus facilities on its roof for use by community center members.

Hop-Skip-Mosey, Figuring The Opportunistic Occupation Of Context

Hop, Skip and Mosey are analytical caricatures of how to occupy the project's context. Each corresponds with a built resource that I propose the school negotiate for. For each resource a series of more traditional maps are made to describe the sites where the assets are located; figure ground, tree coverage, car access ect. The Hop-Skip-Mosey occupational diagrams are derived from these maps suggesting that in order to make use of the resources you need to understand not just what the context is but how it is occupied.

Island hopping [2] characterizes how one would occupy out-parcels in a strip mall parking lot, the unlikely spot in which the local library is marooned. Island hopping describes a point to point experience of separate yet physically and programmatically related spaces. The design incorporates this logic of hopping by shaping a series of islands across the greater site, which physically and perceptually links the existing library to the new construction of the school.

Obstacle skipping [3] describes how one would use the community college's two sites that are split by Interstate 5. This means of experiencing space is described as having similar form and program interrupted by a dissimilar object. This idea is extended throughout the site with a series of paths that cut through parts of the school.

Fabric Moseying [4] depicts the discontinuous and broken circulation through the residential neighborhood where the community center's sports field is enclosed. Moseying is articulated across the site as zig-zag like locker lined hallways.

Spatializing The Logic Of Exchange: A Strategic Reconfiguration Of Existing Patterns

This urban strategy situates the school within the site's occupational context, which is to say that the school's shape promotes moving around and inhabiting the surroundings in order to make use of the resources that it negotiated for. Rather than mimetically copy these means of occupation locally, all three spatial patterns are

70

second level: **privately** run college
first level: **public** school's media and art facilities

community college

second level: **privately** community center
first level: **public** school's classrooms

sports fields

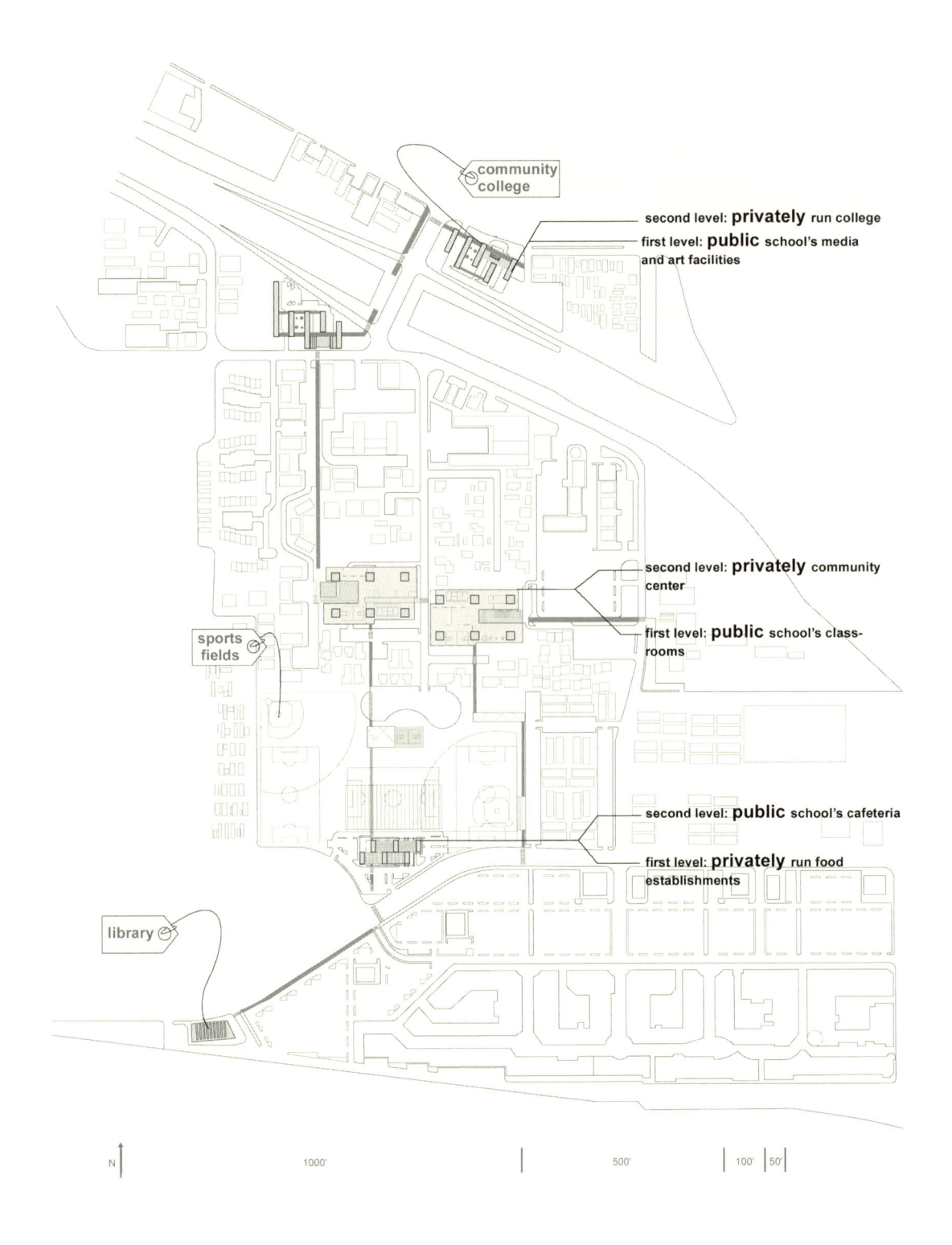

second level: **public** school's cafeteria
first level: **privately** run food establishments

library

N 1000' 500' 100' 50'

5. Site plan

PIPER

extended across the greater site. The pattern of the site is reconfigured through the friction of combination. The nature of this strategy is at once broad, all encompassing, urban as well as minute, shapely architectural.[5] This method of design operates at a mid-scale, where the form making aspirations of architectural intelligence are used to effect the occupation of the broader urban field.

The greater site is organized to establish a distributed network that incorporates the neighboring programmatic resources. Adopting the existing means of occupation and mixing them across the greater site, this network [5] establishes a formal and social mesh that integrates these proximate but currently hermetic uses, creating spaces for synergistic relationships to develop further.

Individual buildings are then shaped to articulate a combination of these three spatial patterns promoting their occupation as integral with the surrounding context and its programmatic assets. For example, in the main classroom building hopping is described in two external courts that are cut out of the overall mat of the building. These cut-out spaces provide defined island-like spots in the mass of the building that both link to other islands around the site as well as provide space for car pick op and drop off. They are crowded with ramps, platforms and a pool to differentiate them physically and programmatically from other islands.

To facilitate skipping through the site a series of paths cut through the open islands and the classroom mat. They link up with sidewalks leading to other spots in the greater site and are programmatically defined as a science super-highway connecting various lab spaces throughout the building and having enough width to be used for outdoor storage or experiments. Formally the paths are defined through linear elements like the glass bottom lap pool on the roof.

Moseying is articulated as a series of locker lined corridors whose continuity is broken and pauses in shared activity spaces. The twelve light-well/tower elements above the activity spaces alternate in height and internal configuration creating specificity to the general shape of the towers.

The overlapping and intermingled occupations that accompany this opportunistic organization establish a logic for articulating form. After first describing these spatial logics individually the site is studied in terms of potential circulation routes and their likely overlaps. Hot spots, or expected points of overlapping circulation are detailed to shape spaces for occupation. Rather than differentially articulate the entire site, or conversely codify details for general circumstances, this method systematically identifies these hot spots yet freely details their material, formal and programmatic make-up. It is intends to create a systematic framework for the willful composition of color, texture and form.

References

> *Harvey, David 1982:* The Limits to Capital. *Oxford: Basil Blackwell and Chicago: University of Chicago Press*
> *Henri, Lefebvre 1974:* The Production of Space. *Oxford, UK: Blackwell Publishers*
> *Soja, Edward 2000:* Postmetropolis. *Oxford, UK: Blackwell Publishers*
> *Tschumi, Bernard 2005:* Event-Cities 3, Concept vs. Context vs. Content. *Cambridge, MA: MIT Press*
> *Whiting, Sarah 2001: Bas-Relief Urbanism: Chicago's Figured Field, in* Mies in America Edited by Phyllis Lambert. *New York, New York, Harry N. Abrams.*

Project Advisors

Sarah Whiting & Ron Witte, Harvard Design School

Notes

[1] *This idea is described as one premise for Bernard Tschumi's Event-Cities 3, Concept vs. Context vs. Content (2005)*

[2] *In an introduction to his book, Ed Soja (2000) reconceptualizes the spatial specificity of urbanism as an infuluential factor in the geo-history of city space, rather than merely an outcome of historical processes(pg 7). He sites David Harvey's concept of the spatial fix, which suggests, in a simplified terms, that economies will seek out socio-spatially different locations to conduct business as a means of fixing economic crisis (pg 99).*

[3] *This concept applies ideas laid out by Henri Lefebvre's conceptualization of space (1974) as perceived (social space), conceived (representations of space) and lived (representations of spaces). My interpretation of his descriptions focus on the idea that that lived or occupied space is effected by its conceived and perceivable characteristics.*

[4] *The idea to analyze a collaborative context of negotiating constituents as a basis for engaging a developer driven context as taken from three academic sources. One: Research I did for Richard Sommer & Laura Miller concerning the various interests involved in the development of the property on top of Boston's big dig (Harvard Design School 2000–2003). Two: a studio I took with Roger Sherman whose title is also the name of a forthcoming book about the same topic: Under the Influence: Negotiating the Complex Logic. of Urban Property (Harvard Design School 2001). Three: Sarah Whiting's description of Mies van der Rohe's IIT campus, Bas-Relief Urbanism: Chicago's Figured Field (2001) which describes how the involvement of multiple institutions in the development of Chicago's Near South Side relates to a shifting reading of it as both object and field.*

[5] *Urban and architectural are italicized here reflecting a generalized, albeit reductive understanding of the terms. This project proposes a practice that combines the two.*

Untitled #19 (Skyways), 2001, Catherine Opie

73

Untitled #23 (Skyways), 2001, Catherine Opie

75

Untitled #16 (Skyways), 2001, Catherine Opie

77

SHAN, Wenhui
Market China Contestation: Purposeful Rationality Versus Value Rationality

In the view of Max Weber, history is a process of rationality and secularization. Purposeful rationality (efficiency) and value rationality (equality) have been the two basic and contrary dimensions of any given social regime since the transition from traditionalism to modernity. Although this immanent contradiction of human society is a source of endless controversy, there is still a consensus that the balance between these two dimensions is the precondition for sustainable development in the long run.

Placing purposeful rationality over value rationality has been the nature of China's economic reform during the last two decades of the twentieth century. As opposed to other post-socialist countries, China's reform has been gradual, experimental and piecemeal. The withdrawal of the central government from heavy-handed economic management to a free market has made a great contribution to economic growth. At present, although the structural disadvantage in the micro-economic realm still remains a major problem for the improvement of economic growth quality and further development, the achievements of economic reform are apparent. The average growth rate of the GDP remains near double-digits and as a consequence, has uplifted hundreds of millions of people out of absolute poverty. China has, in fact, made the largest single contribution to reducing global poverty of any country in the last 20 years.

The concurrent changes in space are the manifestations of significant transformations in the social and institutional dimensions.

Institutional Changes: Authority And Market
The transition of macroeconomic policies

The reform process, which began in 1978, can be described as the decentralization of management, privatization of ownership and marketization of resource distribution. In the early 1950s, the planned economy with its public ownership and powerful central government management of production and distribution made great contributions to nation-wide industrialization and modernization and led to rapid economic growth. This was because the government was able to concentrate scarce resources on the leading industries in a very efficient way during a very short period. However, with the continuation of this kind of economy, the structural economic imbalance gradually became a major problem. In the microeconomic realm, the monopolistic power of the central government resulted in an imbalance of resource distribution, a mismatch of demand and supply, a paternalistic relationship between the government and the enterprises, and organizational inefficiency.

The inefficiency in the micro economy was related to the adjustment of the macro economy, which exacerbated the situation in the micro economy and perpetuated a negative cycle. As with all planned economies, the over-accumulation and widespread shortages became serious problems. By the end of the 1970s, the central government had the great financial burden of maintaining the large welfare system and meeting the need for further investment to stimulate economic growth. The central government became the focal point of all kinds of pressures and conflicts originating from the lower levels. This resulted in a major economic reform initiative, which defined its goals as decentralization of management, privatization of ownership and marketization of resource distribution.

The major characteristics of China's economic reform are internally generated rather than shaped by external elements, in a top-down rather than bottom-up mechanism, and in a gradual, rather than radical, way. Economic reform underwent three key stages—building an economic system with the planned economy as the main body and a limited introduction of market adjustment in 1980; implementing the planned commercial economy in 1984; and establishing the socialist market economy in 1993. The tendency was towards a more open and liberal market economy. The market gradually has played more and more of an important role in social and economic resource distribution. However, a stable circumstance that has good continuity with the former system is also critical for the success of economic reform. This necessitated the coexistence of market forces and strong state control for a rather long period. This is the nature of the Chinese transitional economy: it is neither a western-style free-market economy nor a typical socialist centrally planned economy. The transitional economy has a dual nature. As a result, the year 1984 marked the critical watershed of the urban economic reform in China. The key characteristic function of economic reform in China since 1984 has been to redefine the right of deriving economic benefits, redistributing the right to a lower level so as to increase the incentive for production. The decentralization of power from the state to the local level and the shift of rights and responsibilities from state to enterprise make local government and enterprises more autonomous in allocating scarce resources. Thus, institutional changes originated from the practical recognition of a serious structural contradiction in the economy, and this led to a gradual transformation in ideology. The interaction of institutional changes and ideological transformation not only made great contributions to economic growth, but also brought about drastic changes socially and spatially. Social stratification and spatial differentiation were the major outcomes.

The housing reform: from welfare to commodity

Because housing is the major sector of social overhead capital, housing reform is an important part of macro economic reform. Urban housing was a main component of public welfare in China before 1984. State and city governments were in charge of housing construction, management and maintenance. On one hand, there was a shortage of urban housing. In the socialist planned economy era, production superseded consumption. This policy was dictated by the limited consumption expenditure provided by the central government. A type of consumer good, urban housing was supplied in the most economical way. On the other hand, the rent for public housing was disproportionately lower than maintenance costs because urban housing was regarded as a kind of socialist welfare item. In 1956, the average rent paid by a household living in public housing was only 2.4 percent of the total household income. This system of low rent for public housing continued to be in effect until the late 1970s. This system resulted in many problems, such as government debt, poor management and renovation, and monotonous planning and design of housing estate and housing units. More importantly, this system became the heavy burden of the central government. With the expansion of the urban population, housing shortages became a major problem. Urban housing commercialization has become one of the main objectives of China's urban economic reform in order to rectify this situation. By commercializing urban public housing stock and encouraging the development of new commercial housing, city governments have gradually been relieved of their financial burden. At the same time, mass production of housing can stimulate the development of other related industries and finally revitalize the national economy. When reasonable primary and secondary housing markets are formed, urban residents can have more choices and opportunities to improve their living conditions. Urban housing commercialization, as the major strategy of housing reform, was gradually realized by the reforms of the two interrelated areas of housing investment and distribution.

In the realm of housing investment, the gradual withdrawal of the central government and the emerging role of local governments, enterprises and individuals were the major strategies used to mitigate the shortage of construction funds. Since the Chinese Central Government promulgated the reform policy of urban housing supply and distribution in 1984, the main sector of housing investment and management has been transferred from the central and local government to enterprises. By 1988, the housing investment from the central government had dropped to 3.5 percent and the investment from local government 7 percent, while enterprises were financing more than 60 percent of the total housing construction investment. As a result, collective and private sectors played an increasingly important role in housing investment and construction. In 1988, the central government announced a new housing reform act, which decreed that the housing supply would no longer be a fixed asset investment defined in the planned economy, but would rather be a kind of commercial product. This marked a critical step in the legitimization of private investment. In addition, it pushed reform to a higher level and led to more efficient housing supply dynamics.

In Shanghai, the ratio of basic construction funds from the central government and local government changed rapidly during the 1990s. [1] Although investments from both

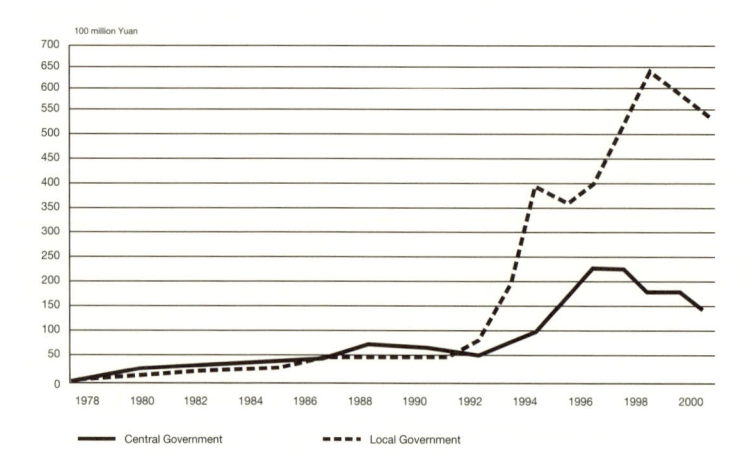

1. Investment on fundamental construction from central and local government, Shanghai, 1978–2000.

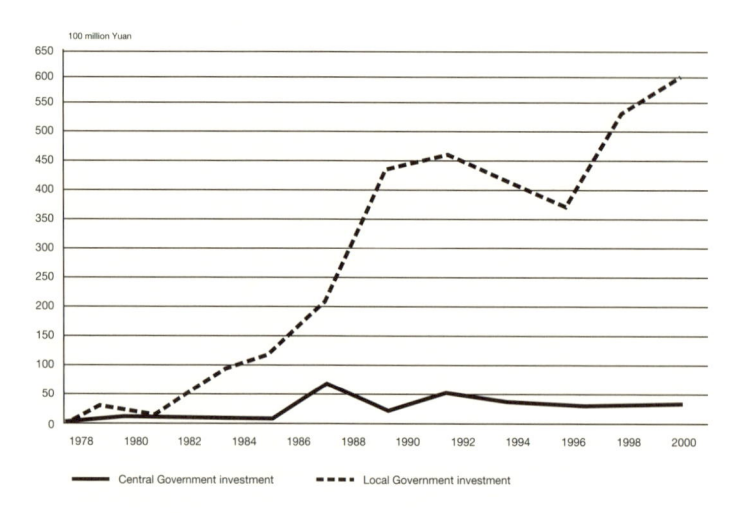

2. The investment structure of commodity housing construction in Shanghai, 1986–2001.

sources increased dramatically during the 1990s, the steeper curve of the local government indicates that its rate of increase was much faster than the central government's investment. By 2000, the fund from the central government was less than one-fourth of the total investment. At the same time, the investment structure of commodity housing construction reflects this same tendency. The proportion of investment by central government dwindled drastically during the 1990s. [2] And this shows us the growing local autonomy that is accompanying the deepening of economic reform and decentralization of management.

The diversification of housing investment is reflected not only in the coexistence of domestic state-owned, collective and private channels, but also embodied in the increasing influx of capital from outside the mainland.

On the national level, following the policy of opening-up, Shanghai gradually has become one of the most important cities for attracting foreign investment. This is especially true since the central government conferred the preference policy on Pudong in 1990, shifting the focal point of development from Shenzhen to Shanghai. As a result, total foreign direct investment (FDI) increased drastically in the 1990s. [3] In general, foreign investors have set up single-owned companies (or subsidiaries), or joint ventures with domestic investors who control the construction of the project. This kind of investment is classified as FDI.

On the local level, the implementation of the land lease system in 1988 stimulated

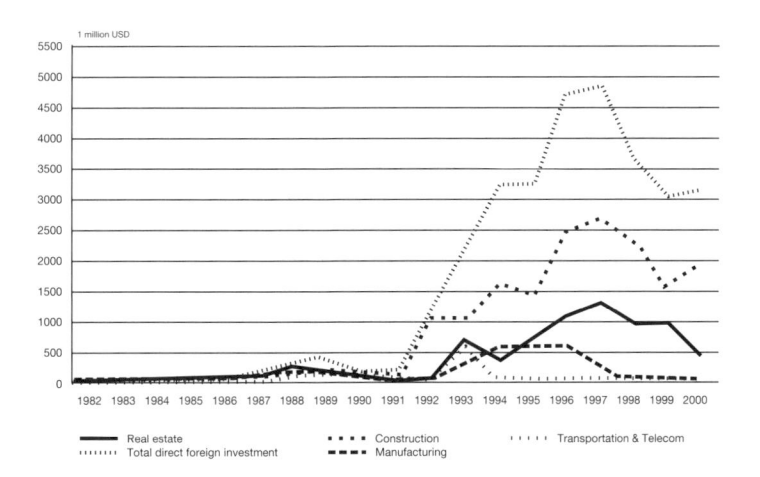

3. The growth distribution of foreign direct investment (FDI) in Shanghai, 1982–2000.

the influx of foreign capital into real estate development. The gradual opening up of the domestic housing development market to foreign capital was also a key element. At the beginning, foreign developers were permitted to build luxury apartments or villas only for the international market. In 1993, because of the shortage of funds for inner city renewal, the Shanghai municipal government announced that foreign capital would be used to develop the domestic commodity housing in some specific dilapidated urban areas. Although there were still some limitations on land acquisition for foreign investors, the new policy basically permitted foreign developers to develop properties for the local market. To attract investors, the municipal government had to permit a mix of commercial and residential properties and increase FAR in order to guarantee a profitable return. The potential rise in property values drew more FDI into real estate development. This was a turning point of FDI distribution in different economic sectors. From Figure 3 we can see that during the year 1992 the FDI in the manufacturing industry was much more than in real estate. This situation changed rapidly in 1993 when the FDI in real estate soared to a much higher level. Much of the FDI in manufacturing was attracted to the real estate. In the following years, the FDI in real estate increased steadily and reached its peak in 1997. It fell due to the Asian financial crisis in 1997 and the gradual ripening of local real estate development enterprises.

By analyzing the historical data, one can see that there were three housing construction booms: the first one in mid 1980s which was mainly initiated by the public institutions; the second one in mid 1990s and resulted from private investment with an influx of foreign capital, and the third one during 2002 and 2004 driven by domestic and foreign floating capital. Through these events, the marketization process of housing supply and distribution has been fulfilled in less than two decades in big cities in China.

The transformation of land use system

It is impossible to separate land use from the housing market, whether in a transitional economy or in an advanced capitalist economy. The major objective of land use reform was to optimize land use patterns and increase profits without changing public ownership of the land, and this was done with the introduction of the land-lease system. Before economic reform, as a kind of public resource, land was publicly owned by either the state or collective ownership and was allocated administratively. Land use reform began to be formulated in the early 1980s, and the idea of introducing a land-user fee was conceived in 1980. In 1988, the National People's Congress amended the Land Management Act. According to the amended act, land use rights could be transferred and a land use fee system would be put into effect. In 1990, the State Council announced the Provisional Regulations on Grant and Transfer of Use Rights to State-

5a. 1990: Transformation of urban fabric in area around People Square of downtown Shanghai (Dark: traditional Lilong housing; Medium: new buildings; Light: others)

owned Land in Urban Areas. It specified the provisions for land use right grants, transfers, leases, mortgages, termination and allocation. Land grants and allocation are the two main ways for land users to obtain land use rights. The granted term for residential land use is 70 years; for industrial land use, 50 years; for education, science and technology, health care and sports, 50 years; for commercial, tourism and entertainment, 40 years; for mixed or other kinds of land use it is 50 years. Land use rights can be granted by three methods including negotiation, tender or auction. This regulation became the foundation for cultivating a competitive land market, thus making the land acquisition process more and more transparent. Since 2002, all the urban lands for profitable uses in big cities have to be acquired by tender or auction.

Shanghai has always been a leader in China's drive to create a system of commercial laws. In 1986, a land use fee was collected from foreign investors. A major change was introduced in 1987, when the collection of the land use fee was replaced by a new system of land use rights transfer. According to this new system, market conditions rather than administrative directives would be the basis for land allocation. In late 1987, the municipal government announced China's first regulations on the transfer of land use right: Shanghai Regulations on Transfer of Land Use Rights for Compensation. In 1988, Shanghai successfully pursued China's first international bidding on land use rights. And in the past decade, by initially introducing the commodity building for overseas sale into the land market, the Shanghai municipal government was aiming to establish a reasonable and stable mechanism for the land market. Realizing that the scarcity of urban land has a determined effect on urban economic growth, the city government managed the land market in a highly rational manner.

Marketization And Its Spatial Manifestation

The reform has not only led to continuous and rapid economic growth, but has also brought forth distinctive social and spatial changes. In the social dimension, urbanization and the cultivation of a market economy have stratified the former dual structure of workers and peasants. And in the spatial dimension, what we have observed is that disparities between regions and cities have grown.

Regional differentiation

On the regional level, there are two trends in urbanization. One is that the population is gravitating towards big and medium sized cities. The other is the increased concentration of labor and capital in the three Economic Zones (Pearl River Delta, Changjiang River Delta, and the Surrounding Bohai Bay Area) which have developed along China's

5b. 2000: Transformation of urban fabric in area around People Square of downtown Shanghai

eastern coast. By the year 2001, there were 25 cities with a population over 2 million, 141 cities with a population between 1 million and 2 million, and 279 cities with a population between half a million and 1 million. With the percentage of cities with a population of less than half a million at only 32.6 percent of the total, the distribution of population is very uneven. Most of the medium and large sized cities are located in the three economic zones. The GDP of the top 55 cities in 2001 was 71.5 percent of all cities above the prefectural level. In addition, nearly all the medium and large cities with a GDP per capita of more than 30,000 Yuan in 2000 were located along the eastern coast, mainly concentrated in the two cosmopolitan zones of Pearl River Delta and Changjiang River Delta.

Although the current population and income conditions have historical roots—the three zones have had the densest populations and the most economic activity throughout history—the economic growth has been uneven and the gap between eastern, middle and western China has been enlarged.

The geographical production pattern indicated that the economic gaps between regions had widened. The highest economic production continued to be concentrating along the eastern coast. Three growth nodes along the coast were emerging. The Changjiang River Delta, where Shanghai is located, became the dominant center.

High-rise-ification and bulkage-ilization of city space

With the impact of intense regional urbanization and economic growth, big cities along the eastern coast have undergone several cycles of boom and bust during the last two decades. The rate of growth was further accelerated around the turn of this century with economic globalization, and the rapid growth of the urban population with the expansion of urban built areas.

The drastic growth of Shanghai during the last two decades can be illustrated as follows: The metropolitan population increased from 11.86 million in 1982 to 16.41 million in 2000, and the urbanization rate increased from 61.9 percent in 1982 to 74.6 percent in 2000; The urban built area expanded from 141 square kilometers in 1978 to 755 square kilometers in 2000. Compared with the expansion of the urban land area, the rate of urban population growth is relatively low, which means a lower population density than before. But this does not lead to a lower density of construction. The fact is that more and more skyscrapers mushroomed in the urban landscape. By 2000, there were about 4000 high-rise buildings with a height of more than eight stories in metropolitan area of Shanghai—most of these built just during the last twenty years. Shanghai has undergone unprecedented high-rise-ification since the 1980s particularly during the late 1990s. [6]

Meanwhile, with the changing land use policy, the growth of new urban areas has incurred great stress upon the preservation of the traditional inner cities. Because of the scarcity of cultural and service resources in the outer-ring area, the inner city is still the ideal place for investment. This leads to large-scale demolition of old neighborhoods and the construction of large patches of new housing. As a consequence, the old urban fabric has been radically altered by profit-driven commercial housing development. (See [5] traditional Lilong fabric rendered in black)

Yi-Cheng-Jiu-Zhen: a spatial strategy for decentralization

Confronted with the pressure caused by continuous concentration, the municipal government of Shanghai started the new process of Yi-Cheng-Jiu-Zhen (one city, nine towns) at the turn of the new century to decentralize both population and industries in the central city. An ambitious metropolitan level mass transit system and an extravagant new port city strategy have also been put into the city's agenda for the next expansion. For westerners, the multinodal city may seem an outmoded concept. But for fast growing mega cities like Shanghai, it might to be too early to predict the effect of Yi-Cheng-Jiu-Zhen. It is possible that a new prototype of urban morphology will emerge, designed to adapt to the many difficulties incurred by the unusual pace and scale of urban development in China. In any case, it seems that the contemporary spatial strategy exhibits tendencies of continuous consumption and expansion rather than demonstrating the initiative of decentralization.

A New Prototype?

The unique condition of the contemporary urbanization process in China is the dramatic time-compressed process of urban growth that continues to occur on the foundation of a highly concentrated management structure. The municipal government has been able to absorb the positive externality of urban growth, which could be considered a highly non-capitalistic result. From this perspective, in fact, the mode of economic integration in China still retains the character of redistribution rather than that of a competitive market. Even with its redistribution-based nature, however, the emerging market forces will further enlarge regional differences and will concentrate resources, including labor and capital, along the east coast of China. It is probable that a new prototype of regional mega-city will emerge, in a way we have just begun to know.

In spite of future potential, we should not become complacent about a contemporary reality driven by rapid urban growth. Drastic growth and expansion of city space can hasten the obsolescence and depreciation of existing buildings. After all, a significant function of urban planning is to slow down the pace of urban growth in order to ensure a stable built environment of high value and quality—Though the pursuit of such an environment becomes a challenge in a rapidly urbanizing landscape where powerful political and economic forces demand a quickened pace of development.

References

> The World Bank, Economic Achievements and Current Challenges (2002), 10 December 2002, <http://www.worldbank.org.cn/Chinese>.
> Shoulong Mao, The Economic Analysis of Chinese Government (Beijing: China Broadcast & Television Press, 1996), 63.
> Fulong Wu and Anthony Gar-On Yeh, Urban Spatial Structure in Transitional Economy: The Case of Guangzhou, China, (Southampton SO17 1BJ, United Kingdom: Department of Geography, University of Southampton, 1997).
> China's Economic Regime Reform Yearbook Editorial Department, China's Economic Regime Reform Yearbook 2000-2001 (Beijing: China's City Yearbook Press, 2001), 302.
> Dianchun Jiang, Jean Jinghan Chen and David Isaac, The Effect of Foreign Investment on the Real Estate Industry in China, Urban Studies, 1998, Vol. 35, No. 11, 2101–2110.
> Fulong Wu, The Global and Local Dimensions of Place-making: Remaking Shanghai as a World City, Urban Studies, 2000, Vol. 37, No. 8, 1359–1377
> Sun Sheng Han, Shanghai between State and Market in Urban Transformation, Urban Studies, Vol. 37, No. 11, 2000, 2091–2112.
> Shuhai Huang, Mu Zhuang, The Collection of Real Estate Policies and Regulations of the People's Republic of China (Beijing, The Law Press, 1993).

> Sun Sheng Han, "Shanghai between State and Market in Urban Transformation," Urban Studies, Vol. 37, No. 11, 2000, 2091–2112.
> "City" in this context indicates a specific administrative territory including both urban area and the surrounding rural area. Therefore the populations of cities include both urban and rural population.
> The National Statistical Bureau of China, The Brief of National Urban Social and Economic Development in 2001 (2002), 15 December 2002, <http:// HYPERLINK "http://www.china.com.cn" www.china.com.cn>.
> According to administrative management hierarchy, cities in China are classified into five top-down levels: municipalities directly under the Central Government, municipalities affiliated with the province government, municipalities affiliated with the prefecture government, cities affiliated with county government, towns.
> Peter Hall, Cities of Tomorrow: An Intellectual History of Urban Planning and Design in the Twentieth Century, (Oxford: Blackwell Publishers Ltd, 1996)

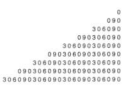

SHAN, Wenhui
Developer Dialogue

Sept, 29th, 2004. 4:00—6:00 PM
Place: Shanghai, Hilton Hotel, conference room
Compere: Wenhui Shan
DDes, Associate Professor of Fudan University
Principal of Urban DATA

Participants:
Dr Jiang Wu, Professor of Tongji University, Deputy Director of Shanghai Urban Planning Bureau.
Dr Huiming Zhang, Professor of Fudan University, Dean of School of Economy.
Jianpin Gu, President of Luxiangyuan Real Estate Co., LTD
Siqi Yan, Deputy Chief Engineer of New Huang Pu Group Co., LTD
Tian Li, PhD Candidate of Land Economy, University of Cambridge

Shan (practitioner): Welcome, guests. We are here to discuss Shanghai as a case, focusing on the new urbanity in contemporary China and its relationship with institutional innovation in real estate, municipal governance, and planning and design. We begin the conversation on the premise that the decline of Keynesian economic ideology and the rise of neo-liberalism since the 1970s has called into question the role of nation states and regions in the global context. In China, emerging regional cities and their consciousness of the necessity of regional autonomy have increasing effect on national and local political agendas, and there are broader collaborations between public and private sectors in investment and maintenance of urban infrastructure. Consider China's unique social and historical condition. Can we identify the characteristics of city governance, development and design of China in this global context? What are the opportunities, challenges and risks with which China might be confronted?

Wu (professor): The shift of social and cultural modes of thinking is very significant in China's reform. A type of privatization that could not happen in the western world is now taking place in China, because the understanding of "private ownership" differs greatly between Chinese and western cultures. Chinese privatization should more precisely be called "marketization." Private ownership in the Western sense suggests absolute domination of the individual's personal terms. Reform in China is neither like this precedent Western mode, nor the former state ownership model. It has its own way, divergent from western methods.

Zhang (professor): From a western perspective, it seems that any action that breaks the monopolization of government can be called "privatization."

Shan: Let's explore this idea of individual versus state interests. Do contemporary public policies on real estate ensure a stable and fair market for developers, or do developers in fact suffer from unpredictable changes of policy? How do developers avoid these risks?

Yan (private developer): Basically, developers familiarize themselves with all government regulations in the initial planning period for a given area, and they maintain regular communication with municipal planners in order to keep a clear vision of future urban development plans. It is understood that the government does make adjustments on leasing lands which have historically had very complex property ownership structures—this is a risk. Indeed, the government has imposed reduction of already agreed-upon FAR in active development areas [downtown Shanghai] during the past two years as a planned solution to the super high-density in downtown areas. But in spite of being unexpected, the lower FAR is not such a bad deal since it tends to introduce a better living environment. The result is higher land value and price of housing—such regulations can benefit developers in the end. I have to say, however, that these days the government is not likely to change the planning and design regulations on lands leased by tendering or auction. A more stable market is emerging.

Shan (practitioner): How is the Bund Area Redevelopment Project pursued by New Huang Pu Group Co., LTD progressing?

Yan (private developer): The Bund Project was initiated in 2000. It's the largest urban renewal project in the historic downtown core of Shanghai. It is also an exploration of urban regeneration. We invited international design teams from all over the world to participate in generating ideas for how to proceed.

Tian (PhD candidate): If the changes implemented by municipal planning affect land value, is there any compensation for property owners provided by the government?

Wu (professor): From theoretical perspective, there is not a direct linkage made between government control, planning changes, and the developers' financial interest. Here's an example: If the government belatedly demands that developers reduce the FAR cited in the original lease documents as a necessity for the macro-level situation, the government recognizes that it should make a reasonable compensation for the losses incurred by developers. And typically the government does prepare the fund—however, the fact is that no developers will come to make claims. The reason is that the loss of income potential resulting from the lower FAR is much less than the cost of communication with the local government that would be necessary in order to make a claim. The communication cost is the greatest cost, yet it is invisible. It is not reflected in the land lease, and this makes it hard for the government to make compensation for it. Developers avoid invisible costs, choosing instead to absorb minor losses. With the further marketization of the land lease system through increased tendering or auction, developers can increasingly avoid having to pay invisible costs at all. Yet the amount of lands acquired by tendering or auction is still relatively small. In contemporary Shanghai, the undeveloped land area owned by developers in stock is 6 or 7 times all the lands developed in 2003. So there are still many problems and uncertainties plaguing the real estate market. We face a critical challenge to manage the conflicts that still persist between the new system and the old one in the short run.

The risks confronting developers are closely related to great opportunities in the contemporary Shanghainese real estate market. Shanghai is historically known as the Eden of Adventurers—so it is today.

Yan (private developer): The central government suggested in a recent conference that the land auction would be a short-term solution. They have said that after they make improvements to the laws and regulations governing the real estate market, negotiation will still be a possible method of land leasing.

What about externalities resulting from government action—like the appreciation or depreciation of land and subsequent profits or losses. What about the distribution of financial benefits? Do you think that disregarding the potential for social inequality will affect the health of the real estate market? What should the government do?

Wu (professor): A very typical case to illustrate this issue is Zhongyuan City. At the time of intervention, the environment in this area had very poor quality. The government leased the land to a developer at a very low price in order to ensure the improvement of the city environment. But the government did not anticipate what happened—specifically, that land value and housing prices in Shanghai would rise so quickly. In the end, the government did not get any return from the developer. In fact, it was not even the developer but rather the home buyers who were the biggest winners in Zhongyuan City.

Tian (PhD candidate): What's the government's opinion on this kind of reaping where one has not sown?

Wu (professor): The government continues to improve the regulations in order to ensure that the return of government's investment will be reaped by the majorities rather than the minorities.

Gu (public authority): All of the different stakeholders, including developers and home owners, can influence the government's decisions.

Shan (practitioner): How much impact can this influence have?

Zhang (professor): After 20 years' development, the real estate market in Shanghai has become the premier market in China. The development in recent years can be understood as an explosive release after many years' restraint. Such an unusual great leap forward is hardly controlled by either central or district government. Most government bureaucrats' vision still lingers in the world of linear management. In this context, the developer can have a very strong influence on the government. Since real estate development is a more complex process, and not at all linear, there are many external variables beyond the purview of this linear management system. Moreover, even developers did not realize the degree to which other stakeholder groups would follow them in order to pursue these interests. It is significant that the inevitable winners would be home buyers. This is a group that has more open attitudes concerning consumption and investment. An open attitude is fortune, especially in the real estate sphere.

Shan (practitioner): Let's talk about real estate trends in Shanghai.

Zhang (professor): As a global city, Shanghai has very limited land supply in contrast to the enormous potential demand. Considering the legacy of "international settlements" [concessions], the housing demand that the Shanghai market responds to is global. Shanghai's housing market has the potential to rise in value continuously, barring a financial crisis.

The municipal government of Shanghai needs to review its policies on industrial structuring, population and inhabitation, education, and so on. An impoverished class will emerge in the city of Shanghai. They temporarily make a living on their houses, selling their apartments in the downtown area and moving to the suburban area to find a lower housing price. Based on development trends in contemporary Shanghai, a large population of such a class will not be able to find their position in the modern metropolitan industrial structure. The housing and education policy must consider the interest of this group. The real estate industry is a complex system; an administration and management mode constrained by linear thinking will cause many problems.

Shan (practitioner): Let's think about this issue from a regional perspective. Because of population migration, some industries have also shifted to suburbia or to satellite towns. Could we mitigate the pressure caused by soaring housing prices in the central city by the simple spatial expansion of city development?

Gu (public authority): Currently, administrative boundaries can prevent cooperation among regions. However, we can expect that emerging market forces will gradually break through this kind of management segregation. We can't ignore the fact that during the 2004 Formula One Motorsport event in Shanghai, a good part of the audience lived in Suzhou or Wuxi, not Shanghai. Considering the relatively recent accomplishment of building the MagLev (magnetic levitating vehicle), I would guess that some Shanghai citizens would actually choose to live in Hangzhou or nearby.

Shan (practitioner): Does this mean that market forces are leading to more regional autonomy?

Zhang (professor): It should be interpreted that marketization has enhanced local official's consciousness of regional collaboration. Also, there can be rewards. In August 2003, regional governments promoted the participants of the Yangtze River delta cooperation conference to a higher level.

Wu (professor): In the context of the emerging market, the drive for regional cooperation has more bottom-up tendencies than top-down.

Zhang (professor): By creating more and more channels for discourse, local governments are guided toward an open perspective.

Yan (private developer): Will this broad regional development affect the price of housing in Shanghai?

Wu (professor): Yes, the scale and scope of the housing market are becoming larger.

Zhang (professor): Clearly, the construction of infrastructure can change the value of a given location. And also, changing lifestyles in China influence people's housing choices.

Shan (practitioner): To what degree is the real estate industry in Shanghai influenced by private firms (rather than by government control)?

Wu (professor): The real estate industry in Shanghai is still in its infancy. The top 20 real estate companies in Shanghai still account for only a 15% share of the total market. Compare this to Hong Kong, where only 10% of the total amount of real estate firms hold more than an 80% share of the market.

Tian (PhD candidate): Can we expect monopolization by several companies in Shanghai through manipulation of the government's policy?

Wu (professor): It should be said that a feasible policy would enhance the efficiency of the market without the social cost of significant inequity. Of course, there is not absolute inequity.

Shan (practitioner): Is fast growth the force driving inequity?

Wu (professor): No—if there is no growth, there is even more inequity.

Zhang (professor): We can only accept this inequity in the short term—we accept it now because we need this difference to stimulate high productivity. However, I believe that after 20 years' growth, the inequity will be mitigated.

Compared with other industries, real estate has little foreign investment outside of the "Chinese troop" (overseas Chinese investors). Why?

Wu (professor): I think the main reason for low foreign investment in Chinese real estate is the lack of foreign investors' confidence in the stability of political and legal circumstances in China. Real estate investment is long-term investment, and has a long financial cycle. Despite this, most of the foreign investment in China is short-term investment. For example, the cooperation that exists between Rockefeller and some Chinese enterprises is very tentative. Since the reform and open policy kicked in, the majority of foreign investors in the real estate industry are from Hong Kong, Macao, Taiwan and Singapore, and have a Chinese background. Even now, they still lack confidence in the future of real estate in China. For this reason, their investment is concentrated in the housing industry—housing investment has a shorter return cycle than commercial or office building investment. Still, we should have an optimistic vision of the future of the real estate industry in China—even while recognizing the existing problems. Long-term investment requires the stabilization and predictability of future development. Our current policy environment cannot ensure either.

Gu (public authority): Another key factor is culture. A mature real estate company wants to be familiar with local culture, otherwise the company could incur a much higher cost of development.

Tian (PhD candidate): Does the uncertainty come out of the artificial action of the government through policies intended to manipulate the market?

Wu (professor): Uncertainty cannot be attributed to government completely. It can also be traced to the psychology of investors. We are learning more now about economic psychology.

In all of the global cities, the direct consequence of globalization is polarization—local groups are marginalized. In Shanghai, a lot of foreign capital and foreign people have flowed into the city fast. In only two years, the average housing price has more than doubled. How can the municipal government protect disadvantaged groups? Will the government introduce an affordable housing policy like Hong Kong and Singapore?

Wu (professor): Yes, it seems that Shanghai is becoming less and less reflective of native Shanghai people. The local government has responded by providing many affordable housing opportunities to local citizens. However, it's likely the problem has been exaggerated—the rate of homeownership in Shanghai is around 70%. This ratio is high not only in China but also in more developed countries.

25% of home buyers in Shanghai are not locals,

5. Shanghai

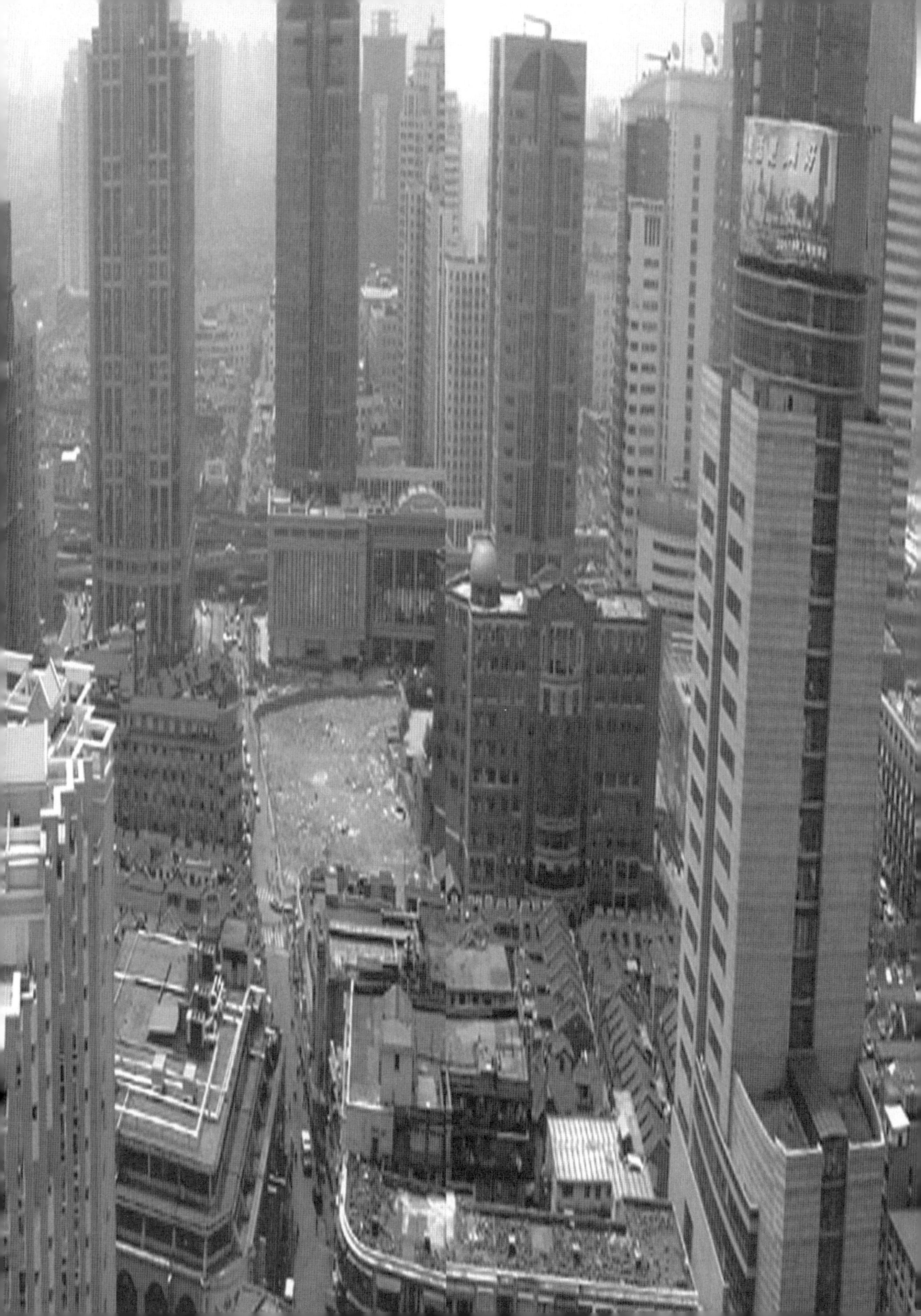

meaning that three-quarters of buyers are indeed locals. Our welfare housing policy has resolved the housing problem for most families, and now the most difficult issue is how to sponsor the residents who were not eligible for the welfare housing because of historic building preservation regulations. The most critical issue currently is not the ownership rate, but the quality of housing. Variation in quality ranges widely—this is worse than western countries. But fortunately, the central government has already realized this problem and is seeking an appropriate policy.

Tian (PhD candidate): The welfare housing policy only benefits Shanghai citizens. We need to ask how to address the needs of floating populations and new immigrants.

Wu (professor): The government is now building various low-rent public housing options to improve immigrants' living conditions. Of course the government hopes to reduce direct public investment—they'd like to attract developers to build these low-profit projects. However, these developments involve some issues regarding land ownership—mainly regarding how to transform collective ownership to state ownership.

Tian (PhD candidate): Does the government have any measures within the land supply policy designed to restrain increases in housing price?

Wu (professor): The problem of housing prices in Shanghai today is linked to the pace of growth, not the scope of growing. Housing prices in Shanghai are not high compared to other global cities—prices here are only one tenth of current prices in Taipei, and one fifteenth to one twentieth of those in Hong Kong. The government policy is therefore designed to slow down the speed of growth rather than to drive housing prices down. It's certain that current prices still have space to increase—whether or not they do depends on the path of globalization and urbanization in Shanghai.

Zhang (professor): The situation in Shanghai is very unique. Shanghai has a big gap in land lease value, which is very different from other cities in China.

Wu (professor): I studied land prices in Shanghai during the 1930s—at that time the housing price difference between the Bund and Xujiahui was a factor of 900. In the market economy, most goods' prices have nothing to do with use value—price is defined by supply and demand.

As a municipal invested company, what does the Shanghai Urban Investment Co. do besides infrastructure projects? What problems do you face? What is your strategy for the future?

Gu (public authority): The Shanghai Urban Investment Co. is an institutional innovation that came out of the government's need to address the problem of insufficient investment in infrastructure. Through this company, the government absorbs enough capital for urban infrastructure construction, operating with a market sensibility.

Many other cities are now emulating this strategy. The company's core business consists of 5 parts: 1. water supply; 2. improvement of environment, such as the Suzhou Creek revitalization project; 3. road and bridge construction; 4. public transportation; and 5. real estate.

The company engages in real estate in order to cover the costs of the previous four project types with profits earned through its real estate investments. This makes the nature of the company as a public entity very unique.

We do have some operating challenges. Thus far, output is always lower than input—but we cannot rely on continual input by government, so we are considering other resources. Of course, we have an advantage resulting from government support—like access to information. We also innovate; for example we introduce market mechanisms to the management and operation of infrastructure. We trade part of the operation and management rights in order to bring in investment for infrastructure construction.

Wu (professor): The public input in Shanghai urban construction is 250 billion RMB annually, including 70 billion in fixed assets, 80 billion in urban infrastructure input, and 90 billion in real estate investment. The direct investment of the government is about 15 billion, which means the government absorbed 93–94% input with only 6–7% equity. These figures reflect even more capital investment than western countries.

Zhang (professor): The toll charge right of Huning Highway was sold to Hong Kong Shanghai Industrial Corporation by auction.

Wu (professor): Even the right to the operation of the water supply has begun to sell.

Zhang (professor): Gas supply is divided into two parts, one of which is sold to enterprises.

Shan (practitioner): Let's discuss the design issues. In the context of continuing marketization, what's going on with the large state-owned design institutes? Do clients have a preference for either privately owned design firms or state-owned design institutes?

Wu (professor): More precisely speaking, these groups should be called the more-and-more-marketized design groups with a state-ownership background. Their status depends on the degree and depth of marketization.

Tian (PhD candidate): Does urban planning leave enough space for design? Also, in the review and approval process, is it possible that a design that meets all planning goals can be rejected for aesthetic or other reasons?

Wu (professor): Relatively speaking, when compared with foreign colleagues, Chinese designers have more opportunities and space for creation. Although government officers certainly can reject one's work, their influence has lately weakened. The developer plays a key role in making design decisions.

Tian (PhD candidate): What about the legal status of development control?

Wu (professor): Development control does have legal status, but there are many difficulties in operation.

Shan (practitioner): In the design review and approval process, does the public authority consider the urban image or some other requirements of urban design?

Wu (professor): Yes, but the issues addressed will depend on the preference of the officers to a certain extent. In America, this power is given to the local [neighborhood or district] communities. In China, many designs are determined by a decision-maker at the municipal level. However, the Shanghai urban planning bureau may transfer the review right of architectural design to a lower level.

Gu (public authority): The factors of marketization and competition promote design quality in Shanghai, not administrative intervention. Of course it is much easier now for developers and officials to communicate with each other.

> Shan (practitioner): The urban fabric of Shanghai has many unique characters. The city is composed of many cells with various scales and characteristics—for example, the sharp contrast we see between high-rise buildings and the fine-grained Lilong houses. What's your opinion about this unique urban landscape?

Wu (professor): Yes, this form is very special. It has resulted from rapid urbanization. From an academic perspective, it adds to the diversity of contemporary city forms. Our responsibility is to conserve this unique morphology without great social cost.

Gu (public authority): Actually, this reflects a problem that the government faced in the early stages of urbanization. Early on, in order to lower the cost of providing relocation, developers would choose cheap land to build relocated housing, creating a block in which new high-rise towers and two-story shanty fabric coexist side by side. When the government noticed this problem, they introduced a "block development" mode, preferred over the construction of a single building.

Wu (professor): Most developed countries have not solved this problem. Some cities in America, and also Hong Kong, have seen the phenomenon of slums and modern urban development coexisting in the city center.

Gu (public authority): This phenomenon of "village in town" is common in Guangzhou and Shenzhen also, but the "villagers" are actually rich there.

Wu (professor): Our government feels confused sometimes. Ten years ago, citizens appreciated being relocated very much, since they felt that it improved their dwelling environment. However, citizens today tend to complain about relocation. The difference is that the dwelling environment was bad 10 years ago, incentivizing moves, but now the city environment has been improved. People don't want to be moved.

Gu (public authority): The relocatees have a very high psychological relocation fee. And there are no precedents to refer to as we try to make a reasonable financial compensation standard for relocation.

What is the government's biggest challenge in regulating the real estate market?

Tian (PhD candidate): Can you make comments on the role of the government in a transitional market? Is it improving the market, or preventing its further development?

Zhang (professor): The mode of development China adopted is government-dominant. It should be said that the administrative skill of the Shanghai government is relatively high, reflecting a good understanding of the market rules. If the government intervenes too much, it risks preventing the maturation of the market. Success of many industries is relative to the radius of government administration. For example, the light industrial products of Shanghai lost every battle in early 1990s—I think the main reason for this was simply too much government intervention affecting the growth of the product market. Meanwhile in Guangdong, Zhejiang, the private enterprises had strong power. This makes a difference. Thus, the role of government is a double-edged sword. The growth of private sectors can be impeded if the government intervenes too much.

> The Bund is the historical financial district and formerly a British concession in downtown Shanghai.

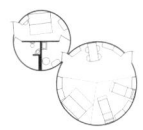

SHANNON, Kelly PhD.

Shifting Norms—The Evolution of Real Estate in Vietnam

Rise of a New Asian Tiger?

The speed, scope and scale of current urban transformation in Southeast Asia is unprecedented. Liberalized economies have propelled pre-industrial agrarian societies into a maelstrom which is mirrored in the spatial structuring of rural and urban territories alike. Vietnam —although late in joining other ASEAN[1] countries in the recent wave of modernization and urbanization—is no exception to the phenomenon. In 1986, the Sixth Congress of Vietnam's Communist Party voted to dramatically change course, effectively ending the country's isolation from the global-economic world. The country adopted a policy—known as doi moi[2]—similar to that of its great northern neighbor (China), whereby it retained communist politics while simultaneously adopting market economics. In its wake, the cradle to grave security of the socialist project has given way to footloose capitalism and rampant real estate speculation; producer cities are rapidly transforming into consumer cities. As Vietnam attempts to assert itself as the region's newest tiger[3], the built landscape is undergoing radical alteration.

1. 1884 French engraving of a village in the Red River delta, with bamboo screen evident and the van chi and mieu located atop a hill

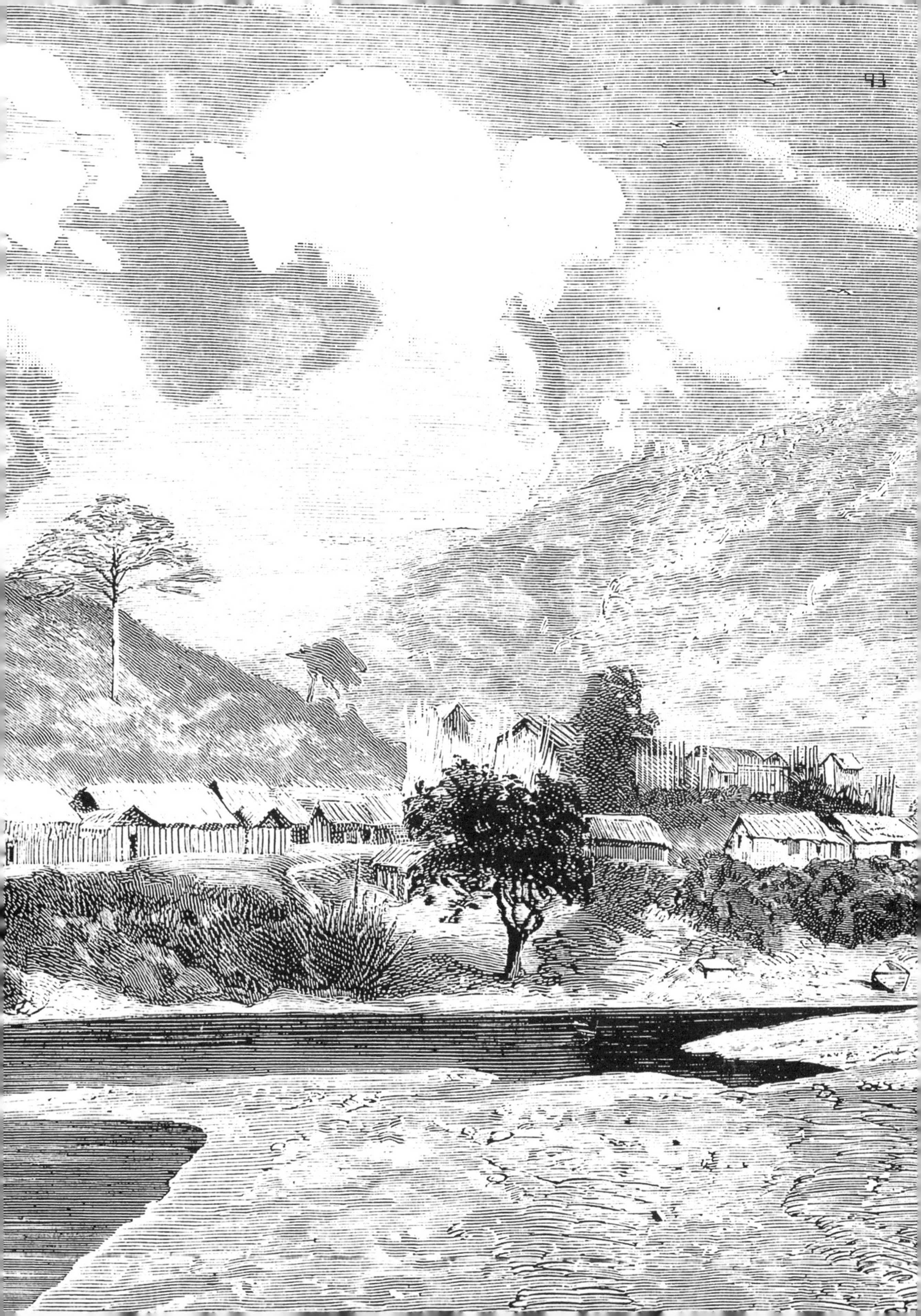

Stringent past policies to control urban growth—restriction of migration, planned decentralization of industry and development of new economic zones (NEZs) in the periphery—have been abandoned. The transformation from a socialist planned economy to a socialist market economy has altered the value of land in that use value has shifted to exchange value. In 1992, the constitution was amended, allowing Vietnam's citizens the right to lease property, to conduct business and to move in search of work.

From Producer Hamlets to Consumer Cities

Historically, settlements in Vietnam were concentrated agglomerations within productive paddy fields. The typical Kinh Viet[4] village was not only an economic unit, but also a cultural community and defensive system within its thick bamboo hedge. Internal organization of villages followed a strict hierarchy of spaces as determined by a series of worship and kinship customs. Power of the reigning dynasties was fuelled by the nation's small-scale agrarian economy in which each household was a production unit. In feudal Vietnam, Mandarins (functionaries appointed by the Emperor) were responsible for coordinating agricultural communities and imposing royal codes upon the peasantry.

Throughout the various dynasties of Vietnam's history, the imperial bureaucracy distinguished four categories of land: state land, land grants, communal land and private land. State lands were directly controlled and exploited by the state. In accordance with an imperial 15th century decree, they were to create land reserves; however, in practice they accounted for small amounts of land. Land grants were allotted temporarily to Buddhist pagodas and Mandarins for public functions. The private, hereditary land parcels of nobility and commoners existed in great numbers but were restricted in size by various statutes and agricultural reforms following wars. Communal land was an ancient land category in Vietnam that was used as a powerful instrument by the centralized monarchy for two purposes:

First, so as not to leave a single inch unplanted nor forget a single citizen, thus alleviating the endemic hunger and misery of the poor and eradicating the scourge of monopolization. Second, so as to be able to levy taxes and men for public works and for the army. To the ancient village custom of distributing land according to kinship structures (age, number of mouths to feed) the Mandarin state added other criteria: taxability and hierarchy of functions. According to the royal code, these lands were not transmissible nor saleable.[5]

Villages were corporate communities that regulated their own affairs and held land for common use. Economically almost self sufficient, the communes paid taxes, provided corvée labor for public works (including the regular maintenance of dykes and irrigation canals) and furnished recruits for the army. Otherwise, the communes had a high degree of autonomy in which structures of kinship, production and religious ties were inseparably linked and developed rich and heterogeneous local traditions.

As an organizer of what already existed, and not by virtue of being the sovereign landowner, the Mandarin state regulated from above and from afar the multi-various activities of a society structured in myriads of peasant collectives and corporations of artisans and shopkeepers. Turned toward the mythical past of a primeval humanity from which it derived its rules of conduct, the celestial bureaucracy gave free play to the earthly affairs of civilian society. Exerting its power as a social regulator for the benefit of its own class interests but also for that of a multiform society, the heavenly bureaucracy knew its own limits.[6]

Initially, the State's grip on the village was loose; however, this tightened with time. Feudalization of the ancient village occurred and simultaneously a network of towns began to develop within proximity of the great rural and regional marketplaces. A number of citadel cities (thanh) were also established at key defensive positions throughout the territory. The Ly dynasty was also responsible for issuing the 11th century royal edict which created the capital city of Thang Long (present-day Hanoi). The newly introduced urban structure was bi-polar and dualistic. On the one hand there was the royal, official city and on the other was the thriving commercial city. The royal citadel and its buildings were set within the midst of rice fields, gardens and ponds.

This enclosed town, staked out in the middle of the open countryside, gave no impression of a city, but rather of an entrenched camp.[7]

On the contrary, the commercial city (Ke Cho, translating to 'market people'), surrounding Hoan Kiem lake, had all the features of an urban agglomeration—uninterrupted rows of habitation opening out towards the streets (pho) and a population whose artisan, commercial and industrial lifestyle was markedly different from villagers. This ancient area, commonly referred to as 36 Streets, was comprised of specialized craft communities (phuong) which resembled ancient villages—complete with their communal houses (dinh), barricades and gates that were closed at night.

In addition to expanding a solidifying settlement control in the Red River delta, from the 15th century onwards, the transformation of communal land into private land increased. Land reclamation made great strides as the hydrological system was extended, uncultivated lands were exploited and new villages were created. During the Le dynasty (1428–1527), the territory of Vietnam was greatly expanded by the March to the South, which provided new lands for a growing population and vastly extended the power of state. The process of southern expansion, begun by the 1558 Nguyen lords, initiated an era of cultural confrontation and the formation of regional identities that would have long-term effects of the development of the nation and its urban places.[8] The traditional, compact village structure was abandoned as new inhabitants settled linearly along the banks of waterways and the rudimentary road networks. Throughout the country a constellation of cities were established, serving as either administrative or military centers for the expanded territory.

The next major transformation of the built environment and notions relating to land value and use came

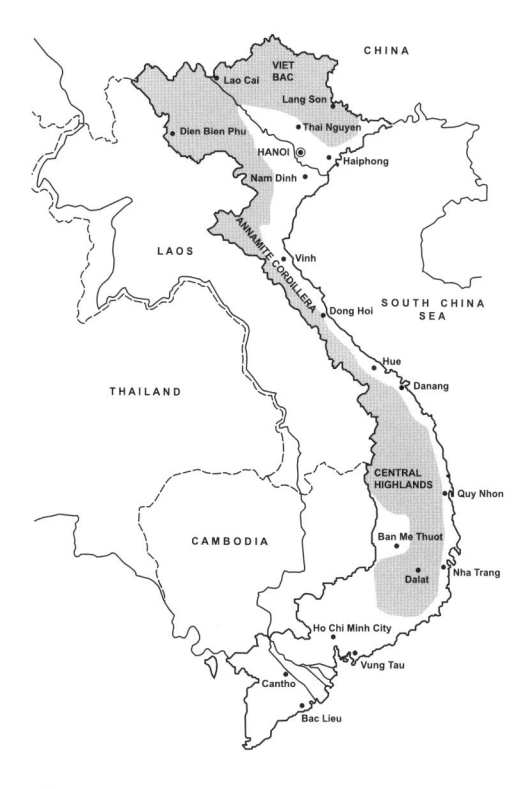

2. Vietnam's southward movement took several centuries to complete. For most of their history, the Vietnamese people lived only in the Red River delta and north-central plains. From 111 BC to 939AD, Vietnam was a directly ruled province of the Chinese empire. The separate kingdom of Champa, south of the empire's border in central Vietnam, existed until 1471, when most of it was overrun by independent Vietnam. The remnant of Champa was absorbed by the Vietnamese in 1720. Thereafter, taking advantage of an extremely weakened Khmer empire, the Vietnamese gradually expanded into the Mekong Delta, completing the conquest by the middle of the eighteenth century and reaching the modern borders of Vietnam.

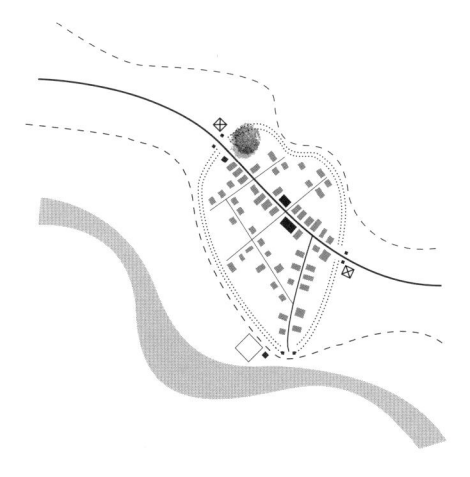

3. Hypothetical spatial structure of a village in the Red River delta with gate and watch station; Dinh—communal house; chua—pagoda; den—temple; van chi—cult of Confucius and mieu—small shrine

4. 1873 French engraving of the Hang Chieu street gate in Hanoi—each phuong was enclosed as a city in the city.

with France's near-century sojourn in Vietnam. The economic prerogatives to exploit natural resources and open up new markets for domestically manufactured goods led to the initiation of Vietnam's transition from an agricultural backwater towards a more internationally-linked, market-driven society. Uncontrolled speculation by powerful corporations and industrialists rapidly transformed town and countryside alike into a fragmented landscape. This was to change in 1922, when Ernest Hébrard was appointed the first director of urbanism for Indochina. He introduced land-use zoning in order to override the individualistic economic interests that heretofore had determined growth patterns. Cities were now planned with five spatially-distinct areas: an administrative center, residential districts, recreational space, commercial districts and industrial sectors. Land-use planning was also utilized as a mechanism for social and racial control. Urban centers were developed as bi-polar, dual cities—the existing, and rarely improved, ville indigène (for locals) was separated by a buffer zone form the newly planned ville moderne (for foreigners).

Existing urban centers greatly increased in size and efficiency and a network of new cities were formed as commercialization of the countryside and land reclamation proceeded. However, as in traditional Vietnam, the concentrated settlement areas continued to rely heavily on the rural countryside. The primary source of profit in Vietnam was the export of rubber and rice. Vast rubber plantations were planted in the terre rouge region along the Cambodian border. Marshlands in the Plains of Reeds (the lower provinces of the Mekong delta) were drained and a dyke, irrigation and water transport system were constructed, converting the previously unusable land into a highly profitable, productive landscape of wet-rice cultivation. Large camps for Chinese and Vietnamese laborers in plantations, agricultural estates and mines (in the mountainous areas) were also constructed. As the formal definition of new areas for development progressed, the tracings of infrastructural lines across the territory were strategically reordered.

The colonial impositions brought traumatic change and created a complete rupture of the traditional Vietnamese society. Modern technology coupled with the impersonal irrationality associated with the competitive market-driven economics radically altered the centuries-old way of production. The development of communication and transportation facilities fostered the diffusion of change, as did administrative and tax reforms and wage labor. A middle class emerged from the increasing number of city dwellers who were exposed to a completely novel social context—one structured by colonial administrators and western-style education. The imposed institutions and associated ethical conventions directly challenged the traditional priorities of loyalty and moral debt to family, village and state. As well, the distinction between urban and rural, town and country, grew substantially during the French era.

The Geneva Conference of 1954 split Vietnam at the 17th parallel with each region having a distinct economic structure, that reflected the competing ideologies in the Cold War. The North, the Democratic Republic of Vietnam (DRV), gradually built-up a socialist economy; the South, Republic of Vietnam (RVN), adopted a modified capitalist system. The subsequent processes of urbanization were as divergent as the ideological/economic models. When Ho Chi Minh and his compatriots returned to Hanoi in the autumn of 1954, they faced a still largely primitive urban sector which had been neglected under the Franco-Vietminh conflict. The builders of the socialist state were handicapped in that their country lacked an industrial base; any large-scale existing industrial centers were damaged in the war.

The goals of Vietnamese socialism followed that of many other socialist countries: state ownership of the means of production, comprehensive planning of the economy, free provision of the basic necessities of life and the "dictatorship of the proletariat." Yet, the means that the Vietnamese Communist Party followed to reach its goals were more pragmatic than many other hard-line countries. Initially, moderate reforms proceeded with the hopes of not alienating the mass population. Private property was abolished, but the more radical policies of the nationalization of industry and the mechanization and collectivization of agriculture were postponed until the late 1950s.

There was concern that the existing cities should not be allowed to grow larger, and a plan was developed to create eleven new industrial centers. At the same time, the over-populated countryside was restructured by a population resettlement program. From 1961 to 1975 approximately 1 million people were persuaded to leave the Red River delta provinces and settle in New Economic Zones (NEZs) in the sparsely populated upland provinces, where they were expected to eke out a living with minimum necessities.[9]

Meanwhile, the South, under Ngo Dinh Diem, started with quite different conditions. The region possessed fertile farmlands, a climate conducive to the cultivation of tropical export products and relatively well-trained industrial and commercial elite. However, the southern regime also faced challenges, including the lack of a resource and industrial base, low productivity and inequality of landholdings in Mekong delta. Industrial development was primarily focused on the production of consumer goods and, with the assistance of US and other Western countries, industrial zones were established on the outskirts of Saigon as well as in the larger cites of the delta and along the central coast. As in the north, there were programs to ease the inequalities in the countryside. In the south they took the form of Diem's unsuccessful "Agroville" program, which forced peasants to live in secure rural small towns, and the partially successful "Land to the Tiller" program of Nguyen Van Thieu, in which tenants received titles to lands without charge and the government provided compensation to the previous large landholders. However, as peasants saw more economic opportunities in the cities, urban populations continued to swell. Despite the urban and rural changes, production levels could not meet the needs of the growing population. South Vietnam progressively became more and more dependent on imports and growing assistance from US.

Both the socialist project of the North and the struggling capitalism of the South were interrupted by the Second Indochina War. In the North, de-urbanization policies were hastened with the accelerated bombing of cities by the US Air Force, which in turn led to the massive movement of populations away from cities. In the south, the cities remained magnets for migration from the countryside, drawn to the commercial opportunities afforded by the presence of the American military in Saigon and as protection from the warfare in the outskirts of the city; thus cities of the south underwent a period of hyper-urbanization. The dispersion of the cities of the north was a foil to the congestion of the cities in the south.

Upon the country's reunification in 1975, the Socialist Republic of Vietnam (SRV) followed a much more vigorous road to socialism, even though the entire country was ravaged by war, industrial and commercial activity was at a standstill, agricultural areas in the south were largely abandoned and there was huge unemployment. Private land owners were expropriated without compensation. In 1978, Vietnam joined CMEA (Council of Mutual Economic Assistance) and the entire country fell squarely in the orbit of the USSR. The classic communist discourse of the structural imbalance between consumer towns and the producing rural areas was found in Vietnam (at least until 1986). But unlike in certain other socialist states, there was not a wholesale refusal of cities as such; the objective was rather to urbanize the countryside, and to achieve a rational and balanced population distribution among the different provinces. Nonetheless, Vietnam concentrated its reconstruction and development efforts in the production sector, to which some 90 percent of the budget was dedicated, and specific emphasis was laid on heavy industries.[10]

In plotting its future, it was decided by the Party that the goal of Vietnam would be to rebuild the north as its industrial base and restore the south as the nation's ricebowl. The repopulation of the southern countryside was therefore mandatory and an intensive period of population reshuffling was implemented immediately following reunification.

During Vietnam's pursuit of socialism, urban and rural landscapes were completely transformed. Urban areas followed the path towards the creation of the City of Socialist Man. Grand, social realist architecture was envisioned—much of which was unrealized due to the impoverishment of the government. Cities focused on production—not consumption—and the resulting proletarian state revolved upon collectivity.

In the countryside, the village stopped operating as an entity of semi-autonomous life in which structures of kinship and production and religious ties were inseparably linked. Instead, it became merely a unit of production, a specialized brigade, integrated into the agro-industrial structures of the district, in turn integrated into the national economic fabric.[11] As the then Secretary General of the Vietnamese Communist Party, Le Duan stated:

> "The entire land is a giant factory in which the state occupies the position of entrepreneur and the people that of salaried workers."[12]

The individual peasant's work in the private or communal rice fields, previously characterized by mutual assistance, gave way to collective exploitation on a grand scale, based on the scientific organization of labor. The thick bamboo hedge that formerly protected the village from the encroachment of the Mandarin bureaucracy was pulled down so that the workers' collective could be transparent to the party-state.[13] Workers' dwellings were organized as microrayons and their architecture mirrored that of the USSR and the Eastern bloc. Mass production techniques were applied to building materials and brick and concrete replaced wood-framed constructions. Architecture became subservient to Party policy.

Despite the objectives and careful planning of the Party, however, difficulties were met on the urban and rural fronts. Production in the industrial and agricultural sectors lagged far behind projections and foreign assistance from the USSR and China was lower than anticipated. In 1982, the party's Fifth National Congress deviated from the Stalinist approach of socialist industrialization and focused on the immediate crisis in terms of food production and increasing the output of consumer goods. Despite the policy shifts, the economic crisis only deepened. Finally, at the Sixth National Congress in December 1986, facing bankruptcy and famine, the Party adopted deep-seated reforms: the planning system and management of state enterprises was decentralized, government bureaucracy was reduced in size, subsidies were eliminated in key commodities and prices were tied to the forces of the market. As well, increased attention was focused on the promotion of agriculture, consumer goods and export commodities, all at the expense of heavy industry. Positive change took a number of years to realize, but by 1989, annual production levels were up substantially, private trade increased and inflation was down. Economic restructuring along the line of industrialization and modernization continues—despite the Party's publicized adherence to their ultimate goal of a socialist-oriented market mechanism under state management.[14] Vietnam re-entered the world stage.

Housing—Registers of Transformation

Throughout the globe, the production of housing reflects broader political, socio-economic and cultural conditions of particular societies at specific moments in time. In Vietnam, the layered narratives of multiple imposed cultural heritages renders richness and diversity in the relation of housing types to the urban fabric. The country's urban morphology is the result of complex spatial translations of different eras and ideologies—from feudal to Chinese-influenced imperial dynasties to French colonial exploits to American military influences and dependent capitalism in the south, to Soviet-block policies and socialism to doi moi and market-based socialism and new industrial zones to modern city extensions. Each of these layered narratives have had recognizable spatial implications that are particularly readable in housing typologies and that reveal specific attitudes towards the development of real estate.

The country's most ancient urban house type is known as the tube house—a long, narrow structure, often only 2-3 meters wide and 50-100 meters deep—believed to have been the result of both lack of space within the urban precincts and the consequence of a tax placed by the imperial government of the width of shop frontage. Indeed, the tube house as it stands today was an evolution of houses that originally began as small hamlets on narrow agricultural plots which became densified as sons inherited property from their fathers. Various rooms/houses were connected by a side corridor and separated by courtyards; as time progresses, the courtyards decreased in number and size. In old days, the tube house was occupied by an extended family, but is now sub-divided and common for a family of four to live in 15–20 square meters. In Hanoi, an entire district of such houses, known as the 36 Streets area, remains relatively intact and is the object of debate and contestation between, on the one hand, developers and entrepreneurs wanting to exploit the central location and, on the other hand, conservationists and local inhabitants who are struggling to rehabilitate and conserve the dilapidated and excessively dense neighborhoods.

The Chinese influence was most evident in the imperial court, urban areas of the feudal period and strict rules revealing a rigid hierarchy enforced in order to maintain the power and privilege of the ruling class. Cities and individual buildings were laid out according to phong thuy—the Vietnamese name for feng shui—creating a new order within nature, whereby the emperor was at the center. At the scale of housing, a system of gian (spans or bays determined by the length of available timber beams) modules revealed the status of families in that commoners were only permitted to build houses of one or three-gian, five-gian houses were for the Mandarin class and seven or more for royalty.[15] All houses were one or two stories high. Today, the pressure on inner-city land is such that these traditional house types are threatened. In Hue (a city geographically in the center of the country), seat of the Nguyen dynasty government from 1802-1945, a large number of such houses exist within its citadel, yet they are also threatened by over-zealous individuals and developers wanting to build higher and more profitable structures. However, since Hue's citadel has been listed on UNESCO's World Heritage list, strict zoning has been established, which restricts heights to two stories. As well, the government plans to reduce the area's population from 70,000 to 40,000.[16] The "imperial scenery" is being re-created since it promises to return ample tourist revenues. Despite the State's restrictions, however, individual initiatives within the historic citadel are evidenced by five (or more) -story structures rising above the sea of low-rise garden and row houses.

The French introduced a completely new housing typology—the villa—which housed the colonists and their servants. The villas were constructed in the urban extensions of cities. Within the existing centers themselves, a hybrid of the urban villa and tube-house/shop-house was developed and inhabited by the upper classes

6. The Soviet era large scale housing estates remain a dominant feature in the urban landscape.

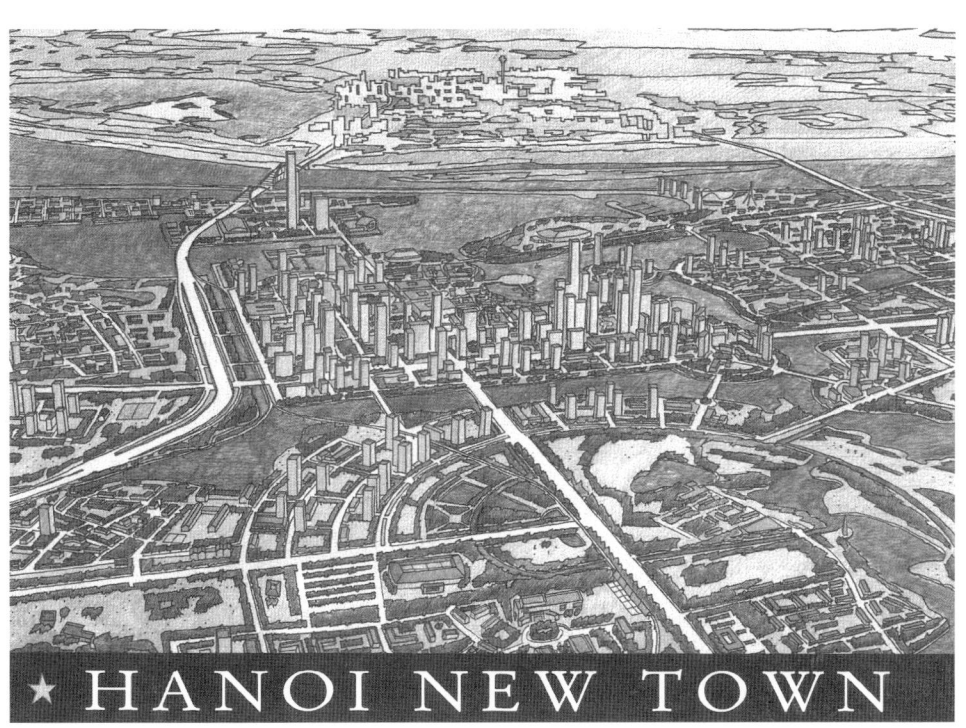

★ HANOI NEW TOWN

7. The project, set to revolutionize the development of Hanoi, was master-minded by a 'dream team' of architecture heavy-weights. The lead was taken by San Francisco-based engineering design consultants, Bechtel, on behalf of South Korea's Daewoo Corporation. Upon completion of a conceptual land use plan, the crème de la crème development of particular areas was left to Rem Koolhaas and OMA (the Dong Anh District), Skidmore, Owings and Merrill (Van Tri Lake area) and Japan's giant Nikken Sekkei consultants (Tu Liem District). In November 1998, Hanoi New Town was approved by the Prime Minister.

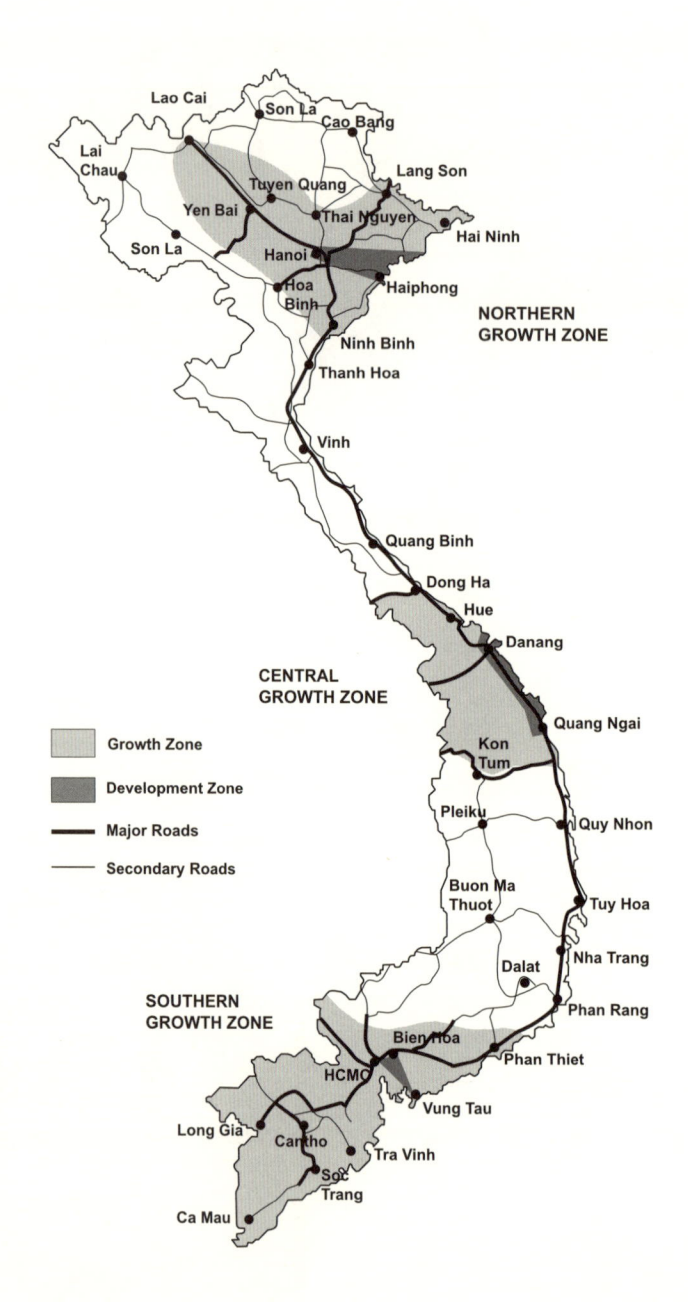

7. The three growth zones with their embedded development poles

of Vietnamese who were collaborating and working with the occupiers. During the socialist era, these houses were occupied by large numbers of Vietnamese families and fell into a terrible physical state. Since doi moi, a series of these villas, particularly in Hanoi, have been refurbished to their original glory and house embassies and institutions such as the World Bank, etc. They are now the most expensive properties in the country.

The Soviet influence may be seen in the numerous housing estates that were developed throughout Vietnam—consisting of fairly homogenous, concrete, five story walk-up apartment buildings, replete with existence minimum typologies. The housing estates were built as autonomous urban entities—microrayons (microregions)—and significantly contributed to the physical materialization of the City of Socialist Man. Estates were built and owned by the state and inhabitants paid token rents, which was not enough to cover the spiraling maintenance costs. Today, the vast yet run-down estates pose one of the largest challenges to the government. The State has stopped providing housing to employees and encouraged people to construct their own houses. The 1991 Ordinance on Housing and a series of related by-laws gave tenants the right to purchase state-owned housing. State/individual cooperative housing is premised on three types: 1) State provides individuals with land, including public utilities and design and construction of houses are financed by individuals; 2) State restores an existing house but the individual pays; 3) the individual is given permission by the State to upgrade an existing house which remains owned by the State and merely rented by the individual. Within the old estates, apartments are now sold to inhabitants; however, the poorest cannot afford to buy. Often, the location of the estates is along major infrastructure lines and therefore the pressure to completely redevelop properties is tremendous. Resettlement policies are still in their infancy and homelessness is becoming a growing reality.

The encouragement of private investment and the permission for an individual economy to flourish independently from the state sector has not only brought an onslaught of international investors, but also encouraged a frenzy of family-run enterprises, resulting in adaptive re-use of imperial and colonial sites and the revival of the traditional private shop-houses into a new distinctively Vietnamese postmodernism, with fanciful facades and frivolous rooflines. The complex system of restrictive residential permits has been abandoned and the country's over 78 million inhabitants are free to move as they please. In urban centers, natural growth is swelled by an influx of peasants lured from back-breaking work in the rice paddies in hopes of richer harvests; there are also numerous urban citizens returning from their forced relocation to new economic zones (the crux of Vietnam's deurbanization policy of the period following the American-Vietnamese War).

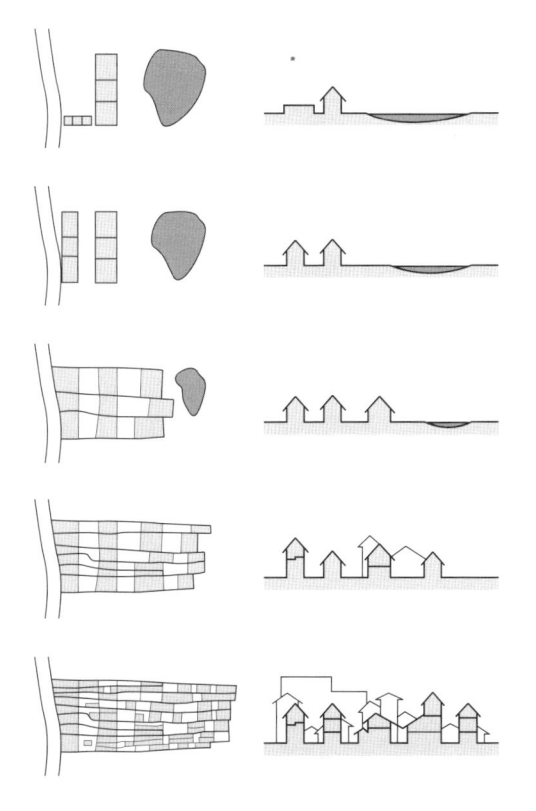

8. The nouveaux riches "tube house" type adaptations are appearing in cities from north to south.

Throughout the country's urban history, housing typologies were to a large extent dictated by imposed models and norms. Yet, these same universal or generic types were also adapted to the Vietnamese lifestyle through local appropriation and adaptation to every-day use. At the same time, the contemporary era is witnessing a revival-of-sorts of the nation's ancient urban housing typology—the tube house, reincarnated today as ever-higher structures many of which also function as mini-hotels. There is circumstantial evidence of the continuity of tradition within the processes of modernity.

Liberalized Land Policies

In absolute terms, all land in Vietnam remains property of the State. However, since doi moi, land ownership has been reformed and a real estate market has been in existence since 1993, following the first Law on Land. The decree gave individuals the following four rights: to exchange, transfer or lease land-use rights; to inherit land-use rights; to mortgage land-use rights to Vietnamese banks and individuals; to receive compensation from the government in the case of expropriation. Ten years later, the 2003 Land on Law, aimed to further improve the investment environment and develop all sources of land for development investment. It clarified discrepancies in interpretation of the previous law and declared equality between different economic sectors. Accordingly, all State-owned and private enterprises are equal before the law in land use, the rights and obligations of land users, administrative procedures for land allocation, land use right reception, and procedures for the implementation of the rights of land users. The State maintains the right to recover any land it deems necessary for such purposes as national defense, security, national benefits, public interests, economic development and construction of industrial zones, export processing parks, high-tech zones, economic zones and large investment projects. These changes were welcomed by investors who, at the time, seek further decrees which would guarantee State non-interference in negotiations between investors and land owners.[17] A new land-use charge policy also gives investors the right to choose to receive land from the State and pay land-use charges or to rent land. They can also transfer land use rights, rent land and stake capital worth land use rights to form joint ventures.

It must be recognized that the real estate market in Vietnam is new and, although it has contributed towards stimulating economic growth and transforming the country's economic sector, there remains a series of shortcomings and weaknesses. Although the Vietnamese Communist Party and State has relatively explicit, comprehensive and coherent guidelines on the development of the real estate market, there is an unusually high level of informal real estate transactions. In fact, Hanoi's Ministry of Planning and Investment (MPI) estimates such informal and illegal exchange as more than 70% of current transactions. Speculation has occurred by national and international investment companies as well as individuals in urban and rural areas simply wishing to improve their housing condition and/or livelihood. Yet, approximately 10% of the households using farmland in rural areas and more that 70% households using land in urban areas have not been provided with land-use certificates.[18] At the same time, the speculation has led to "price fevers" particularly in Hanoi and Ho Chi Minh City, where land prices are considered to be amongst the most over-inflated in the world, rivaling those of New York and Tokyo. The prices are up to 10 times higher than those in large US cities, with the exception of San Francisco or New York, while Vietnam's income per capita equals only a fraction of earnings in the US.[19] An additional problem in the current real estate market concerns a lack of transparency and difficulty in accessing real estate information. Although land laws continue to be updated to deal with deficiencies in the system, many have commented that a competent legal framework, which Vietnam presently lacks, must be implemented in order to effectively manage the real estate market.[20]

By its own assessment, the MPI has claimed that these weaknesses in the system have resulted in several problems concerning development. Firstly, property has often been used inefficiently and the boom of informal real estate transactions has greatly limited resource mobilization for economic development. Secondly, the State has lost important revenues related to land (particularly taxes) since they were not done within the correct legal framework. Thirdly, social inequalities are on the sharp increase as entrepreneurs out-do the average Vietnamese citizen with their real estate savvy. In sum, MPI concludes that the present situation has reduced competitiveness in the global market, thereby hindering Vietnam's international integration process.

In Vietnam, individual and local ambitions have blossomed in the fertile ground provided by liberalized housing and land policies—aided by the shortcomings of official monitoring of compliance with the government's grandiose master-plans. The roll-back of state regulation and economic liberation is equated with a greater expression of societal needs. However, under the new aegis of a still unstable real-estate market, the country is still struggling to find its footing. No doubt, it is merely a matter of time before the country is completely integrated into the pervasiveness of so-called globalization. The challenge that remains is for Vietnam to build upon its rich layered narratives while simultaneously addressing its contested territories. The refocusing of the State's control could work to an advantage in terms of protecting the ever vulnerable public realm and collective concerns from the flattening tendencies of unregulated real estate development.

Notes

[1] *ASEAN (Association of Southeast Asian Nations) includes all 10 countries (Myanmar, Thailand, Malaysia, Singapore, Brunei, Indonesia, Laos, Cambodia, Vietnam and the Philippines) in the region and represents one of the world's fastest growing economies, which in turn has created new geographies of production and consumption.*
[2] *Although Vietnam's doi moi is popularly likened to the Soviet Union's perestroika (meaning restructuring), it is actually a reform*

program of renovation. According to Duiker, in the years following the end of the Second Indochina War, Hanoi became one of the most orthodox practitioners of the Stalinist approach to nation-building—with its emphasis on socialist industrialization. Even after the party leaders decided to embark on the road to reform at the Sixth Congress in December 1986, the new program was not nearly as much a departure from past practice as was the case in Chine or even the Soviet Union. It is equally clear that, for some members of the senior leadership, the ultimate goal of building a fully socialist society has by no means been abandoned. (Duiker, W., Vietnam: Revolution in Transition, Boulder, Westview Press, 1995, p.159).

Asia's "tigers"—or newly industrializing economies—are South Korea, Taiwan, Hong Kong and Singapore. By the 1990s, these countries were the principle investors in Southeast Asia. In a 1993 World Bank report, The East Asian Miracle, highlighted eight so-called High Performing Asian Economies—of which four are in Southeast Asia (Singapore, Malaysia, Indonesia and Thailand). Vietnam is gearing up to compete with such countries.

[4] Kinh refers to ethnic Vietnamese who make up 87 % of population. There are also 53 miniroity groups that live in Vietnam, mostly inhabiting the north and central highlands.

[5] Nguyen Duc Nhuan, "Do the Urban and Regional Management Policies of Socialist Vietnam Reflect the Patterns of Ancient Mandarin Bureaucracy?" International Journal of Urban and Regional Research, 8(1), 1984:75-6.

[6] ibid, p. 87.

[7] ibid, p. 77.

[8] Douglass, M. et al., Urban Transition in Vietnam, Fukuoka, United Nations Center for Human Settlements and Honolulu, Department of Urban and Regional Planning, University of Hawaai'I at Manoa, 2002, pp.1-12.

[9] Thrift, N. and Forbes, D., The Price of War: Urbanization in Vietnam 1954-1985, London, Allen and Unwin, 1986, p. 93

[10] Mathéy, K. and Nguyen Duc Nhuan 1980:277-80.

[11] op.cit, Nguyen Duc Nhuan, p. 81.

[12] (as cited in) ibid, p. 81.

[13] ibid, p. 82.

[14] op. cit., Duiker, p. 156.

[15] Bladerstone, S. and Logan, W., "Vietnamese Dwellings: Tradition, Resilience and Change," Asia's Old Dwellings: Tradition, Resilience and Change, Knapp, R. (ed.), Hong Kong, Oxford University Press, 2003, pp. 137-9.

[16] National Institute for Urban and Rural Planning, 'General Plan for Urban Development, 1997-2020 for Hue, Hanoi, Ministry of Construction.

[17] Nguyen Thoa, "Urgent Issues on Land and Production Areas for Enterprises to be Addressed Soon" Vietnam Business Forum, 10/4/2004 (http://vibforum.vcci.com.vn/the_news.asp?idnews=489)

[18] "Development of Real Estate Market in Vietnam (including right of land use market) to Meet Requirements of Socio-Economic Development and WTO Accession" summary, Working paper No. 3-2004; Central Institute for Economic Mamagement, Ministry of Planning and Investment, Hanoi (www.ciem.org.vn/en/asp/InfroDetail.asp?ID=607)

[19] Hong Ha, "Law to let air out of over inflated real estate," VietNam News, 07/02/2004 (http://english.vietnamnet.vn/reports/2004/02/219866)

[20] ibid; op.cit. Nguyen Thoa.

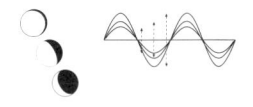

SHERMAN, Roger
If, Then: Shaping Change as a Strategic Basis for Design

In considering the city a stable and controllable artifact, the disciplines of architecture and planning, as traditionally theorized, valorize that very predictability. Today, however, both are practiced in an environment that is increasingly characterized by uncertainty, a product of the constantly fluctuating cultural, political and economic circumstances of contemporary life. In the fast-paced climate of the present, rather than assuming stability and explaining change, one must assume change and explain stability.[1] Indeed, the circumstances upon which most design strategies are based sometimes shift so quickly that by the time a plan is realized, it is often already obsolete. In this ripple-effect atmosphere, a mere election can radically alter the objectives of a master plan[2], just as the advent of new methods of artificial insemination can affect the assumptions underlying a residential remodel[3]. However quasi-real the computer is able to make it appear, almost any design proposal (whatever the scale) is inescapably subject to the vagaries of circumstances and conditions beyond the control of its author. These include, in no particular order: catastrophic change (a single unpredictable event, natural or man-made); ecological/ climactic change; regulatory change (of public policy); technological change (of material/methods); change in market demand (cultural and lifestyle trends); change of land use; even changes in knowledge (where the conditions don't change, but our understanding of them does).

As if to suggest, in response, an alternative proposition, Rem Koolhaas notes of one American metropolis:

"architects (there have) aligned themselves with the uncontrollable. They have become its official agents, instruments of the unpredictable: from imposing to yielding in one generation. Working on the emergence of new urban configurations, they have discovered a vast new realm of potential and freedom—to go rigorously with the flow—architecture/urbanism as a form of letting go." [4]

More than arguing that architects and planners should go with the flow of the market rather than resist it, Koolhaas is also suggesting the importance of understanding the logics that underlie those forces, in order to shape the changes they effect. However, beyond the inertness of the Dutch datascape, which merely indexes these dynamic conditions as if they were frozen in time, what have yet to be developed are more elastic planning strategies able to surf the highly unstable and unpredictable evolution of the contemporary city without merely accommodating them.

It is precisely this question—how to provide sufficient looseness with regard to future scenarios—that constitutes the principal paradox of urban development today. This begins by operating from the point of view that urbanism is fundamentally a self-organized phenomenon, where countless separate plans are carried out simultaneously, interconnected but not coordinated. Comprised, like an ecology, of layered, overlapped and nested arrangements of systems and subsystems organized in scale-hierarchic arrangements, these intangible but actual processes and functions—which are materially manifest in the structure, forms and patterns we observe in the city—once understood, allow architects and planners to get at the operations behind them, providing the tools by which to change urban life.[5] The wicked, change-based nature of most urban problems today suggests that it is only by deriving new urban patterns based upon an understanding of urban processes that one might then proceed to propose how else the city might look. Among other things, this critically hinges on (learning) the ability to operate at the line between control and disorganization. Stan Allen notes that design professionals have heretofore had a tendency to dichotomize these two conditions, aligning with the former and against the latter, thereby artificially limiting themselves from exploring fuzzier, more synthetic, self-regulating planning strategies,[6] which have the capacity to change over time. This is exemplified in the brittle, defensively-minded way in which zoning is used by planners to promote formal homogeneity and segregation of land use, ironically eradicating the very heterogeneity and spectacle of conflict which symptomize the difference that is naturally instantiated in city life. While landscape architects long ago learned to work with this same unruliness in nature, architects and planners have generally failed to understand the city in the same way. Yet the evolution of the man-made environment, like that of its natural counterpart, is a direct function of its ability to survive and adapt to change, whether in response to disturbance events (such as floods), succession, climactic change—or in the case of human ecosystems, as driven by institutional decisions, population growth and economic forces. Rather than practice within the carefully circumscribed bounds of what they or their clients can control, architects must reposition themselves to stand at the very precipice of disorganization, and consider both the perameters as well as the mechanisms, or lever points of their control relative to the self-organized logics of urbanization to be integral to the design task itself. The key question to be asked is: how does one build in resilience to a design strategy such that it possesses the capacity to adapt to multiple contingencies or unforeseeable events?

At present, this dilemma is usually dealt with through a lowest-common-denominator or one-size-fits-all design approach that, as in the case of the generic multi-purpose room or most planning statutes, oversimplifies a complex set of demands whose causes and effects are intricately interrelated. However, over the past decade or so, the attention of complexity theorists—whose interest is in developing methods of describing, predicting and affecting more dynamic, self-organized forms of order—have focused on two more supple models of prediction and control that offer promise as new frameworks for design thinking. The first, the study of complex adaptive systems, or CAS, has rapidly developed as a means of explaining but also predicting behavior in environments characterized by dynamic change, whether natural ecosystems, or more choice-based social ecologies such as the stock market.[7] For architects and planners, it has the potential to provide a means to not only describe and predict the dynamics of urban habitat dispersal and development, but also to loosely control it, using cultivation tactics analogous to those that ecologists apply to animals and plant behavior. As Jane Jacobs first observed more than 40 years ago:

"Cities, too, happen to be problems in organized complexity, like the life sciences. They present situations in which a half-dozen or even several dozen factors are all varying simultaneously and in subtly interconnected ways. The same is true of the.......parts or features of cities. Although the interrelations of their many factors are complex, there is nothing accidental or irrational about the ways in which these factors affect each other."[8]

For all their complexity however, cities, like self-organized systems, are not infinitely complex; their ability to adapt to change operates according to rules-of-thumb, or simplified rules. These rules shape or govern how the system adapts in response to past and present conditions, a type of protocol[9] by which it is able to re-organize itself at critical points of instability (forest fires, stock market crash, etc.). This protocol could be argued to be analogous to constitute a kind of 'soft' planning or design which, rather than seeking to optimize and specify conditions too tightly to the short term, as most zoning legislation does (and which suffers a loss of resiliency as a result), instead builds resilience using tactics which create some slack and flexibility. These tactics, two of the most prevalent of which are overlapping functional diversity and operational redundancy, are directed toward increasing the variety of possible alternative reorganization patterns and pathways. Each has the effect of spreading the risk—not unlike a diversified stock portfolio—thereby lessening the susceptibility of an entire design/plan to failure (or obsolescence) due to an unforeseen disturbance or change in conditions. As complex adaptive systems, human ecosystems, like natural ecosystems, need to develop the ability to not only maintain themselves in the face of change, but to actually take advantage of new design opportunities created by that change—for the two are dynamically interrelated. In this last regard, architects and planners must recognize the constructive role that change, and crisis (known in CAS as a disturbance event) in particular plays in opening the window for renewal, and by extension, novelty. Together with

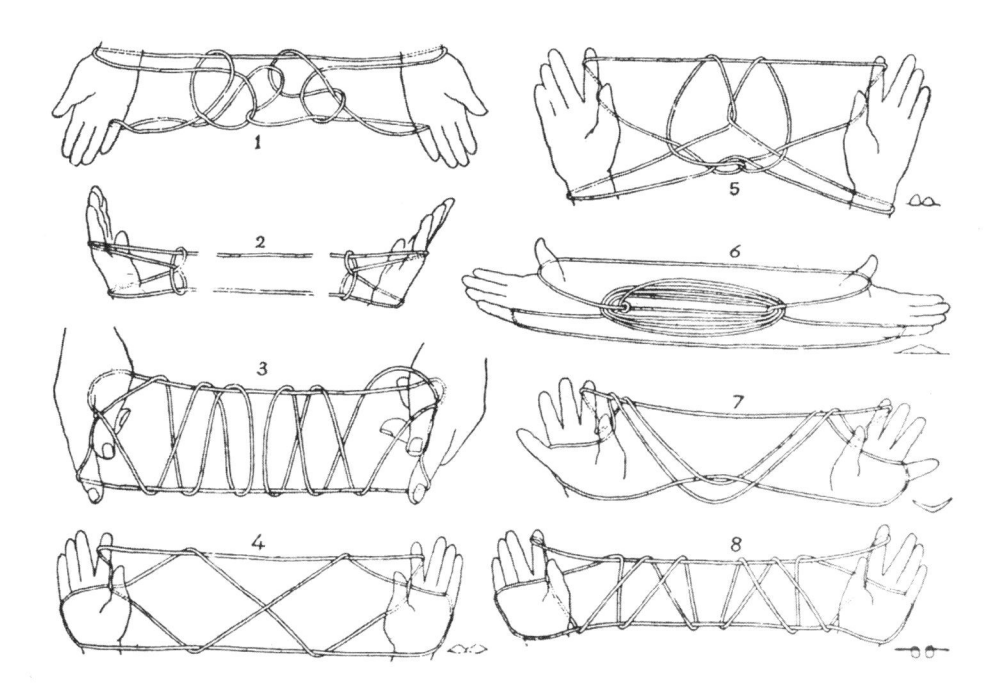

1. Cat's Cradle

the accumulated experience and history of a system (in effect its memory),[10] reinvention is an essential element of adaptability, critical to both anticipating change in order to plan ahead—as happens in the field of ecology through techniques such as controlled burns and conservation patches—as well as to enabling a system to reorganize after a disturbance. Architecturally, this might take the form of careful placement of spec elements which have both a provisional immediate use, yet at the same time sow the seeds for a variety of plausible futures—serving as attractors (in the way that New York's Central Park created value in the real estate around it) which influence (encourage, deter) growth or change in specific directions or regards.

In contrast to the brittle and short-term orientation of traditional notions of control and prediction used today, complex systems thinking begins by identifying a specific change-inducing factor (referred to as an agent), then painstakingly learning its intricate cause-and-effect relationships and interconnections with other factors. This leads to locating key lever points at which a small amount of (design) input can produce a larger wave of changes. By this means, CAS can be used not only to predict, but also to develop protocols of urban transformation and development, similar to the logics of successional dynamics found in natural ecosystems. For instance, one could imagine using CAS as a means of shaping, through a set of simple, pre-tested rules that make strategic use of incentives and deterrents, the seemingly arbitrary but actually density-dependent, use-driven process of neighborhood change. According to this logic, the likelihood of a property undergoing a transition from empty to occupied could depend on the state of the neighboring lots—whether they are devoted to residential, commercial, agricultural or recreational uses. Vacant parcels could also be assigned probabilities for colonization based upon a certain critical mass of properties: is there good drainage, a view of the ocean, an adequate groundwater supply? Developing solutions that address the dynamic nature of today's urban problems, let alone predicting their outcome, means that architects must, like doctors or mechanics, become better diagnosticians, by learning to analyze a problem not merely on the basis of what things look like, but rather in terms of how they actually operate (often out of sync with each other). Given the complexity of today's city-as-ecosystem, it is critical to diagram specific cause-and-effect linkages between urban networks and phenomena as processes occurring over time that are themselves triggered by or a product of other functions or events. Using never-before-available databases such as are now obtainable through mapping software such as Geographic Information Systems (GIS), which has made it more possible than ever before to detect many of the otherwise invisible forces and conditions that shape today's urban landscape,[11] different data sets can be correlated as a means to discover if there is a causal relationship between certain trends or events. Similarly, one can assess whether or not a certain combination of factors suggest the susceptibility of a certain area to change—and thereby roughly project how that change might be likely to proliferate across the larger ecosystem in a non-uniform, complex ripple effect.

The successional dynamics of natural ecologies are also a function of the process of selection as much as of adaptation. This is equally true of man-made ecosystems, particularly those shaped by the free market, in which the determination as to which areas of cities thrive (and in what way) while others decay is driven by the ability of subcultures to compete and/or cooperate with one another. The field of Game Theory[12] studies the dynamics of these alternating behaviors as a means of establishing, like cas, strategies of prediction and control. Though developed several decades earlier, it has in some senses been subsumed as a sub-discipline by cas, since its more statistical, probability-based form of predictive approach still requires the context of the interplay between diversity and disturbance in order to serve as a sufficiently robust model of flexible planning.[13] Its value, however, is in the fact that just as CAS is used to understand and predict the behavior of plant and animal species that compete and cooperate in order to thrive in a natural environment with fixed resources, Game Theory is a framework for studying human players whose interests conflict as they seek to cross their own political and economic objectives with a finite set of available options. In a man-made ecology, the species are the interest groups that organize themselves around and must negotiate with one another for the fixed resources of a given property or lot, represented in a bundle of rights which include air and mineral rights, easements, and profits-a-prendre, amongst others; it is the combined and complex interaction of these localized efforts to assert these rights that is the major force of change in cities. In bargaining, there is as strong an incentive for contending parties to cooperate as to compete, making the process itself extremely fluid and dynamic; this is exacerbated by the contingent (offer/counteroffer) nature of the process itself. Each bargainer must learn how to play

those dynamic logics according to a consistent and premeditated strategy—examples include Prisoner's Dilemma, Tit for Tat, Divide-and-Rule, and Even Up—but one that is at the same time sufficiently elastic that it can be tactically adjusted in response to the other players' own strategies. In the end, the outcome—a kind of equilibrium enforced by each player's self-interest—can only be predicted to the extent that each party will consider it advantageous to its own interests.

The potential value of the rules and strategies of Game Theory to the modeling of more adaptive design and planning methods differs from that of complex adaptive systems in the way they instrumentalize the competition-cooperation dynamic between parties. There are at least two specific regards in which this translates across disciplinary bounds. The first is that as a self-regulated process involving not one, but multiple parties, bargaining represents a unique kind of meta-strategy able to accommodate several separately-sponsored sub-plans, each with its own agenda and objectives. At the same time, these are still able to both affect and be affected by one another. They may be layered, crossed or nested—so long as their possible pathways co-evolve (as do negotiating positions) and incrementally adjust over time. Like the children's game of cat's cradle[1], this evolution is also concomitant with an increase in both social and formal complexity, particularly as pertains to the interrelatedness between the (plans of the) parties. Both CAS and Game Theory consider a system to be complex when there is strong interaction among its elements, so that current events have a heavy influence on later events. It is this latter behavior which leads to the second value of Game Theory: the importance of envisioning and creating diagrams of exchange which exploit the process of quid pro quo as a productive instigator of change (and by extension, design). Used as a form of stimulus that can be used to elicit a roughly predictable response, design can be a means of both staging and creatively working out the cause-and-effect relationships between the various constituencies that comprise the city-as-ecosystem, where the design strategy, as in chess, becomes as much about anticipating (predicting) the uncontrollable logic of the response as about the initial input.

A brief examination of the evolution of two properties in Los Angeles will serve to vividly illustrate the way that the kind of strategic thinking found both in complex adaptive systems (which the first case study better demonstrates) and in game theory (evident in the second), and how those can be used to diagnose and shape the changing urban environment.[14] Both sites could be seen as examples of what could be called planning-in-reverse (the procedural equivalent of Smithson's "ruins-in-reverse"), in that they exhibit a loose but consistent and explicable succession of transformations whose logic only becomes apparent over time.

On the property at 1201 S. La Cienega Blvd., three diverse land uses exist on a single lot—a kind of radical mixed use.[2] The extreme agglomeration of structures stands as a transparent illustration of the real estate axiom of highest and best use: with each successive subdivision of property rights, the overall value of the land and the income derived by its owner increased.[3] The assignment between the uses and their location on the property is both self-organized and hyperefficient in a way that had it been planned, it would never have been able to be: like a jigsaw puzzle, virtually none of the land is wasted, and none of the land uses in any way compromises either the operation or income value of the others [4]. At the same time as they share the property, each party maneuvers in such a way as to increase and extend the value of its own stake: Gannett (the billboard advertiser) through the annexation of air rights above the other two enterprises; the fortune teller through the elongation of her square footage so as to maximize street frontage; and the apartment complex in orienting itself around an internalized courtyard, insulating itself from public disturbances behind a stand of cypress trees. The property owner, who first developed the apartment building occupying the rear half of the lot, later sought, as land values in the area rose, both to maximize the income from of his land—and to diversify his real estate investment—by utilizing the remaining, unused portion of the property, which had considerable commercial value due to its proximity to the well-trafficked boulevard. The street frontage not needed by the apartment building (which is accessed from the alley) was subsequently leased to a psychic reader, who values the visibility as a means of attracting walk-in/drive-by customers. As real estate values rose still further, the property owner again wrung value out of what little land still remained by leasing less than 10 SF to an outdoor advertising company for its stanchion, plus the as-yet-unexploited but valuable air rights. This last tenant brings income to the property owner that is staggeringly large ($250,000/year) in comparison to the amount of land that it occupies, thereby making its future there quite secure.

Cellular Automata, Rule 73 (previous) and Rule 30, courtesy Stewart Smith, stewdio.org.

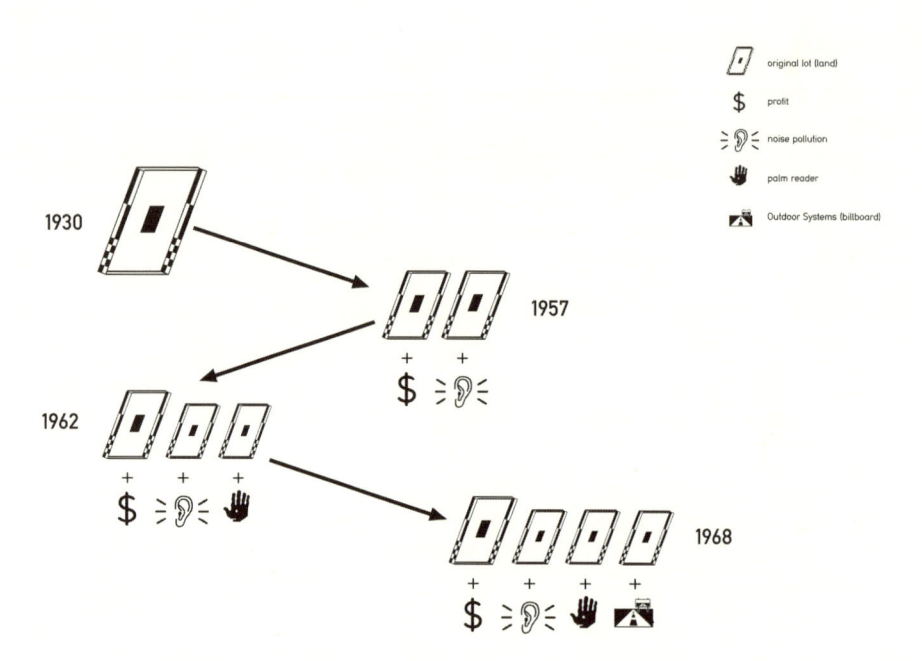

3. 1201 S. La Cienega Blvd., subdivision diagram

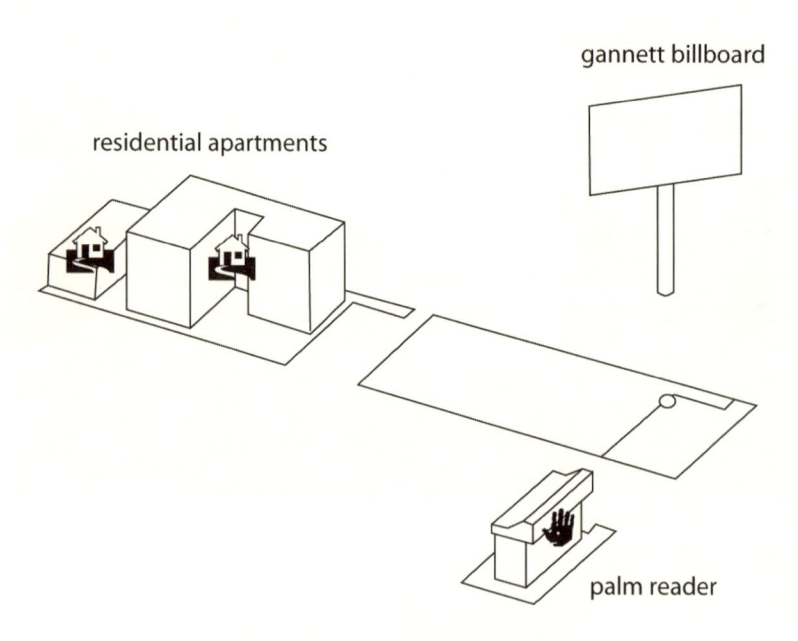

4. 1201 S. La Cienega Blvd., site axonometric and plan diagram

SHERMAN, Roger

2. 1201 S. La Cienega Blvd., three diverse land uses exist on a single lot—a kind of radical mixed use

5. 9865 Olympic Blvd. (Beverly Hills), accidental obelisk

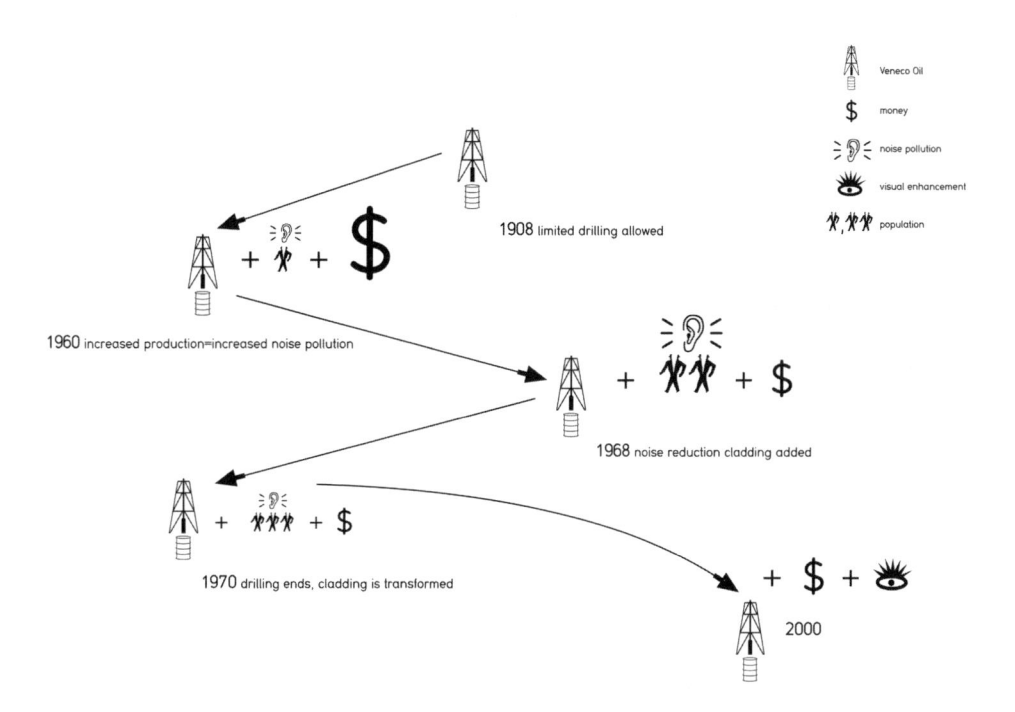

6. 9865 Olympic Blvd. (Beverly Hills), accidental obelisk: interruption diagram

The second site is a tiny triangular patch of land located at the interface of a residential area of Beverly Hills and the commercial towers of Century City. On it stands an enigmatic tower-like structure upholstered in a multi-colored floral pattern graphic [5]. Though a familiar landmark to thousands of Angelenos who commute past it daily on their way to and from work, few could identify what it is or to whom it belongs. In fact, this accidental landmark is an oil derrick marking the drilling operations of Veneco Oil Company, which owns the mineral rights to a roughly 800-acre oil field of which the site marks roughly the center. It has been at the site since 1908, preceding Century City by several decades, though it has been inactive since 1982. It remains on the site, in a twist of irony, only in order to legally enforce the company's interest, reserving its right to drill in the future should they see fit.[15] Until the 1970s, the more recognizable skeleton of the derrick was exposed. It was then, when the development of Century City brought others working nearby, that economic and political pressure was exerted on Veneco, who negotiated to cover the derrick in dull gray acoustical cladding in order to muffle the noise emitted from the drillin. However, since the derrick became inactive and the cladding was therefore no longer needed for acoustical reasons, the tower has undergone yet another transformation of appearance, the result of efforts by a local artist-entrepreneur. The artist opportunistically recognized that a) the cladding still had a value in being retained, now as a form of camouflage for a bare structure that would otherwise be considered by neighbors in toney Beverly Hills to be a public nuisance; and b) that the cladded tower was like a mute 3-D billboard, waiting to be given a new message (especially one terminating a 2-mile long axial view down a major thoroughfare). He bargained with both Veneco and the City of Beverly Hills (representing the high school) to use the inadvertent obelisk to memorialize and call the attention to the plight of terminally-ill children, as represented in the fact that the floral pattern that appears today was painted on the cladding by cancer-striken children. Over the history of the evolution of the site[6], the tower evidenced remarkable resilience in response to the change in circumstances both on-site (drilling > no more drilling) and off-site (neighbors', cancer victims' rights). Through a back-and-forth process, the outcome not only emerged, but moreover reflected the history of the negotiation itself, even to the point of still visually embodying the values that each of the competing parties ascribed to it. In retrospect, it is interesting to note how just as the derrick was attracted to the site by the oil, it itself became both a nuisance and an attractor to others who eventually followed: Century City tenants, who viewed it as competing/detrimental to their own livelihood; and the artist, who saw its visual presence as coincident with his own interests.[16]

Notes

[1] van der Leuw, S.E. "Land Degradation as a Socionatural Process". In R.J. McIntosh, The Way the Wind Blows: Climate, History, and Human Action. New York: Columbia Univ. Press, 2000.

[2] see Adam Gopnik's fascinating recounting of the redevelopment of Times Square in "Times Regained: How the Old Times Square Was Made New", in The New Yorker, March 22, 2004.

[3] In my own practice, I am regularly asked to plan/design for multiple future contingencies. In the case of one small residential project, the clients did not yet know if the latest fertility technology would enable them to have children or how many, but wanted a design that would hedge their bets; at the same time, they were also already thinking about how the new house could be modified when their kids departed for college, and whether it could be adapted for disabled access during their later years!

[4] Koolhaas, Rem. "Atlanta: A Reading". in Bernado, J. and Prat, Ramon. Atlanta. Barcelona: Actar, 1995.

[5] Vasishth, Ashwani, and Sloane, David C. "Returning to Ecology: An Ecosystem Approach to Understanding the City". in Dear, Michael, Chicago to L.A. Thousand Oaks, CA: Sage Publications, 2002. p. 348.

[6] Allen, Stan. "The Logistics of Context", in Practice: Architecture, Technique and Representation. Amsterdam: G+B Arts Intl., 2000. pp. 159-60.

[7] For the best non-technical discussion of cas, see either: a. Axelrod, Robert and Cohen, Michael. Harnessing Complexity. New York: Free Press, 1999. or b. Holland, John. Hidden Order: How Adaptation Builds Complexity. Cambridge, MA: Perseus Books, 1995

[8] Jacobs, Jane. The Death and Life of Great American Cities. New York: Vintage Books, 1961. pp. 432-4. Jacobs is here of course referring not to the cut-and-dried way in which the city is "organized" by planners, but is rather juxtaposing to it the view that cities regulate and organize themselves, in all kinds of complex, interesting ways.

[9] Protocol here is defined as a detailed plan for the course of a scientific experiment or medical treatment, the rules of which are sufficiently open as to be contingent upon the particular feedback/outcome of each stage of the experiment/treatment.

[10] Memory is the property often lacking in most conventional strategies of flexibility, which often use moveability as a mechanism for reconfiguration or, at the other extreme, a "one size fits all" approach which results in a single, generic design response.

[11] The full and proper implications of this information might still be missed by architects, however, unless there is a reposturing of design and planning practice within a larger interdisciplinary context, so as to benefit from, harness and synthesize others' expertise, including that of ecologists, economists, land use attorneys, software-writers, geographers and transportation planners.

[12] One of the most accessible discussions of the principles of game theory, which often gets mathematical very quickly, may be found in S. Heap and Y. Varoufakis, Game Theory. London: Routledge, 1995.

[13] Berkes, Fikret. Navigating Social-Ecological Systems: Building Resilience for Complexity and Change. Cambridge, UK: Cambridge Univ. Press. p. 377

[14] The 2 case studies dealt with here are excerpted from Roger Sherman, Under the Influence: Negotiating the Complex Logic of Urban Property, forthcoming from Univ. Minnesota Press.

[15] There are still 15 active pumps on the site however, which, though not visible from the street, access a vast underground network of wells extending all the way to Wilshire Boulevard.) Under an agreement in which the ownership of the hundreds of parcels of land over the oil field was severed from that of mineral rights below it, the landowners, who are dispersed around the globe, receive monthly royalty checks from the latter, the largest recipient of which is Beverly Hills High School next door, which also owns the small property on which the tower stands, and 5% of whose annual budget is funded through the income from the royalties owed it by the oil company.

[16] Special thanks and credit goes to Alexandra Loew, who put together the story of the site and was responsible for its analysis, including the drawings and diagrams appearing here.

SO, May

Pac Place

As city growth intensifies, social dynamics are becoming deeply polarized in uneven patterns of urban development. Planners and local authorities are adopting a more entrepreneurial approach to urban development aimed at identifying market-led urban projects and assisting private investors in their implementation. Large urban development projects mark a departure of the state from blanket welfare redistribution for local residents to repositioning the city advantageously in the eyes of outside investors, developers, and tourists.

With the advent of new urban policies, architects are operating in an increasingly limited domain. The greater portion of total built production in developed societies involves not the advice of design professionals, but others such as developers, real estate interests, and government officials. These players are most often driven by commercial concerns rather than by local issues. In arguing for the autonomy of the architectural profession from the socio-economic context of its expression, architects are claiming the role of image-makers in close relationship with other arts. However, it is at the very juncture between the framework of non-local forces of urban development and its local specialization that architects can expand their roles and responsibilities in the development of cities.

The Making of a Global City: Vancouver, Canada

In the summer of 1987, a tide of Hong Kong investment capital rolled onto downtown Vancouver's south shore. The result has been the construction of one of the largest redevelopment projects in North America over the last seventeen years on the site now called Pacific Place. Originally part of a distinctive industrial landscape along the waterfront of False Creek, the land fell into decline from the 1930s onwards as Vancouver's economy shifted from industrial to tertiary and quaternary occupations in the central business district.[1]

In the early 1980s, the provincial government assembled the land and, following a five-year conflict between the city and the province over proposals for the site, hosted the World's Fair there, Expo '86. The fair was designed to project Vancouver onto the global investment market. Subsequent to Expo, the site was marketed worldwide as part of a newly initiated privatization program. Concord Pacific Developments, a Canadian company specifically established by several prominent Hong Kong investors to bid for the site, was eventually awarded it. When completed, Pacific Place was expected to provide residential units, including some social housing units, for 15,000 people, and supporting retail space, offices, hotels, parkland, marinas, elementary schools, and daycares.[2]

Since Expo '86, other examples of large trans-Pacific property investment in the Vancouver area have precipitated. Vancouver's latest multi-use development, slated for a prime downtown location, will house the large Asian hotel chain Shangri-la, which was chosen specifically to attract international guests.[3]

The development of Pacific Place reads as a story of how the global flow of capital, people, and information, in concert with local authorities, reshapes urban life. Although Vancouver, being a colonial port city, has had a long history of contact with external forces and diverse cultures, the 1980s marked a decisive shift in the nature of these forces. Vancouver's main economic links had previously been with European nations, but in the 1980s, they shifted weight to the volatile flows of the emergent economies of Asia Pacific nations. With the growth of Hong Kong as an international financial center, some of the most heavily capitalized property development firms in the world emerged. As global capital flowed through Hong Kong, speculative bubbles were created in territorial property, stock markets, and geographic extension of investments.[4] After the bursting of the Asian bubble, a second wave of Asian immigrants and capital flow hit Vancouver, perpetuating the current boom in the housing market. Downtown residential space currently sells for twice as much as office space. The inflated residential market is also leading to a rush of conversions of downtown office space into condominiums.[5]

A New Urban Policy

With the globalization of property markets, the political economy of Western cities has undergone a radical transformation. The mobility of investment has encouraged city governments to market their cities as platforms in an economy of flows. Cities now compete aggressively to attract capital, tourists, and government funds, with the emphasis of urban regeneration policies shifting from local livability to an orientation towards the global market. This is part of a larger trend to use market logic in state actions through the promotion of public-private partnerships, deregulation, fiscal austerity, and cross-subsidies.[6] State resources are withdrawn from socially-inclusive blanket distribution-based policies and redirected into spatially-targeted social policies that support capital accumulation.[7]

Spatial strategies are considered essential, even a precondition, to urban economic regeneration. In Vancouver, the strategic cleansing of public space in the downtown area has been one such strategy. Significant public and private amenities have appeared on the downtown peninsula over the last two decades: a new public library building, the waterfront development along False Creek, and the expansion of the convention centre. In addition, the derelict Downtown Eastside, once the historic site of the business district, is now an attractive site for middle-class residential investment and repopulation due to its relative cheapness, high-density zoning, and proximity to the commercial centre. Urban housing markets are important sites for implementing urban regeneration as they are accompanied by the elimination of rent controls, state withdrawal from housing provision, and the facilitation of speculative inner-city property investment.[8]

Considered by many urban planners as a progressive move, Vancouver's local governing body has used private developments to provide social amenities through legislative incentives and requirements. Several years ago, a development cost levy was implemented on all new large-scale developments. The stated purpose of the levy is to "help pay for facilities made necessary by growth...parks, day care facilities, replacement housing, and sewerage, water, drainage and highway projects."[9] The levy amount is based on the floor space of the development, the use, and the district of the development property. In addition to the levy, a community amenity contribution is required for private rezoning applications to "help address growth costs, area deficiencies, and /or other community needs and impacts."[10] The provision of social and recreational facilities as part of development projects is also encouraged by the exclusion of such facilities from the floor space ratio and by density bonuses. In applying these legislative incentives, urban mega-projects are thus being promoted as fighting polarization, reinvigorating the local economy, and improving the city's tax basis.

Local authorities, along with the private sector, are strongly reliant on the implementation of urban mega-projects to reinforce the competitive position of their metropolitan economies in a rapidly changing global market. Urban mega-projects have become one of the most widely used urban revitalization strategies in large urban centers as their sheer dimension and visual impact elevate them to central icons in the image of the city.[11] *City of Glass,* Douglas Coupland's collection of anecdotes about his hometown of Vancouver, features a wrap-around cover photo of the distinctive marine-style glassy apartment towers of Pacific Place, reinforcing the centrality of the development project in Vancouver's image.[12]

The Fragmentation of the City

Urban geographers have conducted extensive studies on the implications of globalization on city life. Recent literature on Vancouver[13] has focused on the theme of social polarization stemming from development projects. The global flows supporting urban developments are increasingly recognized for their uneven nature; they develop defined project areas while other areas remain underdeveloped.

The use of urban mega-projects as a catalyst for urban regeneration signifies several significant changes

1. Pacific Place, Vancouver

2. Pacific Place, Vancouver, site view

to urban policy. First, urban mega-projects exhibit a shift from a social to a spatial definition of development that targets places rather than people. The assumed trickle-down mechanisms are considered to be of sufficient strength to permit a socially-balanced and successful development. In contrast to universal, inclusive, and blanket support policies, economic regeneration achieved by spatial restructuring casts particular social groups as problematic, excluded, marginalized, and non-integrated. Social segmentation and exclusion are reinforced, leading to the creation of islands of wealth in an impoverished environment. The resulting urban landscape is a patchwork of socio-economically diversified and mutually exclusive areas. Diminishing social redistribution is accompanied by policies that direct funds to social groups identified on the basis of their location, place and characteristics of living environments. According to such policies, it is places that need to be integrated and developed rather than citizens.

Secondly, large-scale urban projects have replaced statutory planning as the primary means of intervention in cities. Against the decline of the comprehensive plan, the large, emblematic project has risen as a flexible and symbolic alternative. Essentially fragmented, this form of intervention supports an eclectic planning style where attention to design captures a segment of the city and turns it into the symbol of innovative and successful urban regeneration. Reinforcing the patchwork pattern of city growth is the project's mode of governance that exercises a degree of autonomy from existing planning instruments and regulations. While the projects are ultimately inserted into existing planning guidelines, the initial conception and design of large tracts of the city often lie outside formal planning structures.[14]

Autonomy, Neutrality, and the Social Nature of Space

In his book, Unsettling the City, Nicolas Blomley argues that the spatial, project-oriented approach to development affords the processes of urban regeneration an air of neutrality and remove from the urban context. Space in Western society is produced and distributed under the ownership model of property which represents property as fixed, natural, and objective—the formal epitome of law. Thus, the system of property distribution is rendered opaque to critical insight.[15]

Treating property as a spatialized phenomenon between an owner and thing obscures the relationship between the owner and other people. Ownership is defined as one's rights over a property against those who do not have rights to the said property. The balance of power in a society is spatially reflected in the balance of property ownership and land control. Access to property, including land, is an important predictor of one's position in a social hierarchy. Property ownership also has cultural meaning associated with the fostering of valued social behaviors like responsible citizenship, political participation, and economic entrepreneurship.[16] Property, then, is social and political in its effects, origins and ethical implications.

The social effects of large-scale urban projects are many, but notable is the accentuation of socio-economic polarization through the working of real estate markets that inflates property value and displaces low-income housing. The objective of mixing social classes is an immensely persuasive concept in large-scale urban developments with implied claims to inclusiveness, tolerance, and social balance. Social mixing is problematic, however, in its implementation because it promises equality in the face of hierarchy. It most often brings back white middle classes into the cultural economies and geography of cities while failing to improve the conditions of the marginalized; it is socially one-sided. Under the guise of social mixing, prime urban land is often subject to being revalued, displacing renters and low-income people.[17]

The expansion of capitalist markets globally and within cultures to the exclusive promotion of economic values has been influential in defining and limiting the present role of design. In cultures dominated by media and the proliferation of images, design is being appropriated as an essential tool for capitalist consumerism by adding style to commercial goods and services.[18] Specifically in architecture, formal innovation has come to be used as packaging, a way of providing photogenic effects to promote both the building and its product.[19]

In an article aptly titled "Can Architects Be Socially Responsible?" Margaret Crawford traces the competing roles of the architect between economics and aesthetic culture, and how that has relieved architects from a focus on social responsibility. She argues that architecture's expensiveness necessarily ties it to sources of finance and power. Many architects, to avoid the danger of incorporation into the dominant economic and political structure, have distanced themselves from contractors and builders. Some have taken on the role of the artist to avoid contamination with the professional world, staking architecture's claim to status on aesthetics.[20] For these architects, architecture first and foremost is an exercise in meaning which issues from the architect. The doctrine of architecture as an autonomous discipline produced a period of great creativity and exploration, but autonomy was interpreted to mean that architecture did not need to respond to its social, political, and economic context.[21]

If social issues were to be considered at all, the Modern project in architecture implicitly premised that the architect could critically engage with contemporary problems through formal manipulation. Instead of being understood as interventions in the environment which bear social, economic, and political programs, architecture today oscillates between self-expression and cultural commentary. Clear aesthetic standards are proposed and then architects and critics explain how a project deals with these standards. A narrowed focus on aesthetics has led to the distinction between what is Architecture and what is construction. Architectural practice, in this model, remains autonomous from the range of ideological, political, social, and economic roles it is designed to fulfill, in the conditions necessary for building.

Notes

[1] *Acknowledgement to Ellen Scobie, Peter Mitham, Bronwyn Maxwell, and Chris Mott for their contributions to the ongoing discussion of sustainable practices for the built environment.*

[2] *May So immigrated from Hong Kong to Canada in 1979 and graduated with an MArch from the University of British Columbia in 2002 after studying drawing and sculpture at the University of Calgary. She is currently interning at a Vancouver architectural practice dedicated to socially conscious design.*

[3] *Cybriwsky, Roman A., David Ley, and John Western. "The Political and Social Construction of Revitalized Neighborhoods: Society Hill, Philadelphia, and False Creek, Vancouver." Gentrification of the City. Eds. Neil Smith and Peter Williams. Boston: Allen and Unwin, Inc., 1986 p 106.*

[4] *Olds, Kris. "Developing the Trans-Pacific Property Market: Tales from Vancouver via Hong Kong." Research on Immigration and Integration in the Metropolis Working Paper Series 96(2) 8-10.*

[5] *Mitham, Peter. "Vancouver Set for Mini Room Boom." Business in Vancouver June 29-July 5, 2004 p 4.*

[6] *Olds 11-14*

[7] *Bula, Frances. "Developers Told to Target Gastown, Chinatown." Vancouver Sun April 23, 2004 B1, B4.*

[8] *Blomley, Nicolas. Unsettling the City: Urban Land and the Politics of Property. New York: Routledge, 2004 p 30.*

[9] *Moulaert, Frank, Arantxa Rodriguez, and Erik Swyngedouw. "Neoliberal Urbanization in Europe: Large-Scale Urban Development Projects and the New Urban Policy. Antipode 34(3) p 547. Blomley 35.*

[10] *City of Vancouver. Development Cost Levies: Information Bulletin 1 p 1.*

[11] *City of Vancouver. Community Amenity Contributions Through Re-zonings: Information Bulletin 2 p 1.*

[12] *Moulaert 543.*

[13] *Coupland, Douglas. City of Glass. Vancouver: Douglas & McIntyre, 2000.*

[14] *See Every Building on 100 West Hastings edited by Reid Shier, Unsettling the City by Nicolas Blomley, "Multiculturalism, or the United Colors of Capitalism?" by Katharyne Mitchell in Antipode 25(4) 263-294.*

[15] *Moulaert 572.*

[16] *Blomley 5.*

[17] *Ibid 38.*

[18] *Moulaert 542-543, 552.*

[19] *Poynor, Rick. "First Things Next." Émigré 59 p 62.*

[20] *Frampton 23.*

[21] *Crawford, Margaret. "Can Architects Be Socially Responsible?" Out of Site: A Social Criticism of Architecture. Ed. Diane Ghirardo. Seattle: Bay Press, 1991 p 31.*

[22] *Gutman, Robert. "Two Questions for Architecture." Good Deeds, Good Design: Community Service Through Architecture Ed. Brian Bell. New York: Princeton Architectural Press, 2001 p 13.*

1. Vancouver waterfront, before and after

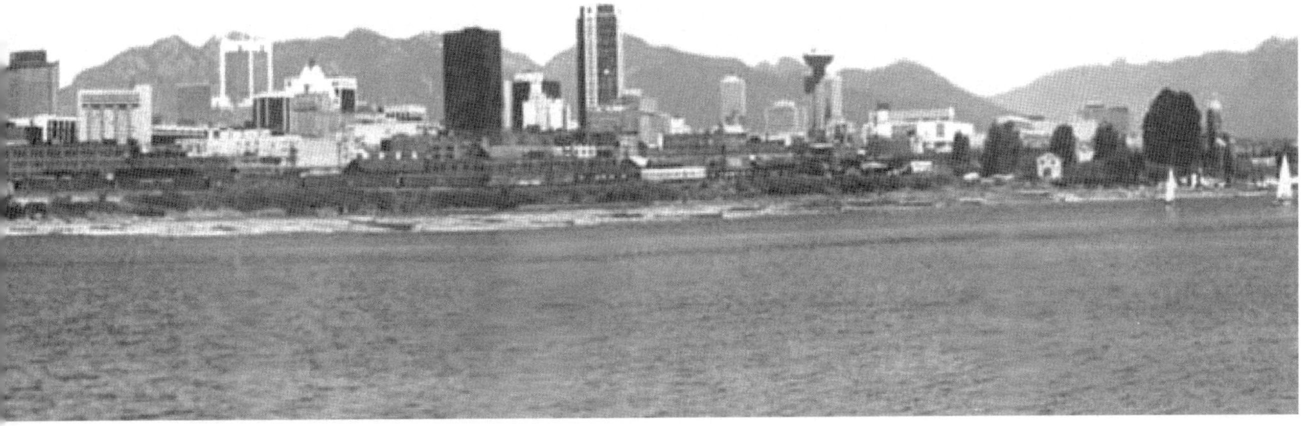

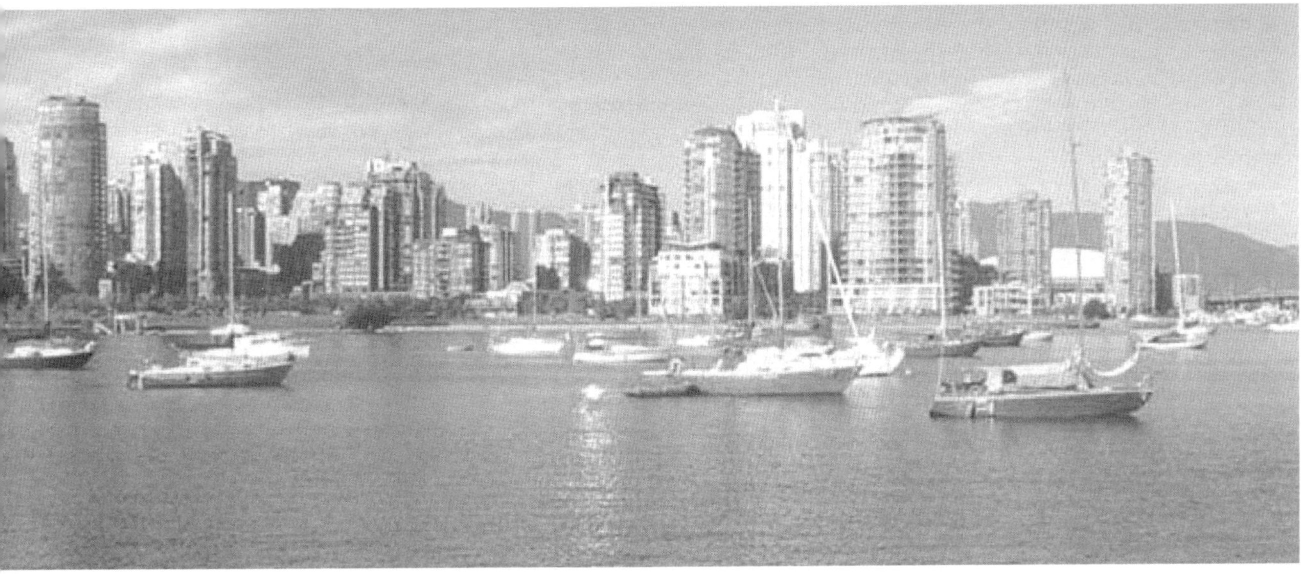

SOULES, Matthew
ON/OFF City Notes from Vancouver

The transition went smoothly, and thus the towers remain as empty as they appear. An occasional landlord will put those $19.99 white plastic stacking chairs out on balconies to generate the appearance of occupation.
–Douglas Coupland. City of Glass.

The questionable accuracy of the above statement doesn't matter so much as what it portends for city making. Let's recount the story:

Sino-British Joint Declaration, 1984... Tiananmen Massacre, 1989... Hong Kong Handover, 1997... 100 thousand Hong Kong immigrants... an endless erection of concrete and glass. The Vancouver story is a sort of poster child for globalization's unleashing of unfettered movement: communication, people, money. It is the diagram of non-local forces radically reshaping the entire image of a city. A bamboo shoot snaps in Kowloon, 14 condo towers are built in Vancouver. At the intersection of anxiety at the prospect of dictatorial rule, open Canadian immigration policies and a strong Vancouver economy, presto, a different city. It all swirls together in a paradigmatic Northwest broth of green cedars, clear waters and an almost unimaginable extension of Garden City modernism. Floor-to-ceiling glass simultaneously opens up to multicultural diversity and disappears in acquiescence to nature. It's exhilarating and healthy, an eco-metropolis playing Shanghai minus the pollution and forced relocations, all construction cranes and kayaks.

Cities have always been at the mercy of non-local forces, but it is the speed and scale of their effect on the Vancouver transformation that harbor new potentials. When the Sino-British Joint Declaration announced that Hong Kong would transfer to Chinese rule in 1997, the ensuing insecurity fueled a mass migration of which Vancouver was a principle destination. It was within this context that Hong Kong's wealthiest tycoon, Li Ka-shing, purchased a full 1/6 of the downtown peninsula and began developing it as Pacific Place. As one of North America's largest urban center master planned communities it covers 202 acres of post-industrial land with slender residential towers. Upon its completion it will include 9,100 dwellings among commercial, retail and public space. In 1994, during the height of the exodus, 61% of new high-rise units in the city were bought by ethnic Chinese. Many of Pacific Place's towers, with names like Columbus, Peninsula, and Waterworks, were essentially marketed and pre-sold exclusively in Hong Kong. While Pacific Place is one of many developments propelled by the influx, its scale and architectural insistence on concrete slabs supporting vast expanses of glass give it its iconic presence, singularly signifying the importance of non-local forces in the shaping of the city.

Not only is Vancouver experiencing the intoxicating effects of horizontal fluidity in global time and space in the form of new buildings, but in the form of an emergent population typology defined by this very fluidity. Already a large number of Hong Kong immigrants have returned across the Pacific as their fears phase-shift into archaic exaggerations under the glow of Chinese economic growth. These boomerang immigrants demonstrate the unforgiving zeitgeist of globalism. If a city can be radically reshaped by a mass arrival so too can it be similarly affected by a mass departure. With the conceptual framework of urban economics and planning tenaciously stuck to unidirectional movement, most often growth based, the instability inherent to globalism exists largely under the radar–registering mainly at the level of mythology, in the realm of anecdotes about plastic chairs. Ultimately, the speed at which Vancouver's new towers rise hints at their flipside reality: their fundamental fragility. Their ease of becoming obsolete artifacts of a specific moment. True, this is always a risk, but those moments may well be more fleeting.

More important than the boomerang immigrant is the increasing prevalence of its exacerbated outgrowth: The half resident that exists in a permanent state of trans-oceanic flow. Equipped, in this case, with the unrivalled liquidity of Canadian citizenship the half-resident moves with enviable ease depending on contingency, a highly evolved global species. Planning and architecture face unique challenges once this heroic nomad of contemporary culture is a model citizen. A vital disposition of the city itself is the confidence to match the agility of the half-resident. Can mechanisms of city management be re-imagined in order to enable rapid reaction to the vicissitudes of increasingly relevant remote forces? A city where rooms, buildings, and entire districts can be reprogrammed overnight, turned off if need be. Can the speed, optimism and excitement of Vancouver's growth-based transformation be mirrored in an innovative and equally optimistic deconstruction in response to shifting global flows? The urbanistic equivalence of half-residency is, as of yet, a faintly imaginable switch. A new on/off city.

Matthew Soules is an architect at Pei Cobb Freed & Partners in New York City and has previously worked at the Office for Metropolitan Architecture in Rotterdam. He received his M.Arch from Harvard University in 2003. Currently he is editing a sociocultural atlas of Vancouver.

SOLURI, Andre
SHoP Interview

Andre Soluri: SHoP has gained a reputation for a practice that actively engages the legislative, legal, and financial structures as part of their critical methodology for designing. Can you describe how these ideas originated and how they affect your practice and design?

Gregg Pasquarelli: I think because we didn't study architecture until later in our lives and we had other careers before going to architecture school, we always understood the act of building to be larger than the act of design. We realized that building and making is not about the architectural object, but more importantly about something that's dynamic and engages within a larger context. We believe that contextuality as an aesthetic model is a ridiculous idea, but contextuality as a performative model is actually a really interesting to us. And so while so many architects use style as an operative term to promote an idea, or themselves, we always felt that the process of architecture as it engages an urban context was more inspiring. That was where we wanted to invest our time and become who we are. This was really was one of the founding principles of the office and why the five of us came together. One of our very strong common beliefs is that architecture lies beyond the façade. We have used the word thickness a lot to try to describe it, although its not easy. We are interested not only in the thickness of the making and what happens behind the building but also thickness as it extends beyond the façade and into the city. And to use thickness intelligently you have to engage other external models. Otherwise that thickness becomes meaningless, it then just becomes form. For SHoP it's that meaning, both from the edge of the façade out and the edge of the façade in—that makes us think architecture's interesting, and that architects have something to offer to our culture. As problem-solvers, architects can engage, refine, and transform all of these simultaneous models. And when architecture starts to present itself as an engaging solutions that are both influenced by and influencing other models, then that's what inspires us.

AS: Yeah. It's funny, because—
GP:—Did I just answer the next question? (laughing)
AS: Well, you led right into it...
GP: (laughing)
AS: Most architects that focus on a critical practice disregard, let's say, the spatial implications of the legislative, the financial, the political, and how these issues affect architecture and design. They see them almost as negative forces that disrupt the design process...
GP:—Right. That's why they don't build very much. Art in a vacuum is a nice hobby. Art that engages can cause revolutions.
AS: I agree.
GP: But let me clarify something, I have tremendous respect for paper architecture, and I have tremendous respect for philosophy and writing and criticism. But we wanted to build, we wanted to take our ideas and see them at work, see them succeed or fail. You know—in site.
AS: Can you describe some examples of how you interpret what [the editors are calling] these "outside forces", like the legal and the financial? How

do they effectively engage and challenge your design?

GP: First of all, it requires an attitude adjustment. I mean, I think we saw a generation of very good architects in front of us who for some reason didn't want any of the responsibility of how do you make and build and make it come together. Many wanted to compose an image of what a building or idea might hopefully be, but when any of the difficult issues came into play, like finance, or legislative, or political, or whatever, the attitude was, "That's a problem that's going to affect my art and I would rather not deal with it." Well, architecture is an art, but it's the art of bringing these things together and coming up with a fantastic solution in spite of these. So the first way to do it is you could either say, "I'm trying to make the perfect image of the perfect object," or you could say, "I'm trying to make the perfect solution for a series of performative models that are simultaneously having an influence over my thought process."

The first thing you have to do is have an attitude that these are not problems, but equally part of what your mandate is: to design, to solve, and to challenge. And no one's saying that you just give in; you have to challenge them. But if you start by saying, "Oh well, I can't design what I want because of this," or, "Ugh, it's a horrible design because, I can only build it this high or this wide," or "They don't understand my ideas." Well, you know what, you're going to be bitter and not build very much. And you're not going to get to try it out, you're most likely not going to have the opportunity to be able to push the limits. At SHoP we try to immediately engage those things from the first step. We begin by saying, "let me find out what every problem is", rather than… "I am going to do my thing and try to fit it in later." It's much easier to make a beautiful object and then look at it and fetishize it. It's much harder to say, "What are all the problems here," deal with them head-on, and still make something that you like or that works or that you think is beautiful.

AS: The East River study. That's a good example of taking an incredibly complex problem, where you have all these competing interests and agencies, and find a solution—working directly with the politics, the financing, public space and private development. Can you talk about how that comes together and how these ideas affected your design?

GP: Well, together with the Richard Rogers Partnership, we looked at the history the site—you know, this 40-year graveyard of master plans for the lower East River. I mean, there are dozens of them. And in many of the schemes the designers made a design object and clipped it on to the side of the island. So you say to yourself, "Well that's great. You either like them, they're either beautiful and sexy and supple, or interesting and dynamic, or brutal and fascinating, or . . . whatever." But to us that's not design. That's making objects; that's making aesthetics. Again, the part that made the project interesting for us, and also incredibly difficult, was we have eight or nine clients. Whether it's the Department of City Planning, or the Economic Development Corporation, or the Parks Department, or the City DOT, or the State DOT, or the Department of Environmental Protection, or the South Street Seaport Museum, or Community Board 1, or Community Board 3, or the LMDC—I mean, each one of these groups has an agenda and has things that they can and can not do. And then you have critical technical difficulties. You have bedrock issues, you have subway troubles, water mains, biological issues with the river, and incredible lease deals that the city executed in the 1970s that have huge impacts, national monuments like the Brooklyn Bridge and the Manhattan Bridge, rusting Robert Moses roadways. I love the way a city works! So the first thing we did was just try and figure out what all the agendas were and what was even possible and not possible. I'm not going to sit and spend three months coming up with a beautiful, supple object that floats over the water if that's an impossible thing to accomplish. That's just folly. And folly has its purpose. Folly can be inspiring, folly can be critical and can challenge us and can do lots of things, but we didn't believe that was our job here. Our job is to try and solve a lot of problems. How does this neighborhood really work? And what would be the most important thing that you can do down there? We came up with a series of issues, and we diagrammed them, and we explained what the problems were and asked for input from each group to make sure we understood the issues correctly. In addition, we had to get all the constituencies to all understand what all the other constituencies' issues were, and why theirs may not be the overriding one, but is a part of a very complex layering of issues—that was the challenge. This was a tremendous amount of work completed before we ever started to "design." Then we came up with a series of a dozen short-term solutions that would make the waterfront better without upsetting the balance of each group and that would immediately make short-term impacts and improvements. And then we felt that we would have this foundation and trust and then we could study what would be the bigger thing that you could do that would really radically change the place, after you finish the short-term solutions and everyone gets a taste of how great this place could be.

AS: The image that stuck in my mind after your presentation of the East River Study at Cooper Union, which seems to encompass what SHoP does, was that very simple diagram where the larger the development—
GP: (laughs)
AS:—the larger the park. Can you talk about that?
GP: The fact of the matter is that the community boards, and many government agencies are wary of architects and urban designers because they think they're just trying to impose their own vision to build an edifice to themselves whatever the consequences are. One of the most aggressive proposals we had was to float four to seven skyscrapers over the FDR Drive and really invent something new there; a completely new thickened waterfront where the city structure and the water's edge would be totally integrated in a way that it doesn't happen anywhere else in this city. At the same time, we didn't want to say that we were imposing this big vision. It's their community and we were trying to demonstrate how a performative model would work. We tried to demonstrate to them what the impacts were and what benefits they could get out of the proposal. We were very proud

that we found a way to give lower Manhattan a 20 acre park that wouldn't cost the taxpayers one cent. Interestingly, every time we presented this to the community, they said, "how big do the buildings need to be?" And we said, that's not the question. It's how much park do you want. You tell us how much park you want, we'll tell you how big the buildings need to be. If you want a small little green triangle park like Duane Park, they don't have to be very big at all. They can be very small; we can build one four-story building. If you want Grammercy Park, we need four ten-story buildings. If you want, you know, Bryant Park, we need fifteen-story buildings. If you want twenty acres of park, we need seven thirty-five story buildings. You tell us. What does the community want? The process for us was how you make a design that can take the reciprocal action of all of these constituents and still maintain its integrity no matter what the external decisions are. At the end of the day, you could get an incredible thickened edge, with a programmed waterfront, with a new kind of connection between the water and the city, providing amenities for free—an incredibly different park—a different place than any other place in the city.

AS: So it's a mix of public and private development.
GP: That was our hope.
AS: Are there other projects that SHoP is working on that have a mix of public and private?
GP: Well, Greenport was a public project—which was a waterfront park which where we recently completed the final phases of construction—and our new building for FIT, which is a public institution, but, you know, there are institutions that contain programs that are semi-public and semi-private; for example, having a for-profit carousel house and a skating rink in a public park alongside a municipal ferry terminal, or, spaces for fashion week inside a community college. So, I think that there is that idea of both things. I think we really try and bring the public—we bring a little taste of private to the public and a little taste of public to the private, as much as possible, and watch how those two interact.

AS: One negative issue for many architects and designers is how the market affects what the developers want and hence what the architects can do. What are your thoughts on this issue of how the market affects what we do? How do you navigate this issue? Is it an issue or is it reality?
GP: It is an issue. But the anger or the blame from the architectural community in general is not aimed at the right person or people. There are bad developers and there are good developers. There are bad clients and there are good clients. There are clients who have taste and intelligence and who are articulate, and there are clients who are less so. That happens in anything you do. There are government agencies that spend their money wisely and ones that don't. I do not believe it is necessarily the development community that is at fault. The developers actually have their own burden that they have to deal with, beyond education and taste and their lack thereof. And their main problem is that they have to satisfy their lenders and their investors. The people having a larger influence on the quality of design is not the development community, it's really the lending community. It's the system by which a lender will verify the viability of a project. Because the only way they'll verify the viability of a project is through what are called comps (comparables). And the concept is they'll only lend it if they can say, "Well, here's an example of the same thing

1. Fashion Institute of Technology, North Façade, SHoP Architects

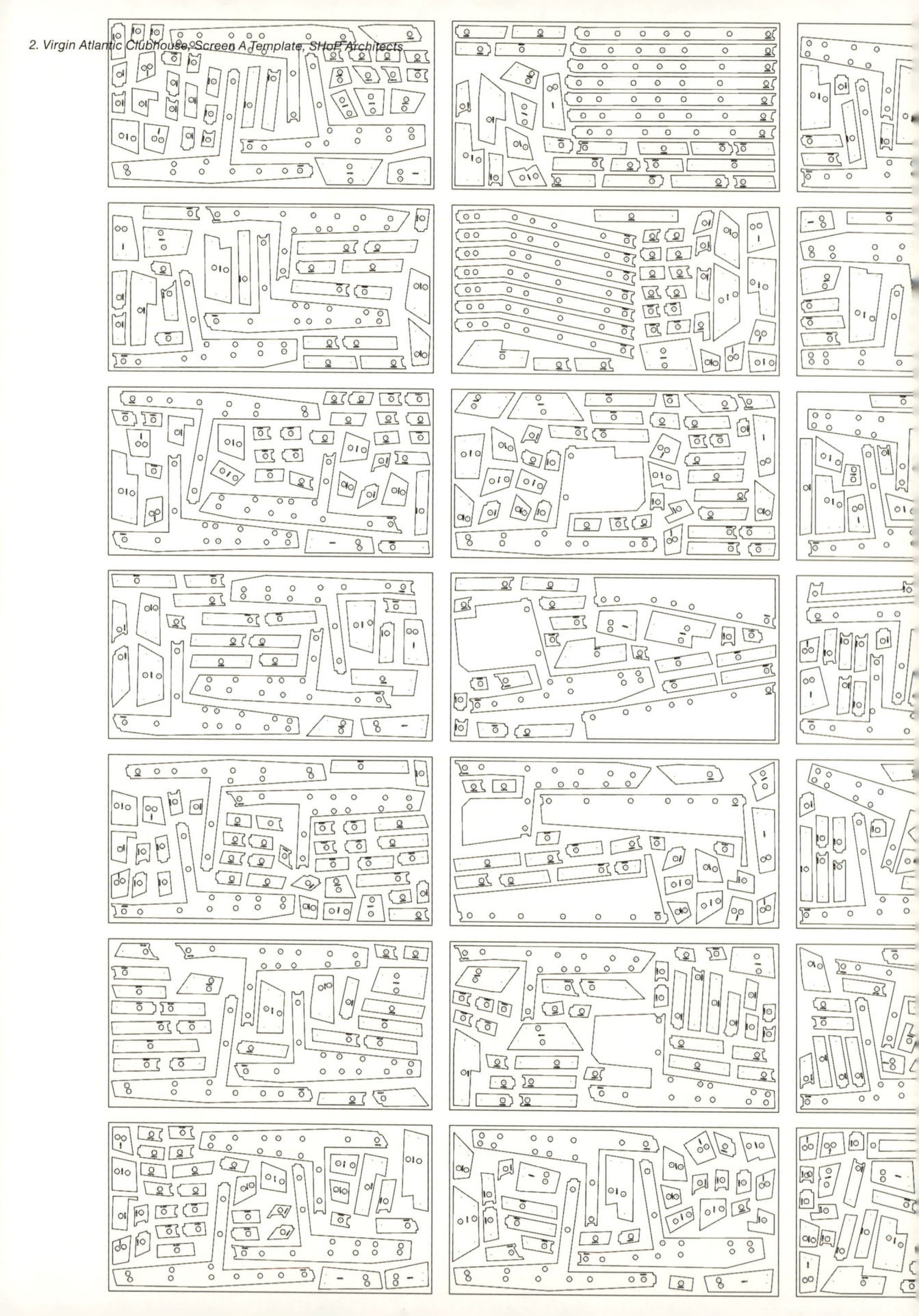

2. Virgin Atlantic Clubhouse, Screen A Template, SHoP Architects

127

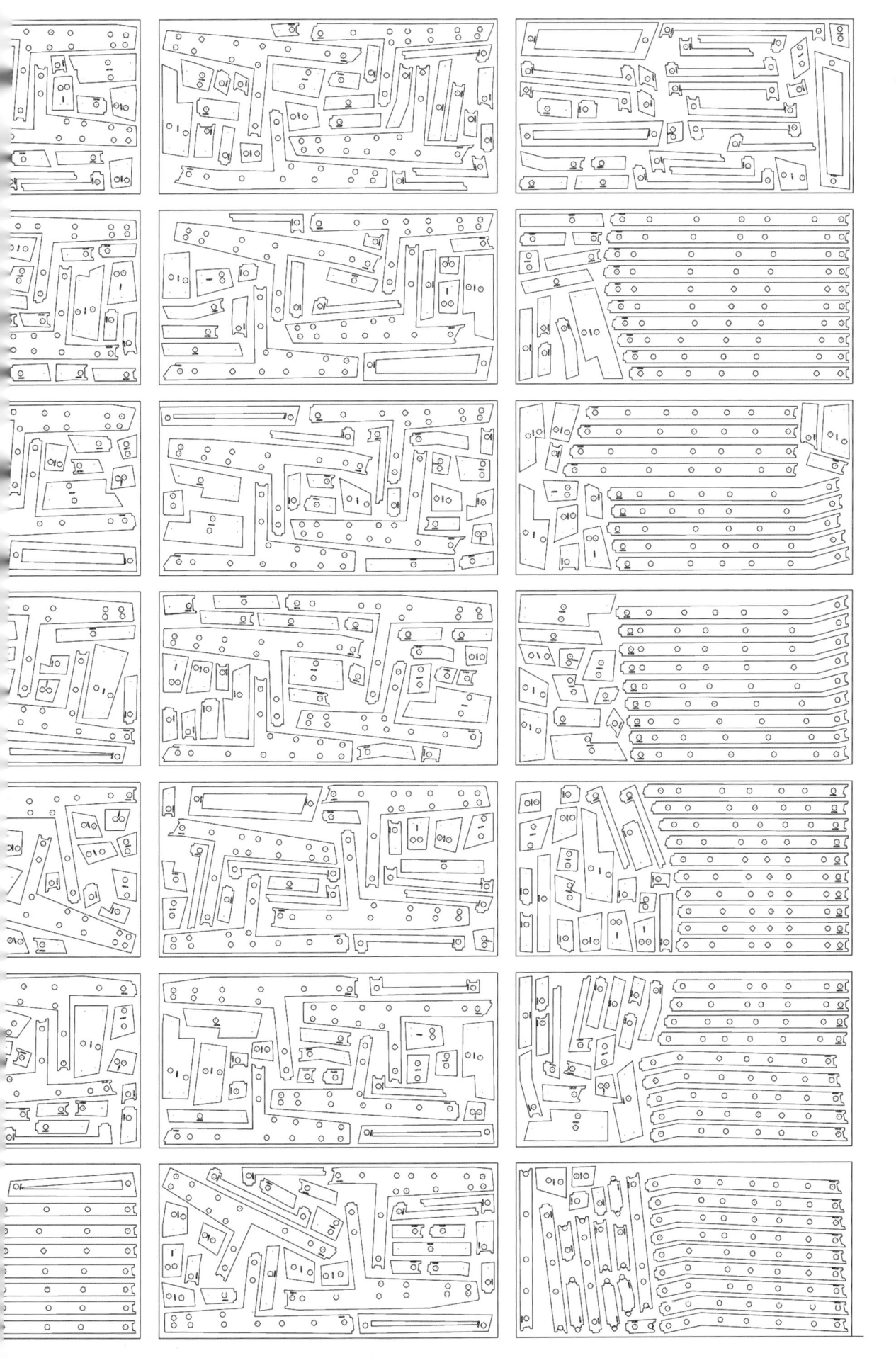

that's been done before and here are the revenues generated by that." So if that's the only thing that they'll lend against, it creates what I call the cycle of mediocrity. Because the developer goes to the broker and asks, "Well, what sells?" And the broker says, "Well, two bedrooms that are 1600 square feet with x, y, z amenities." Well, the only reason that sold is because it was the only thing available on the market. The only reason the broker sold that is because that was the only thing they had to sell. And it was the only product that they had to sell because that was the only thing that would get financing, and the architect is told by the developer to do what he can get a loan for. So it becomes this feedback loop that is very difficult to change.

AS: It sounds like—and this is what I think SHoP is doing—that it's really up to the architect to navigate that as their terrain, and use that as a tool to develop their projects.

GP: Well, I think you do. I think incremental change is your best hope in that system, or you have to put up your own money. That's it. Those are the two choices. You either incrementally nudge it and then you hope over ten generations of design it changes the typology, which would be a career, or you have to find you own funding, either personal or other people's money, and get someone to believe in you and say that by making this design change it's going to radically alter the profitability model. And believe me, if you do one and it works, the lenders and developers will all follow. They're just looking for... It's a biological model. You know, suddenly one animal has the bigger claw and so he can eat more fish, and they get to reproduce the most.

AS: Is that what happened at The Porter House?

GP: Well, The Porter House... yes, in a certain respect. I mean, we had a partner... we found the project but brought one of our clients in because together we believed in the same ideals and were willing to take the chance of altering the typology. At the same time, The Porter House did not radically alter the typology; it's a medium sized incremental shift. And now we're working on half a dozen other development projects that are all incremental shifts, because there's only so far that you can push the market. But hopefully we'll continue to prove the model and have the opportunity to exponentially enlarge the incremental shifts.

AS: Right. Because The Porter House is a good example of taking zoning legislation and the transfer of air rights to influence an architectural design, can you specifically talk about how SHoP creatively uses them to affect your design?

GP: The Porter House's massing is a pure performance and zoning model. We just said, "Let's take the purity of the idea, link it with the financial model, and link it with a structural and a constructional technique, to... You know, there were more than half a dozen competing developers going after the site but there was a limit to what you could do, and without changing the financial model through the cantilever and the air-rights transfer, you wouldn't win the bidding war for the site. And the other guys—I'm sure other developers thought about the cantilever, but not in exactly the same way and not with an intelligence of design that would make the cantilever a profit center rather than a cost center; at the same time, using the emerging technological construction methodologies to make a daring and dramatic building that

3. East River Waterfront Comprehensive Study, Pier 35 Overview, SHoP Architects / Richard Rogers Partnership

would in and of itself become a kind of marketing profit center rather than a cost center, allowed us to pull off that design. Our favorite part of that building is that it's a pure performative model that is completely orthogonal. I mean, performance models don't always have to curve!

AS: Are there any projects in the books where SHoP is doing something similar that you could talk about?

GP: I can't really talk about it, but there are about a half dozen or so, actually. (laughs) It's working. Our own slightly deviated self-generating model is working.

AS: Can you talk a little bit about "tools"? Would you consider Versioning to be a tool for design? Could you say that SHoP has developed its own proprietary system, software or methods of working?

GP: I would say it starts with an attitude and it continues with how we adapt existing technologies. It's now moving into us developing our own proprietary software systems. So we are starting to consider writing our own code. And, you know, we're working with people outside of architecture to do that and it's starting to bring some really interesting ideas to the table. I mean, it might take a couple more years to really develop it but that's definitely the goal of the office is to move more and more in that direction.

AS: Does it have a name?

GP: —No, not yet.

AS: Is that something that you're just going to use internally, or are you going to try to—

GP: —We'll make sure it works before we (laughs) before we let anyone else hurt themselves with it (laughs)—we have always been pretty open with the techniques we have developed. In general, the techniques are not what are most interesting to us.

AS: If this is what I think it is, it sounds like something our profession desperately needs.

GP: Well, we'll see what happens. We may not be able to do it. We may be too small and we don't have the resources to do it. But definitely part of the office is working on that. You know, it's just interesting because I think that some people see it as technique and some people see it as theory and other people see it as design and other people see it as being really savvy and smart and other people see it as being a total sell-out. I hope it's all of the above.

AS: It sounds like it's the way to really practice. To work within the world that we really live in. How to actually—work.

GP: I think the people who are the most outspoken critics are the people doing the least in their life. So, you know, it's not easy. It's not easy, and we don't say we have the answers at all. We're just trying out a few different things and trying to have fun and still make really beautiful buildings.

AS: Last two questions. One of the interesting things that seem to have brought SHoP to where it is is the fact that all of the partners have very diverse and unique backgrounds academically and professionally. With reference to what we've been discussing, are there particular things that you think young architects or students should think about? Or courses that students should be taking that can bring about this more diversified look at practice?

GP: Well, I think there's a big difference between

4. Camera Obscura, Shell Under Construction, SHoP Architects

being educated and being trained. And if you only take courses in one field I think you may lean more towards the training side of the equation. As you diversify the kinds of experiences in your life the more educated you become. I think that it absolutely has helped—I think that having different backgrounds helped the five of us be a little bit freer, or... we had an easier time adapting other methods or modes of thinking into architecture. We went to Columbia at an incredibly exciting time and we had phenomenal faculty and incredible leadership out of Bernard. He provided an remarkably diverse environment where so many agendas could be worked on. Each one of the five of us has different but overlapping skills and that has helped us. I think there is also is sacrifice—there's a definite sacrifice that all of us take for the benefit of the group. And that it's never about one of us. It's always about the five of us. Which I think helps tremendously too, that you're willing to realize that it's more important for the group to do well than for any individual to do well. And it's just unbelievable commitment between the five of us. You know, we really feel incredibly lucky to have each other. Maybe the most important part of the small success of SHoP is the way in which the staff works, the way that it's a non-hierarchical office, that everyone pitches in, that it's not a studio system. There are not defined teams. Everyone works on multiple projects. I think because the partnership was a family where there was always a sacrifice for the good of the group, we think of our staff as just an extension of that family. It sounds cliché, but it's true. And we have excruciatingly low turnover because of that. And we have fun. And we have a total open-book policy with all of our fiscal information. Everyone knows exactly what's going on and why we make the decisions that we make. And, you know, we really see the staff as the greatest asset. So I think it's about an environment and an attitude, more than what you can learn in a class. But I think diversifying the kinds of information that you take in, the kinds of experiences that you have and the kinds of organizations... You can sense how they work, and pulling out what works and doesn't work in a performative model aspect, and trying to build your own vision of what you think might work, is always a positive way to go about it.

AS: So your final thoughts or advice for, say, young architects, would be to diversify their experiences and a self-check on their attitude about how they go out and look at the world and look at what they're doing, how they're approaching things...

GP: Precisely. As we were just talking about before, take as many projects as you can, figure it out, get dirty, see what influences all different kinds of people, don't worry about some kind of pre-determined path, and take responsibility.

AS: Don't be afraid of these outside forces—

GP: Embrace them. See if you are smart enough to get around them, or use them, to the benefit of both sides. It's not getting around it in the sense that "I beat them," or "I was able to outsmart them," but it's, "Let me satisfy them and us." And then you really win. And I think you learn how to do that by going out and taking responsibility for each one of those things rather than sitting in an office and blaming other people, or not even engaging. Engagement. Risk—that's what matters.

André Soluri holds a Master of Science in Advanced Architectural Design from Columbia University and a Bachelor of Architecture from The Cooper Union. He currently lives and works in New York as a registered architect and is a frequent contributor to 306090.

Special thanks to **Caitlin Connors** of Yale University for transcribing the interview.

THEUNIS, Katrien

The Rise of the Private Developer and The Fall of the Designer

After WWII the private developer became an increasingly important player in the urbanization process, primarily with regard to housing construction. Since that time, the relationship between designers and private developers has been rather conflicted. Most designers adopt a negative attitude towards private developers. The relationship between these parties has grown into a rivalry instead of becoming a synchronized action in the (sub) urbanization process. In Belgium, tensions between designers and private developers (commonly referred to as "promoters") in residential development have been outspoken since private promoters entered the scene at the beginning of the nineteen

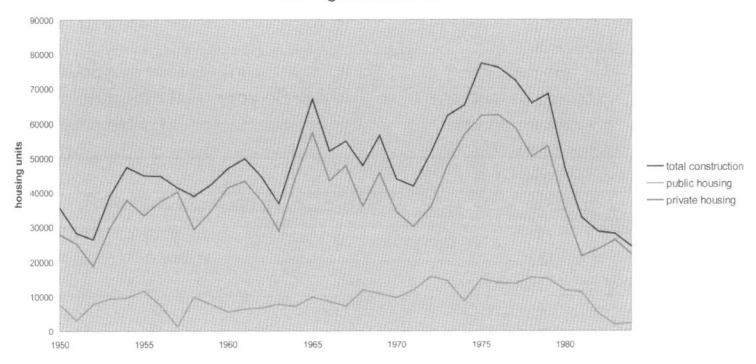

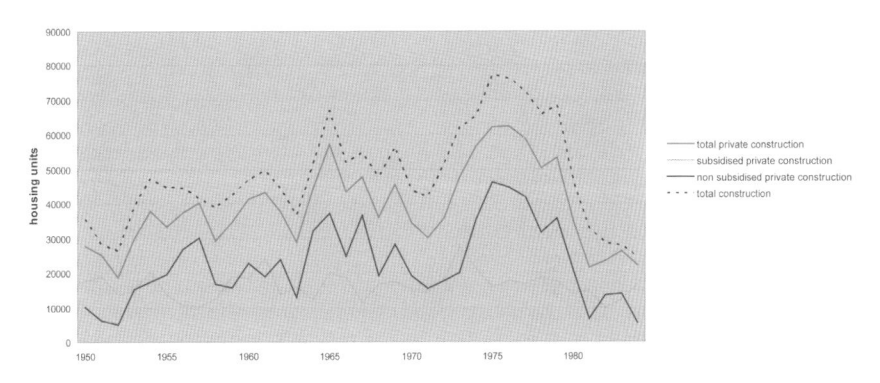

1. Housing construction, total and private

seventies. "It occurs all the time more that the building contractor, often upgraded to promoter, takes care of the entire construction process, including the choice of the architect and the control over the design."[1] As such, private developers are often accused of facilitating the uncoordinated colonization of our territory by low density single-family-house developments. They are held responsible for fragmenting our open space and provoking land speculation.

State as a provider or as a facilitator?

As modern architects stated in the Athens Charter in 1941, modern architecture and urbanism would provide the conditions necessary to create a new classless society. In this progressive idea, the government was imagined to be the initiator and administrator of ideas and projects, providing its citizens with infrastructure, employment and housing. In short, the common view was that the state should take care of the well-being of its society. During the post-war period, in most countries of Western Europe (the Netherlands, France, United Kingdom, etc.), leading architects were soon preoccupied with extensive public housing programs initiated as part of the establishment of the welfare state.

Belgium, however, did not fully adopt the modern principle. The government decided to take up the task of social provision only partially. They did initiate large infrastructural projects for the (re-)construction of the country, but the main provision of housing for middle-class families was left to the citizens. The authorities focused on stimulating private initiatives in the construction of individual houses by establishing financial measures such as low interest loans and building gratuities (De Taeye Act, 1948). In this structure, the state became only a facilitator and the market itself turned into the provider. Later, at the eve of the 1973 oil crisis, the central government's incentives for private housing were no longer sufficient to help middle class families buy a home. At this point, the government enacted legislation to enable the construction of large-scale private developments. This move was in contrast to the 1948 Act (what 1948 Act?), which only subsidized the construction of freestanding single-family houses. The central government outlined standard contracts for public-private collaboration in residential development in 1971. The standard contracts mainly define tasks, rights and obligations between public and private partners, thereby setting up a legal framework for collaboration.[2] Secondly, the government constructed the expanded Brunfaut Act[3] in order to generate more benefits to generate incentives for the private promoter. The expanded Act regulates the provision of subsidies for partnership covering 60% of the infrastructural costs through public funding, leaving only 40% of the cost to the private developer. In return, the municipality—in case of being the owner of the building site—ceded the right of construction to the private developer, who is responsible for the housing production. In this public-private structure, each partner could expect to receive remarkable returns; the municipality reduced its expenses to a minimum and enlarged its housing stock while the private promoter was offered buildable land for free and only paid 40% of the investment required for development.[4] Also in 1971 the Breyne Act was introduced; this was a law outlining a minimal binding contract to regulate the accord between consumer and private contractor regarding housing development. The Act normalized conveyance of property, the content of sales agreement and determined when an advance on the purchase prices may be asked. It was enacted primarily to protect the prospective buyer against questionable point-of-purchase tactics used by real estate agents and contractors, but it also reduced suspicion of private contractors, enlarging the trust between the individual buyer and the private promoter. As such, the private developer was consciously introduced to the housing production process in a coordinated effort organized at the national level.

  The Belgian government acted out of the conviction that providing a public supply of housing would be financially difficult for the country. The point is well demonstrated by the case of Hoboken and its failure around this time to solve its housing problem through public initiative. In 1966, the town council of Hoboken decided to urbanize a polder located on its territory and build a new town of approximately 10.000 inhabitants, named Polderstad. The town council—known to be a socialist strong-hold—hoped to meet several objectives at once: coordinate the expansion of Hoboken, create a substantial number of housing units and counteract land speculation.[5] In spite of good intentions, the town council encountered financial difficulties in meeting its responsibility to develop the new neighbourhood. The infrastructure cost; road construction and utilities were to be partly funded by the municipality. An even larger problem was the inability of the Social Housing Association to deal with such a large building program. In fact, it was only authorised to receive and allocate credits for projects reaching up to 100 housing units. As a result, the development of the new town on public initiative encountered a financial deadlock.

Supported by the recent legislative framework, the municipality of Hoboken decided to continue the development of its polder in collaboration with a private contractor rather than on public initiative. The municipal executive signed a joint venture agreement with N.V. Ipeo, a private association for project development. N.V.Ipeo was one of the companies that made up N.V.Groep I, an umbrella organisation financed by several insurance companies,[6] and an initiative of the Bank of Paris and the Netherlands (Paribas). N.V.Groep I could rely on a whole range of specialised companies for construction, centres of study, planning and control, as well as commercial management centres.

Contradictions between the model of public and private housing

Besides the structural problem of public initiative, the modern housing typology itself seemed to be inappropriate. A consumer-oriented suburbanization model challenged the model of high density residential housing promoted and defended by the modern architect. The sixties and seventies was characterized by the emerging clash of competing ideologies: the concept of equal society versus rising consumer culture. Mass housing strategies as promoted by modern architects conflicted with the production of a new way of life rooted in consumerism—low rise and single-family houses stood in opposition to high-rise.

This tension is present in the case of Polderstad. Initially, the socialist town council commissioned the project of the new town to modern architect Renaat Braem, defender of socialist values. Braem saw in the project "the opportunity to accomplish a coherent urban structure, large enough to create an organic entity with the necessary social equipment."[7] According to Braem, these social services are only feasible in dense agglomerations. Therefore, Braem argued that the neighbourhood should house approximately 25,000 inhabitants.[8] This model of living in high density with all necessary services can be interpreted as a materialization of the modern idea. Braem described the Polderstad project as a reaction to "the extended neighbourhoods disposed of any soul, any cosiness or any conscious social cohesion."[9] As such, his project can be interpreted as a critique of the private development of freestanding single-family homes. The

2. Birds-eye view of the neighborhood

3. Diversity and personal expression in dwellings was the design goal.

THEUNIS

design clearly opposes scattered housing, fragmentation of open land, and reduction of collective space.

Braem's project was received with scepticism by both town officials and developers. For technical and financial reasons, most building contractors preferred rectangular buildings over the proposed round towers (are there images of both plans? If not, we need further descriptions here). They also argued that the plan contained too few single family houses.[10] The dogmatic discrepancy between what Braem considered being a quality project and developers considered to be good coincides with the financial deadlock in which the public authority found itself.

In the end, the deadlock was released when the new private investor, N.V.Ipeo, endeavoured to prepare a new plan of development for the polder. The new project proposed 1000 new housing units with single-family housing planned for the main part of the territory and semi-high-rise units on the boundaries of the site. The project was to be executed in several phases. The neighbourhood would be comprised of a central shopping area with public facilities and collective space. Between the residential areas a small local center with a primary school, playground and a popular bar would be integrated. The public authority wished to avoid extensive repetition of identical housing types, and insisted that a comfortable diversity of buildings be achieved. Since unique architecture per parcel was not feasible, a modular system was utilized. A set of model unit types was developed, which differed from each other in typology, comfort and price. The dwellings were grouped in small rows, and there were never to be more than six identical housing units in a row. These rows were cut and rotated to create diversified street sections and favourable living environments. These rows of dwellings were positioned around green strips that directly connected to the large green space at the edge of the neighbourhood.

This second design for Polderstad was successfully executed. This achievement can partly be attributed to the presented urban form and typology. It responded to the ambition of each Belgian citizen: to become an owner of his/her single family home. The grouped housing typology utilized in Polderstad is neither the impersonal high-rise of the modernist project, nor the expensive individual house built with the personal architect. In fact, grouped housing construction benefits from the advantages of serial production but in this case breaks from monotony and repetition by working in limited series of no more than 6 similar houses in a row. The provision of different housing types ensured that a broad layer of society could be reached, while simultaneously providing them with means to distinguish between one home and another. In this vision, everyone could find a housing type that corresponded to their own aesthetic values and financial position. The grouped housing typology is the contribution of private developers. Its intention is to correspond to the aspirations of a new consumer society, promoting values of individuality, personality and freedom.

Development in capitalist culture

Structural and ideological discrepancies between designers and developers describe only part of the overall difference in vision and approach evident in Polderstad. Also important to consider are financial strategies, non-local forces dictating prices and markets, project management, and marketing.

Grouped housing typologies reflect a lower selling price than typical homes on the market. In itself, this lower cost can be considered an important result of type innovation. The type is less space consuming than the freestanding single-family house, thus avoiding price inflation linked to the rocketing cost of land acquisition. Moreover, at their origin, the urban design and housing typology are conceptualised to use a rationalised repetitive construction system. The Dutch construction company N.V. Breevast executed the project. They used a system of in-situ concrete between prefabricated steel slabs that are re-used for each dwelling. This method reduced material and labor costs, consequently remaining below typical free market prices where labour-intensive conventional construction methods significantly raise the cost to consumers.[11]

Another decisive factor leading to the success of the project can be attributed to promotion. N.V. Groep I had a special division, N.V. Icasa, responsible for promotion and sales. N.V.Icase implemented several promotion techniques. A number of large consumer-oriented advertisement panels were located in and around the community of Hoboken. Advertisements were also published in a number of popular newspapers. At the beginning of the first phase, one example of each housing type was erected and opened to the public for visiting. The exhibited houses attracted numerous curious visitors and

villa « rietzang »

Bent u gewend slechts genoegen te nemen met het allerbeste ? Stelt u altijd de hoogste eisen ? Dan is villa Rietzang iets voor u. Want deze vorstelijke villa biedt nu werkelijk alles op het gebied van topkomfort.

Riante ruimte, 180 m² woonplezier. Wat denkt u, zou een living van 46 m² groot genoeg zijn ? Groot, maar gezellig. Want de eethoek en open keuken liggen iets lager dan de living zelf. Dat schept sfeer. Vooral omdat de scheiding tussen beide elementen zo elegant is uitgewerkt : televisiehoek - open haard - plantenborder - trapje. De ruimteschepping door het schuin oplopende dak geeft een eigen karakter aan het geheel van de leefruimte.

Alles in villa Rietzang is royaal. Zo biedt de garage plaats aan twee wagens. Tussen de beide slaapkamers van de kinderen een fijne, praktische doucheruimte. De andere twee slaapvertrekken grenzen aan de luxueuze badkamer.

Nog even potten kijken in de keuken. Ook hier valt de zeer verzorgde afwerking op. Plus de komplete inrichting. « Rietzang » een indrukwekkende villa, zowel binnen als buiten.

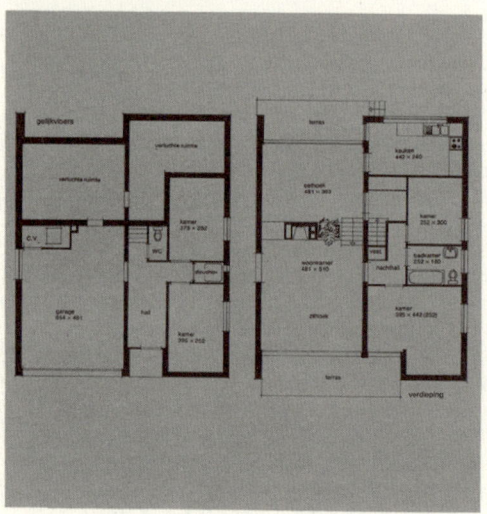

villa « zandweel »

Half open bebouwing in villastijl. De verzorgde buitenafwerking met strakke vlakken en modern lijnenspel maken van villa « Zandweel » een architektonisch geslaagde realisatie. Ook van binnen voldoet deze woning aan alle criteria voor modern woongenot. De gastvrije inkomsthal geeft meteen een prettige indruk van het huis. Woonkamer (30 m²) en volledig ingerichte keuken vormen één geheel ; een groot schuifraam maakt van tuin, terras en woonkamer één grote, natuurlijke ruimte : een origineel-praktische vorm van ruimte-indeling en -aanwending die het enthousiasme wekt van wie het ziet ... of, nog beter, er in leeft.

De garage, helemaal buiten de woning, is groot genoeg voor uw wagen plus fijne hobby-hoek én werkplaats én berging.

Boven, drie aantrekkelijke slaapkamers met een juweel van een badkamer. Nog hoger komt u op de grote zolder, nuttig in te richten voor alles en nog wat. De villa « Zandweel » heeft verrassend veel te bieden !

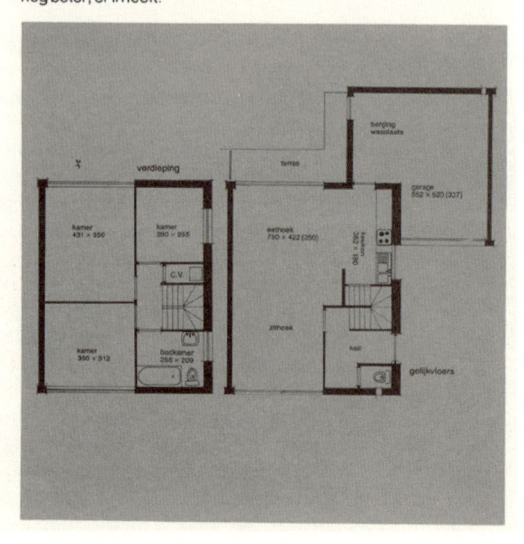

4. Detail of the Polderstad brochure, showing two prototype dwellings

THEUNIS

residentie « ter leie »

De appartementsgebouwen in Polderstad bieden met 4 verschillende types van appartementen een zo ruime keuze dat aan vrijwel elke wens « op maat » kan voldaan worden. Per residentie zijn er tweeëntwintig appartementen : twee op het gelijkvloers en vier op elk van de vijf verdiepingen.
Naar wens :

Het 130 m² appartement met drie slaapkamers.
Living van liefst 38 zonovergoten m² met terras op de Zuidkant. Een pracht van een keuken die geniet van een heerlijke voormiddagbezonning. Drie slaapkamers waarvan de grootste met een oppervlakte van meer dan 14 m², de beide andere groot genoeg voor elk een dubbel bed en dito kast. Badkamer en afzonderlijke WC piekfijn afgewerkt. Een indrukwekkende inkomhal verbindt het leefgedeelte met het slaapgedeelte, en biedt plaats te over om meer dan een paar gasten tegelijk te ontvangen. Appartementen met zoveel stijl en standing, zó ruim bemeten, worden meer dan zeldzaam !

Het 106 m² appartement met twee slaapkamers.
Living in L-vorm, meer dan 32 m², met terras op het volle Zuiden. Ruime praktische keuken.
Van de twee slaapkamers meet de grootste méér dan 14 m², maar ook de kleinere is voldoende groot voor tweepersoonsgebruik. Daarnaast . . . de fraaie badkamer en afzonderlijke WC. De royale inkomhal, met dubbele glazen deur op de living, accentueert nog de biezondere ruimteindruk van dit standingvol appartement.

Het 96 m² appartement met twee slaapkamers.
Ook in dit appartement heeft de living een oppervlakte van meer dan 32 m², met terras op het volle Zuiden. De keuken, funktioneel zó opgevat dat zij één geheel vormt met de living, is een droom voor een moderne huisvrouw. De twee slaapkamers hebben dezelfde vorstelijke maten als deze van de grotere appartementen. Badkamer en afzonderlijke WC kompleteren dit attraktief geheel.

Het 58 m² appartement met één slaapkamer.
Pittig ideaal voor elke alleenwoner (ook voor vijftig-plussers). Living en kitchinette vormen één geheel, met liefst 22 m² woongenot. De slaapkamer van 3 bij 3,50 m is zo groot dat deze studio terecht appartement genoemd wordt. De inkomhal heeft ruimte over voor een grote bergkast en geeft toegang tot de living, slaapkamer, badkamer en afzonderlijke WC.
Klein maar fijn . . . en heel wat ruimer dan u denkt !

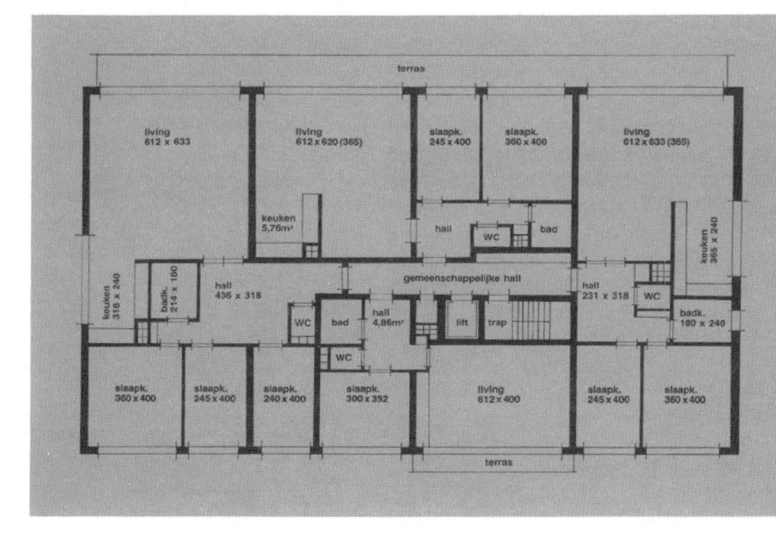

Elke residentie beschikt over volgende gemeenschappelijke lokalen : ruime inkomhal-met-sas, uitgebreide fietsenbergplaats, afzonderlijke bergplaats voor kinderwagens. Bovendien beschikt elke verdieping over een diskrete vuilschuif, in verbinding met een containerlokaal.

Bij elk appartement hoort, naast brievenbus, parlofoon en boodschappenkast, een private bergplaats op het gelijkvloers. Inzake modern woonkomfort werd niets over het hoofd gezien : individueel centraal verwarmd, ruim, logisch, funktioneel, af... een Polderstadappartement is werkelijk anders. Het is beslist de moeite waard er één te bezitten, ook al hebt u voorlopig niet de bedoeling het zelf te bewonen.

eliminated the stigma attached to buying on plan. Moreover, attractively designed flyers promoted the advantages of the modern single family house, comfortable and fully equipped: kitchen with the latest appliances, bathroom, central heating, decoration with wallpaper and paint, and a connection to cable television.

N.V. Groep's purposeful analysis and understanding of the market enabled them to manoeuvre within market forces in order to produce a typological response. They proposed a feasible project with competitive prices and consumer advantages in a short time, and they invested in acquiring the knowledge and resources necessary to sell their product fast. These are factors the single designer cannot control, and in many cases chooses not to engage.

The first phase (250 housing units) of the Polderstad project under N.V. Groep I was an undisputed success with long lists of potential buyers and all dwellings sold. The realisation of the second phase (333 housing units) followed suit, generating the same flood of applicants. It seemed as if the perfect design and financial formula had been found for successful further development of the project.

No compromises

The financial and structural power of the private developers left the designers in this case feeling completely marginalised. N.V. Ipeo demanded to be in charge of the conceptualisation of the urban plan in order to guarantee successful operation. Consequently, the project conceived by the urban designers was completely discarded and replaced by a new urbanization plan conceived by an anonymous architect embedded in the machine of the company. In reaction, Renaat Braem and his colleagues immediately dissolved their contract with the municipality, arguing that their responsibility had been marginalised because of the agreement between the municipality and the private promoter. Moreover, they argued:

Our concern as urban designers existed in creating something large at Polderstad. To what extend are we still able to participate in this? Until where does our responsibility stretch? Indulgences have been made for economic as well as social and financial reasons; we are no longer designers.[12]

In his autobiographical book published in 1987, Braem called the project in Hoboken "a failure for those who hoped to build a real piece of urbanism in this country. A failure, although the bank director was socialist, the alderman of the municipality was socialist and the town council as well!"[13]

Redefine tasks or redefine territories?

The occurrences of the seventies were a foreword of the reshuffle of tasks and domains between architects and private developers in Belgium. First of all, for structural reasons; the Belgian government became a facilitator and created a framework that allowed the private developer to control and take over the field of housing production. The agency of the modern architect was structurally and institutionally marginalised. Secondly, it seems that the housing production model proposed by the modern designer has a social, urban and sustainable concern, but disregards the needs and desires of intended inhabitants. The housing production model of private developers is, by comparison, less urban, less social, and less sustainable—but the happiness of the inhabitant is assured. One can argue that designers significantly underestimated the power of market demand as a factor in urban design. The product put forward by the architects did not correspond to the needs and taste of the market. Thirdly, the managerial skills of the private developer fit in with the new consumer way of life—developers pursued the art of selling the house as a consumption product, marketing homes in the same fashion as the TV or the car.

And finally, designers simply gave up; they did not want to make compromises and refused to resign their ideology. By effectively withdrawing from the suburbanization process, architects themselves seemed to remove all obstacles from the path of developers and their continued dominance in defining the evolution of housing production.

In retrospect, one might say there was a fight over territory in the sixties and seventies. Both designers and developers were trying to claim housing production and urbanization as their own domain, and they became rivals instead of collaborators. The discussion remains open as to whether designers and private developers should collaborate in the field of housing production or not. Perhaps there should not be redefinition of tasks, but of territories. In 1978, Luc Deleu proposed to abolish the title and profession protection of the architect, arguing that "people should have the freedom to build their farmhouses if they feel like it. They don't even need an architect for it, what they build themselves doesn't look worse then when an architect first makes a design for it. We architects should concentrate on the public space."[14] Or even more striking, as Philip Johnson said in 1946, "Let Bucky Fuller[15] put together the Dymaxion dwellings of the people so long as we architects can design their tombs and monuments."[16]

Notes

[1] G. Bekaert, F. Strauven, Bouwen in België 1945-1970, Nationale Confederatie van het Bouwbedrijf, 1971, p. 12

[2] More specifically, the main ideas of the contracts were: "the town council will not act as the contractor of the entire action unlike what happens in the case of public housing. Instead, it provides support and supplies in real estate. The engagement of the town council had the main task of conveying trust among future buyers. Moreover, the local authority should not run any risk since the promoter accepts all risks linked to the promotion. He must be able to offer all technical and financial guarantees, in accordance with the Breyne Act and execute the plans as approved by the municipality." From: Belgian Association of towns and municipalities (VBSG), National Federation of Construction Industry "Concerning the collaboration between municipalities and private sector regarding housing construction" (unpublished document), in: Archive AG Vespa, s.d.

[3] At the beginning of the seventies, the Brunfaut Act of 1949 was expanded to the development of neighbourhoods in private construction while maintaining the requirements to qualify for subsidy; the commissioner should be a public authority or service, the ground has to be sold for a reasonable price, the ground should be exploited immediately by a fast execution of the project in order to avoid land speculation and the blocking of building land, the houses should be erected in grouped construction, the contractors should give the guarantee that the ground will be sold without speculation, the houses are to be sold for an affordable price to families with medium-sized or modest wage.

[4] In case the private promoter would work alone, he would have to pay 100% of the urbanization costs and purchase the building land. His initial expenses would be remarkably higher.

[5] X., "Instellen administratieve procedure voor het verwezenlijken van het Polderproject" (unpublished document), in: Archive AG Vespa, May 1965

[6] The capital of the company was of 236.250.000 Belgian francs (almost 6 million euro), founded on initiative of the Bank of Paris and The Netherlands, and was endorsed by important national and international companies, such as Cobepa, Assubel, De Volksverzekering, La Royale Belge, Securitas-AG, Mercator, Assurantie van de Belgische Boerenbond, La Mondiale, La Prévoyance, De Nationale Investeringsmaatschappij, De Verenigde Bedrijven Bredero.

[7] R. Braem, J. Wittocx, M. Wynants, "Hoboken—Polderstad. Elements of justification" (unpublished document), in: Archive AG Vespa, s.d., 19 pages

[8] The architects made an extensive study on needed social facilities by drawing a comparison to a middle large town; civil services, cultural and religious services, commercial equipment and parking facilities.

[9] R. Braem, unpublished letter addressed to alderman 'Wyninckx' of the town of Hoboken, in: Archive AG Vespa, 9.10.1972.

[10] X., unpublished report of the meeting between architects, secretary of Hoboken and services, in: Archive AG Vespa, December 11th 1967

[11] X., unpublished report comparing selling prices of Polderstad with market prices. The houses of the first phase were sold at the price of 1.275.000 BEF (31.875 euro) to 2.300.000 BEF (57.500 euro). The building ground was sold at the price of 200.000 BEF (5.000 euro) up to 500.000 BEF (12.500 euro) according to area of building lot. In: Archive AG Vespa, 30.01.1979

[12] R. Braem, "Argumentation of the urban designers to break the contract between them and the town council", (unpublished letter from R. Braem to the town council), in: Archive AG Vespa, 21.02.1973

[13] R. Braem, Het schoonste land ter wereld. Leuven (Kritak) 1987.

[14] X., Luc Deleu & T.O.P.Office 1967-1991, Antwerpen, MUKHA, 1991

[15] Buckminster Fuller was a Kansas aircraft manufacturer that retooled his factory after WWII for the fabrication of low-cost metal houses. By 1946 his Dymaxion prototype was readied and exhibited to an enthusiastic public.

[16] Joan Ockman, Architecture Culture 1943–1968, Rizzoli, 2000, p. 15

1. The design uses a module of 2.4 m2 of pre-cast concrete panels allowing for an industrialized production process while providing diversity of the different apartments.

VERBAKEL

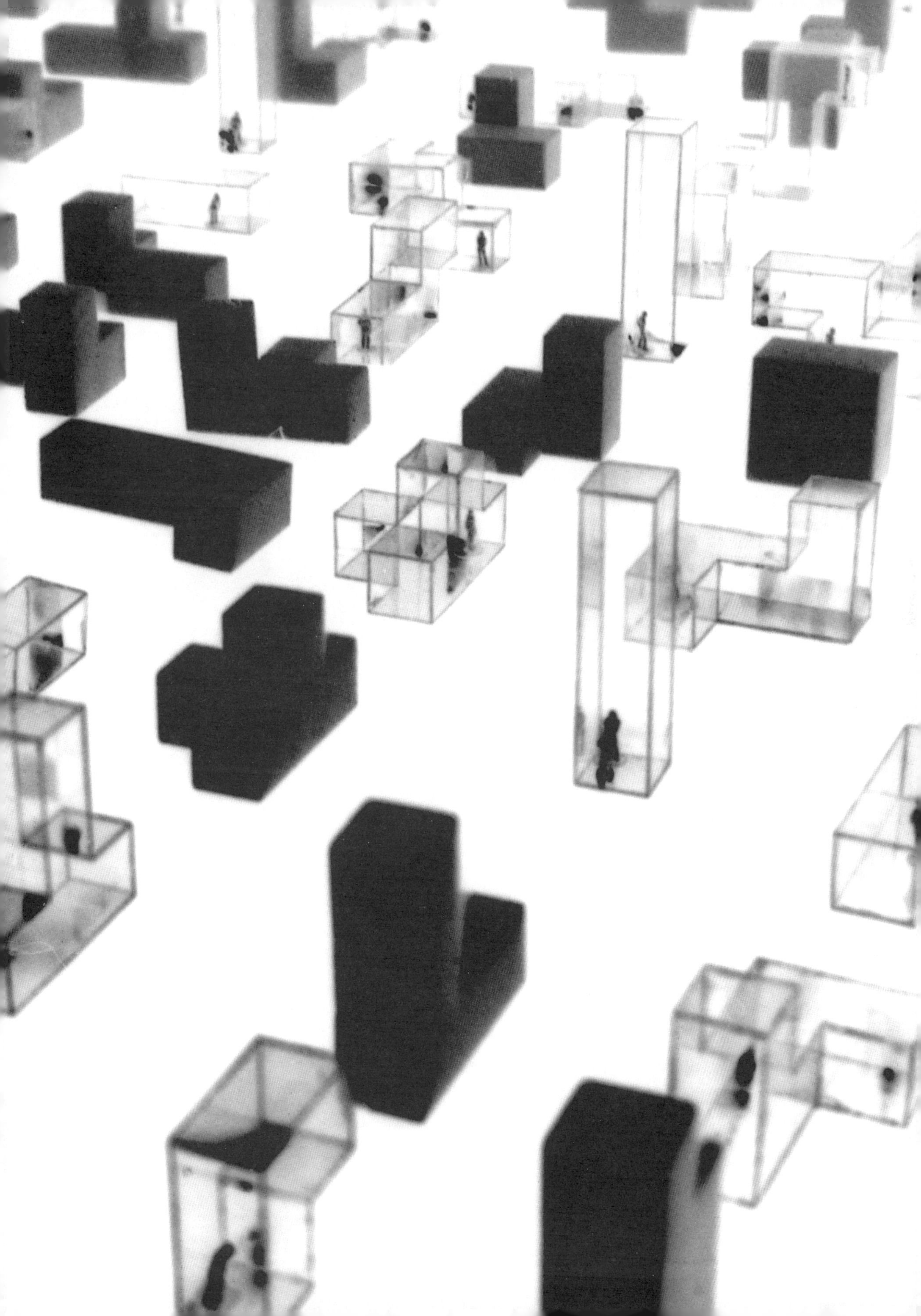

2. By implementing the low cost building using a high level architectural language, the project turns the disadvantage of the small apartment units into an extra asset of the project's design.

VERBAKEL, Els

Space Blocks and Other Transnational Strategies for Urban Habitation

The following reflections have grown out of the curatorial research I carried out for an exhibition and web platform titled Urban Life: Housing in the Contemporary City at the Architectural League of New York. This project resulted in a traveling exhibition and website bringing together contemporary multi-family housing from cities around the world, and allowed for the creation of a catalogue of strategies offering new insights for housing design in American cities and beyond. At the same time, this spectrum of strategies functions as an indicator of current and future urban conditions not only in the US, but in a globalizing or even transnational urban world.

This catalogue of design strategies is a crucial element in moving from the specificity of the buildings to a realm of future potential in which the collection of tactics can inspire other cities in other places. It is only possible by thinking of the network of cities as a transnational one, in which elements can travel from one to the other unlimited by state borders. This transnational network participates in another system of distance and proximity.

In order to construct the catalogue, operating between the specific and the generic, the projects were studied using six perspectives: Body, Building, City, Environment, Technology, and Implementation. These six filters 'distill' a range of strategies from the collection of examples, stretching beyond the specifics of the projects. Rather than being a prescriptive design system, this catalogue can be thought of as a remodeling of the role of the architect's profession, as a challenge for design professions in general to engage in a transnational housing market.

The first part of this article introduces one of the

housing projects, namely the Kamishinjo Housing Project in Osaka, Japan, as an example of how a project can function as a generator for future cities. The second part will look in more detail at the six housing perspectives explored in the exhibition as a useful format for thinking in terms of transnational design research.

Kamishinjo Space Blocks

The Kamishinjo Space Blocks are a compelling example of the way in which a project can generate new urban conditions by achieving a close harmony between socio-economic parameters, building system technologies and urban design strategies. By designing a complex configuration of basic 8-foot cube modules, the project successfully combines a diverse range of individual units, an articulated building profile and a new type of urban condition characterized by small grain fabric and semi-private views and passages.

Except for a commercial ground floor, the building exists exclusively of studio rental units for singles, a frequent typology in this district of Osaka, with an average apartment floor area of 200 square feet. The high-density neighborhood near the center of Osaka is made up of a mixture of low cost apartment buildings, small factories and bars. This creates a crowded urban condition and an incoherent low-rise fabric. This urban context led to a design approach combining methods of mass production, maximum profit, minimum risk and energy efficient construction. Although the project responds to these very specific conditions, a parallel can be drawn with the design of SRO (Single Room Occupancy) housing in American cities, in which a different set of social demands could be met with similar building strategies.

The modular design creates a new type of urban condominium based on the stacking of 'space blocks,' allowing for diversity, flexibility and an articulation of the human scale. Twenty two apartments are laid out over four floors, with eighteen different types ranging from 180 to 375 square feet and with eight roof terrace units. The building module allows for an open and simple plan organization while non-structural concrete block walls can be recombined for future rearrangement of the apartments.

In order to adequately respond to the socio-economic considerations and the need for standardized production, Architects Coelacanth & Associates and Kazuhiro Kojima developed a building system called Basic Space Blocks for which this project served as a prototype. Basic Space Blocks are standardized cubes of 95-inches wide that can be puzzled together in many ways creating a distinctive composite building form. In the meantime, the architects have implemented a similar concept in a housing project in Hanoi, Vietnam. This new approach to the 'existenzminimum' unit produces an unexpected spatial play based on a building technology of precast concrete panels composed into a variety of single and double height apartments. Although the modules create units that are small even for Japanese standards, the standardized production, not of dwelling units but of smaller components, permits a freedom of design at the scale of the unit. This strategy provides diversity while at the same time meeting the demand for low cost industrialized construction. The system also uses a minimal number of continuous top to bottom walls, which are reduced to core positions. Avoiding structurally unnecessary walls, the organization of units creates a more dynamic configuration. Because of this tight linkage between program, technology, spatial insight and aesthetic sensitivity, affordable and efficient housing can be combined with a high quality of architectural language.

Finally, this arrangement not only creates an innovative approach at the scale of the unit, but, by defining a combinatory logic for the dwelling units, the project generates possibilities for a future city. The fine-grained modular system is also an appropriate urban approach, inscribing itself well in the irregularity of the narrow building site of about a tenth of an acre. Five service cores structure the conglomeration of units, with exterior stairs and corridors accessing the apartments, creating an interesting semi-private space of interaction. By carefully positioning the modules and by thinking in volumes rather than planes, an interesting articulation of the urban and collective space is achieved. An existing public passage from one side of the site to the other is maintained, and together with the multiple small open spaces created all over the building the design produces a new type of intimate public space. The project thereby employs a high density scheme while at the same time creating openness in its urban and interior configurations. One could say that the space block system almost works as a fluid building, poured into the site, able to adjust to difficult and irregular site conditions.

This innovative approach in which socio-economic conditions serve as an opportunity to develop a design approach in which building technology, architectural language and manipulations of urban form are closely tied together, can be taken as an example of how to imagine future cities.

What is the future of our cities? Or should we ask: what will our future cities look like? These two questions do not necessarily address the same issue yet they are often confused. While one looks back, the other looks forward. Learning from truly innovative housing design strategies, the second question can be investigated in more depth. Innovative strategies do not operate from a motivation of nostalgia for the lost splendor of existing cities but instead they are able to imagine not yet existing urban futures. These future cities fully take part in current socio-economic tendencies of privatization and globalization, which require new urban formations of built and open space.

Six Perspectives on Housing

The six perspectives developed for this research are a way to redistribute the information gathered, moving from project to perspective and eventually to strategy. In that way it is a transformational device that allows us to create a spectrum of transnational design tactics that at the same time respond to local conditions. The research of these projects thereby shows how transnational urbanism is not necessarily disconnected from place, site or locale. The strategies that can be extracted from case projects reveal ways of responding to locale rather than being non-local.

3. Views, top to bottom:

Street: Public passage is very narrow creating an intimate relation with the commercial functions on the ground floor.
Interior: The single-room units are designed so that different areas within the unit can easily be delineated.
Open Air Corridor: A semi-public space is created by leaving the building circulation open to the air.
Roof: The roof units are given a wide view over the city, enlarging the space of the living unit to the larger urban field.

4. The small dimensions of the units create an almost 1 to 1 proportion between the horizontal and the vertical plane.

The first three perspectives relate to different scales and are delineated not as merely the mathematical ratio between relative and real size but as the relationship between physical, economical, political and social meanings linked to different fields of reach. The second group of spectra is related to the ways in which the projects are implemented, the processes in which they take part.

Body: Flexibility and Experience

How does the organization of a domestic space unit relate to a body's needs, limits and desires? Is the dwelling flexible enough to be adapted to different and changing household configurations? How can architects respond to the apparent opposition between specific individual demands in a world of heightened diversification and the need for universal housing standards in an increasingly rapid turnaround of occupants?

In the context of housing, body can be understood as the individual experience of a person's inhabitation of space. Sheltering people not only answers physical ergonomic demands, it fosters the experience of habitation. As versatility and polyvalence become increasingly important, housing design requires a better understanding of how they can operate within the intimate relationship between bodies and domestic spaces. Bodies reside not only in housing units but also in buildings and cities. As the smallest molecules of the urban fabric, they take part in urban life through the dwelling unit as a mediator. Contemporary processes of social atomization, diversification and acceleration challenge designs to provide spaces to facilitate and support those dynamic interactions. A habitat thereby occupies a new position as a space of withdrawal and at the same time as a modulation of the multitude of daily dialogues occurring between bodies and cities, physically and virtually.

Building: Privacy and Collectivity

Can a building incorporate spaces that negotiate between public and private? How can the design of collective space create a sense of community? How are building functions distributed between private and collective? Does the design allow for different degrees of isolation and interaction and what does this mean for the transitions between them?

At the scale of a collective housing project, privacy and collectivity enter into an interesting dialogue between an individual and a group of inhabitants. At medium or high densities, social boundaries between private and public operate at the critical edge between intrusion and alienation. It is in this context that the

IMPLEMENTATION

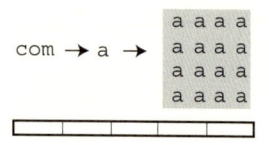

com → a →
```
a a a a
a a a a
a a a a
a a a a
```

MASTERPLAN COMPETITION

The Zaanwerf
Zaanstad, The Netherlands
Tania Concko, Pierre Gauthier
2000

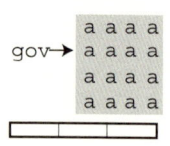

gov →
```
a a a a
a a a a
a a a a
a a a a
```

GOVERNMENT REGULATED NEIGHBORHOOD
REGENERATION

Rue de l'Ourcq Postal Workers' Housing
Rue Oberkampf Postal Workers' Housing
Paris, France
Frédéric Borel, Philippe Gazeau
1993

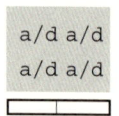

```
a/d a/d
a/d a/d
```

DEVELOPER-ARCHITECT

Merrimac Housing
San Diego, California
Smith and Others with Lloyd Russell, AIA
1998

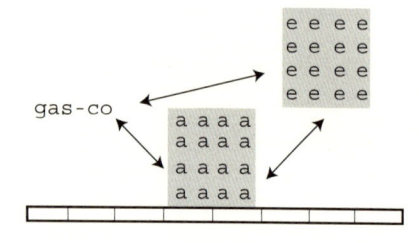

gas-co ↔
```
e e e e
e e e e
e e e e
e e e e
```
↕
```
a a a a
a a a a
a a a a
a a a a
```

LONG TERM HANDS ON COLLABORATION
AND PARTICIPATION

Osaka Gas Experimental Housing Next 21
Osaka, Japan
Committee for the Osaka Gas NEXT 21 Project
1994

GOVERNMENT	gov
COMPETITION	com
ARCHITECT	a
EMPLOYEE	e
ARCHITECT/DEVELOPER	a/d
MULTIPLE	▦

VERBAKEL

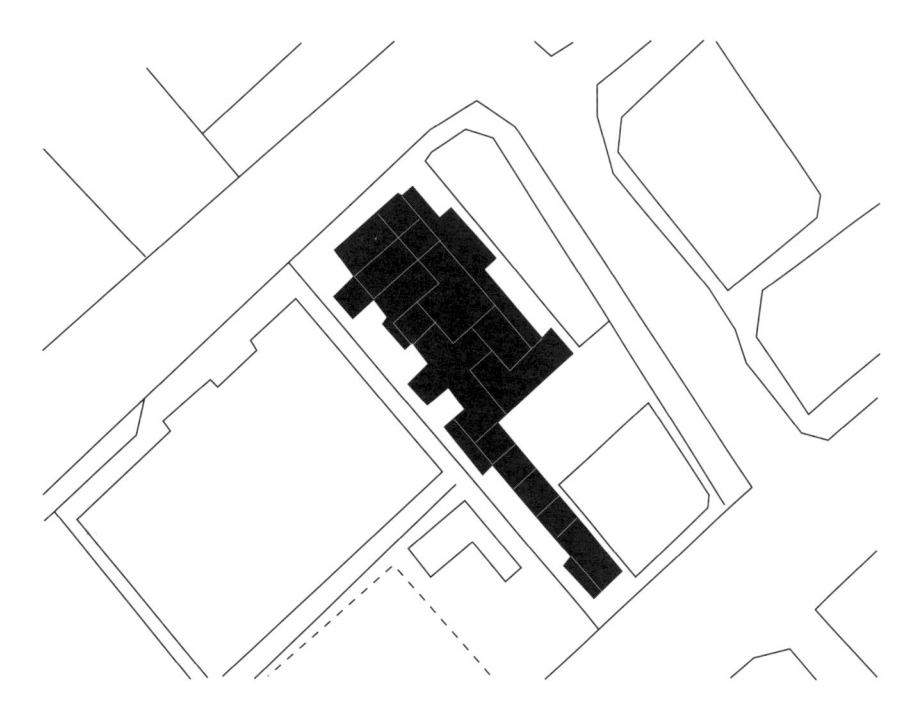

5. Site plan

6. The narrow street façade was given its shape based on the smallest modular dimension, creating an interesting addition to the street wall.

design of intermediate, semi-private, transitional spaces needs special attention. The balance between introverted and extraverted spatial relationships can reach a moderate collectivity ensuring the inhabitant's safety and protection and at the same time allowing for social interaction. These are aspects of housing design that address a larger question of the way in which a building can be a generator of urban space. Considered this way, housing design not only addresses the needs of a specific project but more broadly, it can contribute to new ideas about the forms and processes of the contemporary city.

City: Transforming and Connecting

How does a housing project respond to the urban fabric? How does the project participate in urban transformations, how can it be a generator of new urbanities? How is the dweller connected to the immediate surroundings, the larger city and the global network?

The city's historical layering and urban transformations offer the long-term as well as immediate context for intervention. As contemporary cities adapt to postindustrial economies, their physical and functional densities shift significantly, which directly affects the search for appropriate housing configurations. A housing project's ambition to provoke urban change places housing design at an interesting junction between action and reaction. As travel, transportation and communication speeds accelerate, housing designs become nodes in far-reaching networks, connecting inhabitants to the rest of the world. These spaces of flow develop in parallel with a fragmentation of the city, in which mixed-use programming and self-sustaining housing complexes are gaining importance. Housing when integrated with other functions can thereby become a piece of city itself.

Environment: Sustainability and Landscape

How does housing design address environmental issues such as climate changes and energy use? How does it support or question the relationship between inhabitants and nature? Can nature become an integral part of the city?

The environment, understood as the ecological system in which we live, can be incorporated into housing projects through landscape and sustainability strategies. At high densities, a closer attention to the environmental aspects of housing stimulates strategies of transplanting landscape to the building in an attempt to activate an intimacy between inhabitant and nature by blurring the separation between building, city and environment. These strategies range from treating the natural environment as an additional building component (green roofs, vertical gardens, etc.) to thinking of the building as a micro-ecology which bridges the distinction between landscape and sustainable design. This can happen at different scales; from soil remediation and self-sustaining energy households to the recycling of unused city fabric such as the redevelopment of brownfields (formerly industrial sites) and grayfields (formerly commercial sites). This implies a more profound understanding of the creative design of alternative energy sources in the building's construction and maintenance and the manipulation of biological processes as alternative technologies.

Technology: Efficiency and Innovation

How can technological innovations be implemented both at the scale of the building industry as well as the ad hoc scale of an individual project? How can a balance be reached between traditional techniques and technological innovation that permits the experiment of the new as well as the refinement of the old? How do these improvements in building technology facilitate a better housing condition?

New methods of construction, production and the implementation of new materials allow for an increase in cost-efficiency, design flexibility, construction speed and low-energy consumption. Technological innovation is a particularly challenging aspect of housing design because of the complexity of inherent financial mechanisms, the resistance to fully embrace mass production, the inertia in adapting to changing labor markets and the importance of cultural norms for domestic space. Technology transfers from other fields, including material research and methods of mass production, can offer new possibilities for housing production. For instance, the system of prefabrication is being reinvented to a form of semi-fabrication, a combination of on-site and in-factory production. This balance between module and variation facilitates coherent yet diverse building schemes and urban environments. In order to respond to the accelerating transformations of the urban fabric, faster construction processes drastically change the housing production methods, which need to be incorporated in the design. The demand for environmental and cost-efficient solutions requires an integration of high tech applications of energy-reducing construction and maintenance processes.

Implementation: Policy and Regulation

How do changes in financial flows, zoning regulations and interdisciplinary collaborations influence the implementation of housing production? How can those processes be controlled in order to achieve higher architectural quality? How binding are zoning regulations and building codes; how might they be rethought to facilitate more and better housing production? How can affordable housing be combined with high design standards?

As housing markets privatize and greater numbers of people need housing, certain vital components of successful urban housing are overlooked. Affordability, livability and the quality of collective and open space are threatened by a reduced understanding of housing in cities as production cost or revenue per square foot. This condition calls for alternative attempts to ensure basic housing needs in situations where resources are scarce or inequitably distributed, particularly at medium or high densities. In addition, planning can play an active role by creating building regulations and codes that are more comprehensive, less limiting and more quality assuring. The rise of collaborative efforts and cross-disciplinary processes—new constellations of public, private and not for profit organizations—involve increased or changed roles for various actors in the process: inhabitants as self-builders and clients; architects as developers and financial strategists.

These six perspectives were derived from an initial study of a large number of housing projects. As a set of lenses through which the projects can be understood, they operate as a generative tool for housing interventions in the expanded field of transnational architectural operations. As a method, this range of perspectives allows for research over a large territory without loosing connection with the specificity of local conditions. Thereby they are also an indicator of current and future urban conditions in which localities such as high density leftover spaces, large peripheral brownfields, obsolete commercial and industrial complexes are interchangeable over large distances.

WALL, Ronald

Archinomics: An Investigation Between the Disciplines of Spatial Design and Spatial Science

Driven by an expanding population with rising demands, a highly sophisticated, worldwide urban system has emerged which supplies our ever growing demand for material and immaterial resources. This global network economy increasingly fuels the process of urbanization, rapidly producing physical spaces and infrastructures, where powerful firms have greater influence upon the development of cities within this system. This economic-spatial interdependence carries prospects and predicaments, where private corporate interests often clash with the local public realm. On one hand it generates unprecedented wealth and material opportunity; while on the other, it perpetuates immense disparities between people in different parts of the world. These segregating forces are found both at the worldwide level and within individual cities, where rapid private corporate developments often result in isolated, low-grade urban spaces. It is evident at global to local scales that the benefits of globalization are mostly to the advantage of the minority and in general lead to increased segregation and discontinuity in cities, dividing and disabling many communities and hereby creating increased uncertainty and insecurity[1].

For the first time in history it seems that we are influencing the environment more than it influences us[2]. Our complex world city network is the product of an age old process and will remain an inevitable part of our future. Therefore, the most critical question for our future is how to make this globally integrated network sustainable in which individual cities and communities can flourish. The world city network and the cities within this system are becoming increasingly unsustainable, which challenges how the world's limited resources will be managed, but also how cities will be designed and developed in future. Therefore it becomes vital that we better understand the structure, operations and performance of this highly complex system. This calls for an interdisciplinary approach which can lead to a more integral understanding and possibly improved urban interventions.

Confronted by the increasing upsurge of global spatial transformation, complexity and the blurring of control and certainty, the established foundations of architecture and related fields are becoming obsolete. Where previously the role of architects and planners was simply to translate local information into design, leading to suitable solutions to a given context, it has now become evident that local information is increasingly multidimensional, requiring that architects comprehend and engage with different scales of this extensive spatial system.[3] If it is true that network assets are as important as territorial assets to a city, then it follows that we need to acquire as much knowledge of a city's external linkages, from local to global, as we traditionally have of the internal composition of a city. This requires a large-scale monitoring of multifarious flows.[4] Architecture should become an exercise between the worlds of everything and something requiring that we operate beyond the conventional paradigm. Possibly archinomics can contribute to this endeavor, where an integration between architecture and spatial science (economic geography) is sought, motivated by the assumption that this intersection will eventually lead to improved sustainable urban development.

The Interdependence of Cities and Firms

World cities are not simply places; they are processes—hubs through which flows are articulated with power residing in the flows themselves. These bring forth shifts in governance through entities such as multinational corporations, while nation-states have less and less power to regulate these flows or exercise authority over the economy. Powerful firms determine to a strong degree the actions of cities and nations. The top two hundred multinationals in 1999 accounted for almost one third of world GDP and of the world's 100 largest economies (multinationals plus countries), 50% are multinationals, controlling 70% of world trade.[5] It appears that globalization and urbanization profoundly influence each other. On one hand multinationals provide money, jobs, knowledge and technology to cities; on the other hand, cities compete to attract these firms by means of adequate resources, human capital and infrastructure. It therefore seems that a city's development depends on a high correlation between its external network (relation to other cities and firms) and internal urban properties (relation to intrinsic assets). Knowledge of this interdependency, it is assumed, would lead to more effective programming and planning of cities resulting in more sustainable urban development. This would require an integrated approach between spatial science and spatial design disciplines, in which analytical description and visionary prescription are combined. The following research projects serve as initial attempts to tackle this interdependency and have been developed together with researchers and designers. These explorative investigations have been organized into macro, mezzo and micro scales, assuming that these scales are integrally related and that future sustainable urban development will depend on strategic interventions at and between these scales.

Macro scale

At this scale a research project called Field Optimizer was carried out concerning the interdependence between multinational firms and urban areas at the global scale. [1] It is shown that the global urban system relies on the increasing competitiveness of urban areas and their necessity to attract and maintain multinationals, through the development of strong urban identities and specializations. Spatial planning was elaborated into a tool which keeps urban fields functioning and attractive to global enterprises, which prove to be vital indicators of the global economic system. Cities within the system manifest themselves spatially through degrees of competitiveness and collaboration; defined by human capital, network connectivity and population density. This follows that the ultimate urban area is one with high education, good connectivity, and large populations. In this project, these three parameters were indexed into the attractiveness coefficient, (AC) which correlates highly with the number of multinationals per location. Based on World Bank data the AC of the world was calculated and mapped using GIS mapping techniques. From this a map depicting the current situation has been shown and also a future prognosis generated, in which today's Western-oriented economy gives way to an extremely polarized Eastern economy after 2030, due to economies of scale and cheaper production sites. In these maps we see that the economic agglomerations of South East Asia, Europe and the USA are competitive with each other, but collaborative within the internal structures of each particular agglomeration. The expected prognosis for Europe is that its attractiveness will weaken due to its decreasing population growth and the resulting depletion of human capital.

This analysis was followed by a simulated scenario, in which the reduction of political borders allows for the calculated redistribution of populations into weakened urban fields. In this way, a sustainable urban system is pursued. The future is perceived as the densification of urban fields and the intensification of the voids in-between, defined as areas with low global power. These voids exist next to the fields of attraction and corporate investment. This extreme scenario allows for the thinning and rejuvenation of other

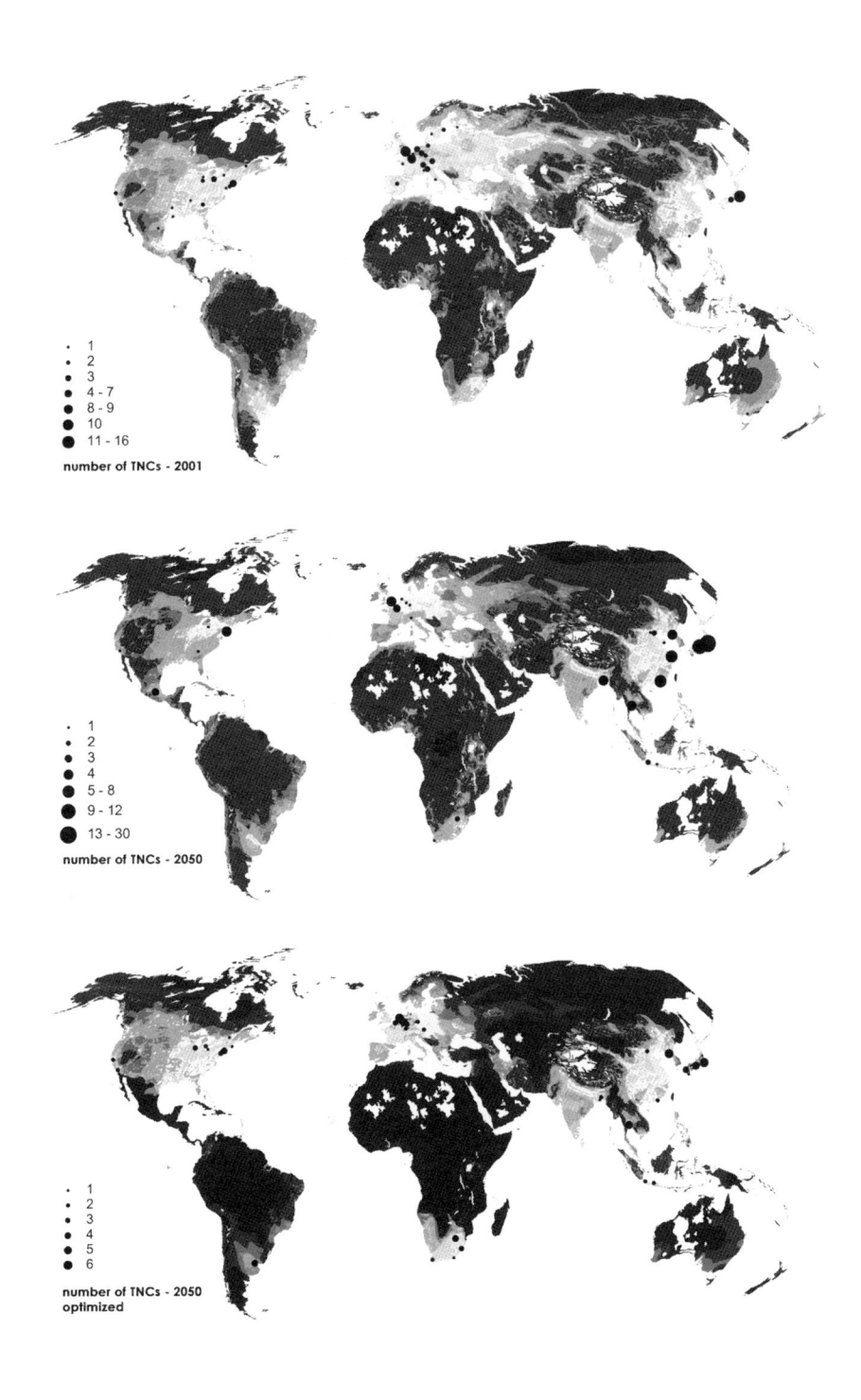

1. Field Optimizer (2001)

Based on World Bank and UNDP sources, GIS maps in which geographic 'attractivity coefficients' for transnational corporation (TNCs) are calculated, based on human capital, network connectivity and population density. The top and right map represents 2001. The middle map represents World Bank expectations for 2050. The bottom left map represents a manipulated outcome, based on liberated migration flows, in which a more optimised world urban system is achieved.

parts of the world into ecological and agricultural zones. The result provokes a conception of what a sustainable world might be—however unlikely this may seem to us today. Furthermore, the project challenges current policies concerning migration and state borders; the West's political and economic hegemony over poorer regions; the implications of a global village; the necessity to globally invest in education and entrepreneurship; improving access to networks of information, communication and transport; and the necessity to provide a broad spectrum of attractive dwellings and living environments. By intervening with the spatial and economic parameters of this model, guided by a desired vision, a step has been taken further than mere geographical analysis. It may even be argued that this engagement towards a more qualitative and sustainable system demonstrates an architectonic intervention at the global scale. However, this elementary model serves merely as an experiment.

Mezzo scale

Based on the headquarters (HQs) and affiliated firms of Europe's top 100 multinationals, empirical research was carried out to map the network and interdependency of these firms with European cities. Based on this, GIS mapping [2] and statistical analysis was undertaken. The first map depicts the number of multinational headquarters in each European city, depicting that for instance London, Paris and Frankfurt are primary global cities and that Dublin scores low. Because the HQs are highly dependent on their collaboration with networks of smaller businesses in various cities, the dataset was elaborated to include all the affiliates and subsidiaries of these multinationals. This led to the second map, depicting that smaller cities play a more significant role as centers for the subsidiaries and affiliates of top multinationals. Dublin in this case is a primary centre and the Ruhr-Randstad-Flemish Diamond region has the highest agglomeration of such firms. Following this a matrix analysis was done to find the inter-urban network intensities between HQs and their subsidiaries and affiliates.

In the first map we see that London and Zurich have the highest interdependency, followed by Düsseldorf to Frankfurt and so on. The core global business region of Europe is situated between London, Paris, Brussels, Amsterdam, Zurich, Frankfurt and Düsseldorf. Similarly, research was carried out to map the bandwidth intensities between Europe's major ICT hubs. The core information region of Europe is London, Paris, Frankfurt, Düsseldorf and Amsterdam, and is strikingly similar to the core business region, roughly indicating the dependency of core business to internet technology. Furthermore, the similarity between these prominent zones and the highest European regional intensities (light blue areas) of the previous project [1] can be seen. From this we can deduce that Europe's core business region also depends on a high score of human capital, network connectivity and population density and a strong degree of collaboration between cities. This alliance allows it to compete with other parts of the world as seen in the first project.

In the project Redefining Regions an analysis is carried out concerning regional networks of specialization and profiling, so as to stay in competition with other global agglomerations. This is done by the specialization of cities and regions in different sectors, such as trade, insurance, banking, transportation, R&D, and cultural specializations such as art and fashion. This project concerns a strategy of profiling several European regions, consisting of the areas Randstad, Ruhrgebiet and Belgatri, through the use of specialization profiles for the different sub-regions around the cores (cities) and the connection on the different relevant networks. This, to point out the best locations for further urbanization and specialization, so as to generate an integral competitive supra-region. This qualification, being expressed by the interrelation between the indexes of economic production, connectivity, technology, human resources and knowledge, for instance the specialization of the sub-regions of Randstad for high-tech services, Belgatri for knowledge intensive services, and Rhine-Ruhr for high-tech manufacturing.

Micro scale

In this integral spatio-economic system, where agglomerations tend to compete more than collaborate at the global level; and collaborate more than compete at a supra-regional level, it becomes important to question the position and potentials of individual cities within this system. From the HQ, affiliate, and subsidiary datasets we compiled, it was possible to derive the hierarchy of connectivity (number of inter-firm linkages) for all European cities. This was done by looking at the economic sectors of manufacturing,

CITY LINKAGES

Subsidiaries and affiliates of Europe's Top 100 companies
(Berlage Institute research based on Financial Times, 2001)

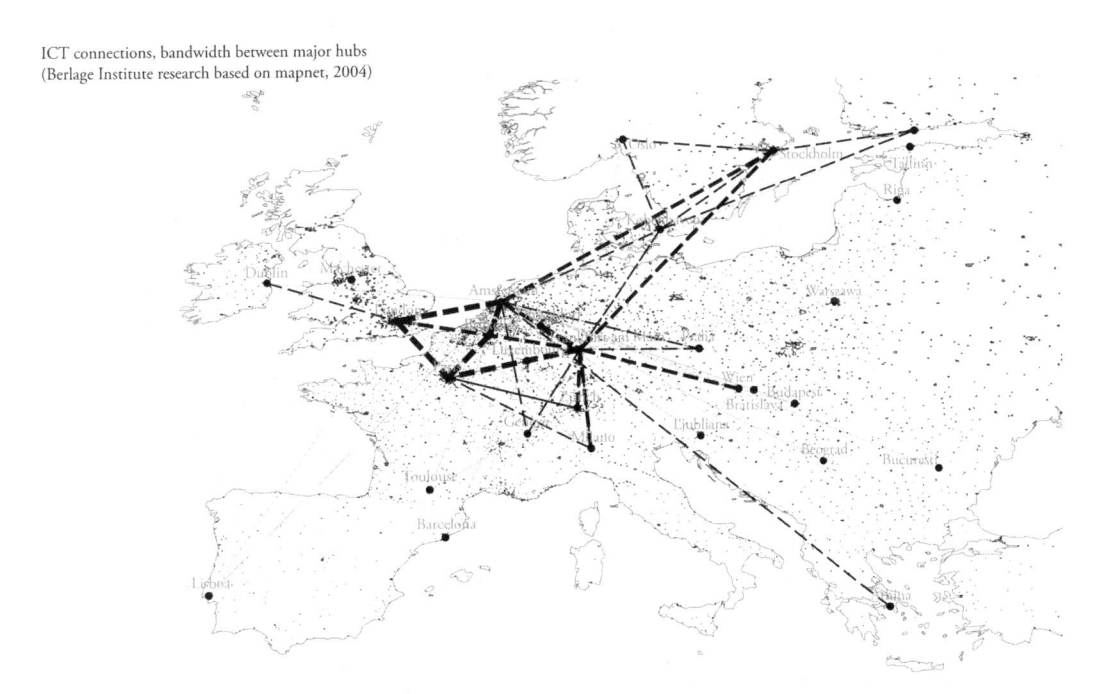

ICT connections, bandwidth between major hubs
(Berlage Institute research based on mapnet, 2004)

2. Rotterdam Metanational Corporation (2004/2005)

Based on Financial Times and Berlage datasets, GIS maps depicting the clustering of Europe's top 100 multinationals (headquarters) in cities and the intensities of headquarters and their related subsidiary and affiliated firms. These maps show where Europe's primary global activity is located.

trade, information, public services and basic materials. From this primary, secondary and tertiary cities were derived. For instance, London, Paris and Frankfurt have primary connectivity but there are only a few of these; Dublin, Luxembourg and Munich are secondary, but their group is larger; while Rotterdam, Helsinki, Essen and Bucharest are examples of tertiary connectivity, which fall into the biggest group of comparable cities.

Based on the five sectors, city profiles for all cities were derived. For instance, London, Paris and Amsterdam score high on information and public services, proving that their profile is specifically knowledge oriented. Eindhoven scores extremely high on manufacturing, but poorly on all other sectors, proving its high dependency on Philips electronic manufacturing. Looking at port cities, Rotterdam and Antwerp both score high on basic materials (mostly goods related) and information (mostly insurance related). Antwerp has a zero score on trade, where Rotterdam has an upcoming potential. Both score equally on public services. From these profiles we can derive that for instance Rotterdam should compete more with cities like Antwerp and collaborate more with dissimilar cities like Cologne, Luxembourg and Amsterdam. From this the question arises, how Rotterdam can improve its urban qualities, so as to attract more business from these sectors (or hybrid combinations between these sectors) and alternatively how these economic potentials can be used to further improve urban and social conditions in the city.

In this essay, it is argued that within our globalizing world, sustainable urban planning will depend on a dual approach, in which a city's internal fabric must be analyzed in relation to its external linkages to other cities, and across different spatial scales. In the following scheme [3], Rotterdam's interscalar challenge is depicted. The bottom map represents two important local nodes, which connect various scales of networks. The first is the new to-be-built port area on the Maasvlakte (MV 2) which caters to Rotterdam's port functions, like cargo handling and logistics. Rotterdam Central Station is the second node, which is being developed into a new station on the soon to be completed High Speed Rail and Randstad Rails. This will efficiently connect Rotterdam at a supra-regional level, to other European stations; and will in a sense bring Amsterdam Schiphol Airport closer to Rotterdam, giving it a more global business potential. Combining the economic sectoral research and this scheme, a design strategy has been made, in which these two nodes will be boosted. [4] This is done by strategically developing these nodes; by instigating an increase of flows (people, goods, information and money) from different spatial scales (global, regional local). These directed interventions would have spillover effects for the surroundings, stimulating further formal and self-organizing processes. This can be seen in six stages of development, which would exist within an approximate 30 year period. The main causal intervals are R0=now; R1=the completion of the high speed rail in 2007; R2=the completion of the monorail linking Rotterdam, Delft and The Hague; R3=the completion of the port area MV2; R4=the addition of a cargo airport above MV2. The development of these two nodes is interrelated and stimulates cross-over activities. Rotterdam, a once united portcity, is today splintered into port and city, which have little to do with each other. The proposed strategy suggests the reuniting of port and city in a socio-economic sense, but not spatially.

The last scale of discussion, namely the site, concerns a project called Supernode whereby an alternative architectural-economic methodology is demonstrated to develop Amsterdam as an invigorated global city. In this project, a second economic development strip is proposed, in which new potentials are to be generated. These allow Amsterdam to compete better internationally. This is necessary because Dutch cities, which are extremely dependent on export, are becoming less attractive for high-value businesses. To restrain this weakening performance, the improvement of urban qualities and the generation of new potential areas are fundamental to recovery. A new alternative hub can emerge—a city of progression, an alternative to the historical Amsterdam, the city of resistance. The project gives insight into the complex relationships between planning and designs at the local level, but with linkages to the higher scales. A model has been made, indicating how interscalar influences from the macro to the micro level are interlinked and affect the development of urban projects. These influences have been empirically researched into statistical data and mapped using GIS, so as to determine the potentials and predicaments of this area. The maps indicate the intensity, identity, connectivity and accessibility of this site. The performance of these parameters is expressed in the score-diagrams on the right. A vision of enhancing Amsterdam as an amplified socio-economic node, in a worldwide urban network is put forward—where architecture, urban planning, GIS cartography and geography interact.

In this essay, several projects are put forward, which are highly explorative and

SPATIALISATION

INTERSCALAR NETWORKING

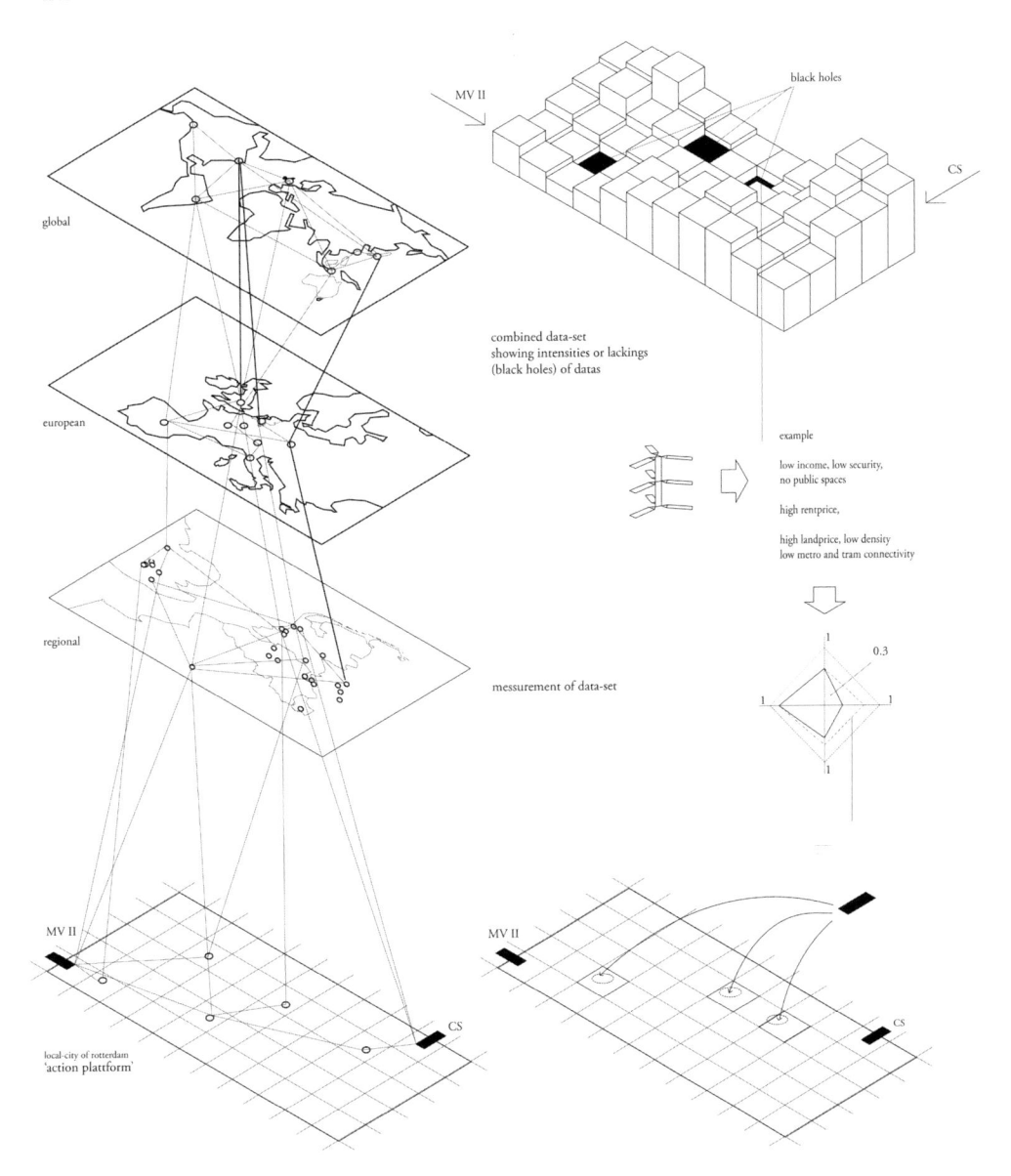

global

european

regional

MV II

CS

local-city of rotterdam
'action plattform'

data-set collection of nodes, flows, MNCs and site

INSERTING PROTOTYPE IN "ACTION-PLATFORM"

MV II

black holes

CS

combined data-set
showing intensities or lackings
(black holes) of datas

example

low income, low security,
no public spaces

high rentprice,

high landprice, low density
low metro and tram connectivity

messurement of data-set

MV II

CS

3. Rotterdam Metanational Corporation (2004/2005)

Based on Financial Times and Berlage datasets, GIS map depicting Rotterdam's interscalar network relationships.

NODAL INTENSIFICATION

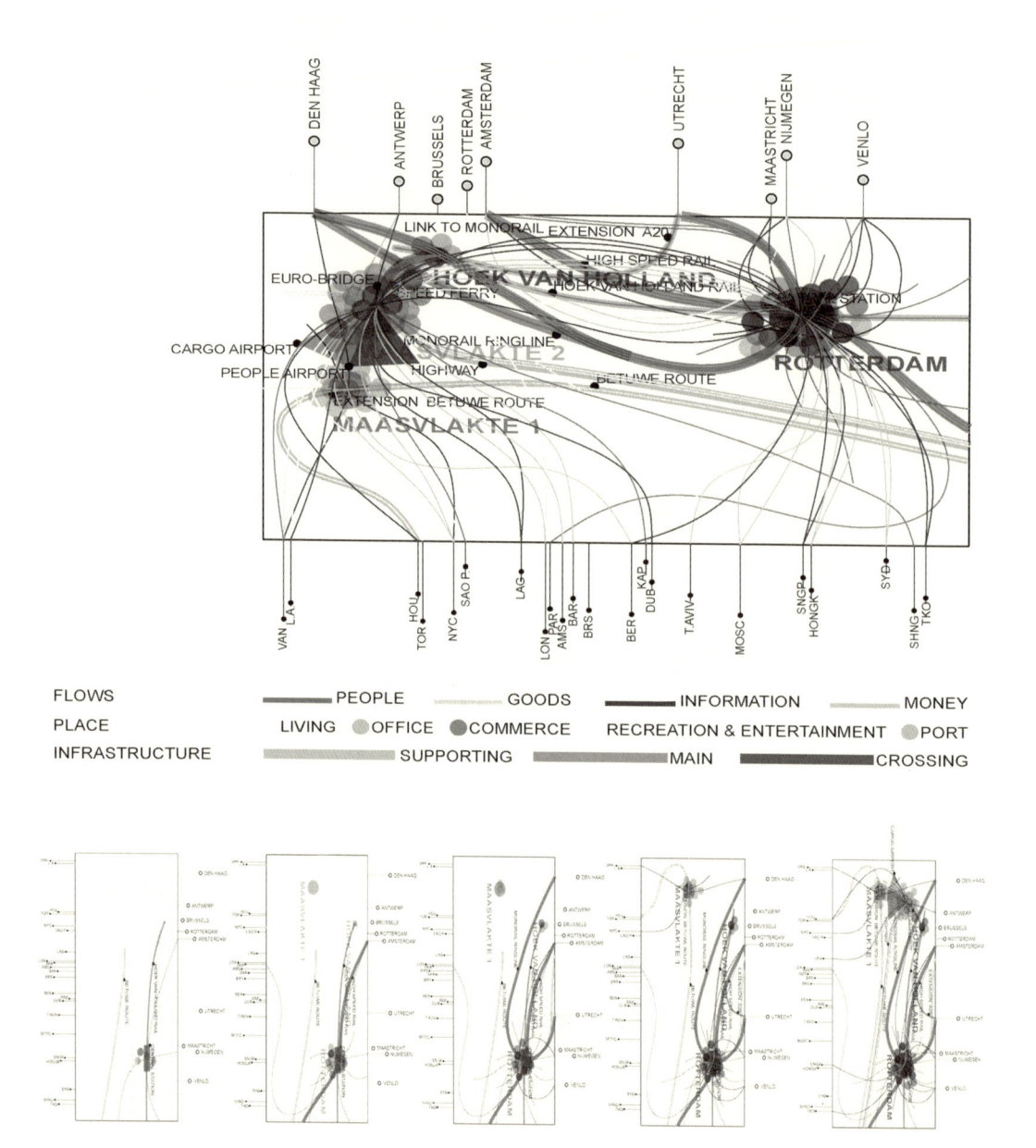

4. Rotterdam Metanational Corporation (2003/2004)

Rotterdam's two major 'local' nodes were developed. The first is the Maasvlakte, which will become an intense goods nexus. It is strategically designed to become an integrated port, cargo airport, passenger airport and multinational logistics centre. The second is the development of the central station area into a information services and business-public trade fair.

WALL

empirical (to a certain degree) and engage with topics, methods and spatial scales, not usual to design professionals. Due to the nature of complexity of the assignments, the results do not provide hard solutions or recommendations. This however is not the objective. Instead, the intention has been to investigate various issues within the contemporary paradigm as thoroughly as possible, so as reveal partial understandings and propose plausible interventions and alternatives. It is intended to inspire new ways forward, raise debate and even criticism, so that it contributes to the future of the architectonic disciplines. The essay challenges the role and identity of the future architect and the boundaries within which she or he will operate, in pursuit of a more sustainable and diversified context. It is suggested that a more conscious engagement must exist between the spatial sciences and spatial design disciplines. If the future matters to us, then some degree of foresight and innovative strategies seems appropriate.

Notes

[1] *Graham and Marvin, 2003*
[2] *McNeill, 2003*
[3] *Beauregard, 2000*
[4] *Taylor, 2002*
[5] *The World Bank, 2000*

Credits

Figures 1 & 2: Rotterdam Metanational Corporation (2004/2005)
Mentor: *Ronald Wall, Faculty of Economic Sciences, Erasmus University Rotterdam*
Assistant mentors: *Im Sik Cho and Suitbert Schmitt* **External advisors:** *Bert van der Knaap, Wilfred Sleegers, Faculty of Economic Sciences, Erasmus University Rotterdam.* **Students:** *Ross Adams; Florian Heinzelmann; Rolf Jenni; RenÈ Kuiken; Stephan Mehlhorn; Duöanka Popovska; Chintan Raveshia; Ivonne Santoyo Orozco; Canan Saridal; Chang Ho Yeo* **Institution:** *Berlage Institute.* **Client:** *Jacco Hakfort, Ministry of Economic Affairs* **GIS mapping:** *Suitbert Schmitt*
Image editing: *Andrea Fiechter.*

Figure 3: Metanational Corporation (2003/2004)
Mentor: *Ronald Wall, Faculty of Economic Sciences, Erasmus University Rotterdam*
Assistant mentor: Im Sik Cho. **External advisor:** *Bert van der Knaap, Faculty of Economic Sciences, Erasmus University Rotterdam.* **Students:** *Alexa Neurnberger, Bart Melort, Bernardina Borra, Celine Jeanne, Cristina Garcia, Hideyuki Ashii, Martin Sobota, Miha Cebulj, Nick Veelken, Tom Weiss, Uli Franzel, Weerapat Chouebeetaweeanan, Ying Zhu* **Institution:** *Berlage Institute.* **Client:** *Jacco Hakfort, Ministry of Economic Affairs* **Image editing:** *Andrea Fiechter, Im Sik Cho.*

Figure 4: Field Optimizer (2001)
Mentors: *Ronald Wall and Duzan Doepel* **External advisor:** *Bert van der Knaap, Faculty of Economic Sciences, Erasmus University Rotterdam.* **Institution:** *Rotterdam Academy of Architecture and Urban Planning.* **Students:** *Jeroen Zuidgeest, Joris Vermeiren and Ivar Branderhorst*
Image editing: *Andrea Fiechter, Im Sik Cho.*

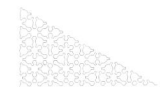

Permissions & Source Notes:

pp. 2-8, 26-29 / OPIE
All photographs courtesy of Regen Projects, Los Angeles.

pp. 14-19 / DUVAL / MONSON
All images courtesy of the authors.

pp. 20-29 / DUARTE / CONTRERAS / CABALLERO
All images courtesy of the authors.

pp. 30-34 / HADDAD
All images courtesy of Solidere.

pp. 35-38 / HARRINGTON / LEE
All images courtesy of the authors.

pp. 39-33 / JOACHIM / ARBONA / GREDEN
All images courtesy of the authors.

pp. 44-49 / KELLY
All images courtesy of John Portman & Associates Inc.

pp. 54-65 / MARTENS
All images courtesy Atelier Van Lieshout.

pp. 66 / MOSKOW
All images courtesy Moskow Architects.

pp. 78-84 / SHAN
Drawings and photos courtesy of UrbanDATA, Inc. Graphs courtesy Shanghai Statistical Bureau.

pp. 91-103 / SHANNON
Engravings courtesy Nguyen Khac Can & Nguyen Ngoc Diep (1997) Viet Nam.
Promotional graphic courtesy Bechtel.
Graphics based on Khawatmi, Asma (2001) 'Le Compartiment Hanoi: Structure/Usage/Temporalit?' in Pierre Clément and Nathalie Lancret (eds.) Hanoi, le Cycle des Metamorphoses; Paris: Editions Recherches/Cahiers de l'Ipraus.
All other images courtesy of the author.

pp. 104-116 / SHERMAN
All images courtesy of the author.

pp. 117-121 / SO
All images courtesy of the author.

pp. 122 / SOULES
Before and After Photos of Vancouver skyline courtesy The City of Vancouver. All other images courtesy of the author.

pp. 123-129 / SOLURI
All images courtesy of SHoP Architects.

pp. 130-143 / THEUNIS
Cartoon drawings (p.132-3), Braem courtesy AAM, Brussels. Plans, photographs courtesy Stadsarchief Antwerpen. Brochures courtesy Archief Stad Antwerpen. All other images courtesy of the author.

pp. 144-149 / VERBAKEL
Plan courtesy Coelacanth & Associates
3D cubic volumes graphics by Els Verbakel, based on architects' drawings
All other images courtesy of the author.

pp. 150-157 / WALL
All images courtesy of the author.

Forthcoming in September 2005

306090, Architecture Journal, Volume 9
306090 09, Regarding Public Space

Cecilia Benites, Julie Flohr, and Clare Lyster, Design Bureau for Public Space, guest-editors

306090 09, Regarding Public Space, focuses on the materialization and meaning of contemporary public space, through a framework for debate that highlights how its ethos, conception, production, aesthetics, appropriation, identity and dissemination perpetuate its existence in the neoliberal order. This volume will compile the work of design professionals, teachers, students, policy thinkers, environmentalists, artists, activists and the public with proposals that react to, illustrate and/or challenge how the public realm is understood and approached in the 21st century.

Including:

GAMBLE, Michael
Emerging Public Realms in the Contemporary City—Catalogues and Projects

SHEPARD, Mark
Tactical Sound Garden (TSG) Toolkit

SLASKY, Gavri E.
Public Inverted: Hans Haacke—"And you Were Victorious After All"

WHITE, Mason and SHEPPARD, Lola
Flat.space: Ex-urbanism+Infrastructural Landscape

SEAVITT, Catherine
Atlantic Intracoastal Waterway: Kayakers Guide Series

LAN 3016H, University of Toronto
Public Park: The 5th Model

REED, Chris
Performance Practices

JAUREQUI, Jorge Mario
Public Space in Contexts

VEKSTEIN, Claudio
Social Invisibility

WALDHEIM, Charles
Re-calibrating Milwaukee

TARKOWSKI, Christine
Working on the Failed Utopia

MCGRATH, Brian
Bangkok (CSD) Central Shopping District

DURATE, Gabriel N.
Infrascapes: Interstitial Enclaves of the Unplanned

Call for Submissions

306090, Architecture Journal, Volume 10
306090 10, Decoration

Emily Abruzzo, Alexander Briseño, Jonathan D. Solomon, editors

Decoration

As we shake off the restrictive remnants of 20th Century theories on the subjects of ornament, pattern, and decoration, we find these elements are everywhere in contemporary architecture. From inventive uses of color, to material applications, to structural systems, architecture and decoration are inseparable. Decoration — we are not afraid to say it — is essential for the survival of our art, and responsible for much of its current acclaim. Building on our conviction that architecture, as a profession, must necessarily be multi-disciplinary, we ask:

How does architecture decorate? How can architectural systems be decorative? Can decoration be structural or programmatic? At what scales can decoration operate? Importantly, how does today's decoration defy identification as such? How do Pattern, Appliqué, Color, Relief play into contemporary design? How do new methods of construction and digital production open up new opportunities in decoration?

Volume 10 of 306090 will compile contemporary attempts to incorporate, address, and define decoration within the practice of architecture.

...How is decoration better integrated today or alternately related to architecture than it has been since being so vilified by our Modernists?

...How has decoration today surpassed the applications of the post-modernists?

...How has decoration triumphed over the later derisions of deconstructionists and critical theorists to become a meaningful element of contemporary practice?

Please submit projects, essays, or commentaries that address decoration in architecture, as architecture, of architecture.

Submissions are Due October 1, 2005

Submissions Requirements:
Text: Microsoft Word format (500–2000 words using MLA Standards)
Images: 300 dpi grayscale TIF files.
Images will not be enlarged from submitted size.
Drawings: Process Black EPS files.
Method: PC formatted Compact Disk in duplicate mailed to address above.
No electronic submissions permitted.

Emily Abruzzo received a Bachelor of Arts in Architecture from Columbia University and a Master of Architecture from Princeton University, where she was the recipient of a Certificate in Media and Modernity as well as a project grant from the Center for Arts and Cultural Policy Studies. She is an architectural designer with Balmori Associates in New York, and has worked with AtopiaUK, SHoP, Acheson Doyle Partners and Eisenman Architects. She is a collaborator on an upcoming book from Agrest and Gandelsonas on their Des Moines Vision Plan.

Alexander Briseño received a Bachelor of Science in Architecture and a Master of Architecture from the University of Michigan and has also attended SCI-Arc. He is a licensed architect and senior designer at DMW in New York and also runs Sohbr Studio, with partner Cara Soh. Briseño was the 2003 recipient of the Booth Fellowship for his research titled The Palimpsest of Parma. He is a frequent critic at Pratt Institute and CCNY.

Jonathan D. Solomon received a Bachelor of Arts in Urban Studies from Columbia University and a Master of Architecture and Certificate in Media and Modernity from Princeton University, where he was the recipient of a Suzanne Kolarik Underwood Prize and a Howard Crosby Butler Fellowship. He is an architect with Reiser+Umemoto RUR Architecture in New York and teaches design at the City College of New York. Solomon is the author of Pamphlet Architecture #26, 13 Projects for the Sheridan Expressway.

Send all submission materials to:

306090, Inc.
Attn: 306090 10 Submissions
350 Canal Street Box 2092
New York, NY 10013-0875
US Postal Service deliveries only

No overnight or courier deliveries accepted.
No submissions will be accepted via email.
Contact 306090 with any questions
at info@306090.org or visit www.306090.org